A DECISION MAKING PRIMER

G. CLAUDE WRIGHT

Copyright © 2023 G. Claude Wright.

All rights reserved. No part of this book may be reproduced, stored, or transmitted by any means—whether auditory, graphic, mechanical, or electronic—without written permission of both publisher and author, except in the case of brief excerpts used in critical articles and reviews. Unauthorized reproduction of any part of this work is illegal and is punishable by law.

ISBN: 979-8-88640-699-3 (sc)
ISBN: 979-8-88640-700-6 (hc)
ISBN: 979-8-88640-701-3 (e)

Because of the dynamic nature of the Internet, any web addresses or links contained in this book may have changed since publication and may no longer be valid. The views expressed in this work are solely those of the author and do not necessarily reflect the views of the publisher, and the publisher hereby disclaims any responsibility for them.

One Galleria Blvd., Suite 1900, Metairie, LA 70001
1-888-421-2397

CONTENTS

Introduction vii
Acknowledgments xi

I. SENSIBLE DECISIONS MAKING 1

Relinquished Decisions 3
Everybody Loves A "Yes" Man 6
Is Celebrity Endorsement Reliable Advice? 9
Ready-Made Wisdom 11
Only Fools Accept Dares 14
Check Your Focus 17
Assumptions Can Be Dangerous 21
Don't Bet Heavily on the Untried 25
Tempted to Take a Break? 28
Not Deciding is to Decide 32
Buy Time! 34

II. INSIGHTFUL DECISION MAKING 37

Seek a Small Victory 39
Reassess Your Resources 43
Backward Steps Can Produce Progress 46
Filter Your Decisions 49
Decisions Don't Exist in Isolation 53
An Unusual Crystal Ball 56
Jump the Fence 60

III. ELIMINATING WASTE 63

First Things First 64
Misplaced Items Waste Time, Cost Money 67
A Costly Memory Lapse 70

IV. EXAMINE YOUR SHORTCOMINGS 73

Do You Twist the Truth? 75
Control Your Anger 79
Unbridled Greed 84
Seeking the Easy Way Out 87
Procrastination Causes Problems 91
Repeating the Same Mistake 95
Do You Bore People? 99
I'm Bulletproof 102

V. PERSONAL IMPROVEMENT 107

Become a Positive Person 108
Invest in Others 111
Traits of the Successful and Great 114
Guard Your Mind 117
Do the Right Thing 120
Protect Your Reputation 123

VI. DEALING WITH PEOPLE 127

It May Be Legal, But is it Right? 128
Protect Your Own Interests 130
There Are Givers...And Takers 133
Investigate Any Potential Associate 138
Guard Against the Inside Job 140
Beware the Charmer 143
Is He Really Your Friend? 146
He's Your Competitor...Don't Forget It 150
Identify the Dominator 153
Don't Burn Bridges 156
Trade Viewpoints 159

VII. SUCCESS AND GOAL SEEKING 161

Make Setting Goals A Habit 163

To Get There, You Must Begin 169
Goals You Shouldn't Pursue 172
How Much Pressure Can You Stand? 175
Is Your Commitment Strong Enough? 179
When in a Battle, Fight to Win 182
Expand Your Options... 188
Focus on Your 'A' Skills 191
Passion Separates the Best From the Rest 194
Stepping Outside the Box... 204
You Will Pay a Price to be The Best 208

VIII. BUSINESS AND INVESTMENTS 213

There Ain't No Free Lunch 215
Getting in is Often Easy...But 219
Is It Too Good To Be True? 223
How Much Do You Deserve To Make? 226
Unrealistic Expectations 230
Understand the Nature of Opportunities....................................234
People Value Things Differently 240
Partnerships? 243
Value Your "Trump Cards" 247
The First Rule of Risk-Taking 251
Overlooked Wisdom 253
Know When to Hang in There 257
Know When to Retreat 263
The "End Game" Strategy..268

IX. ATTITUDES AND HABITS 277

How Do You Know It's Bad? 279
Surprises in the Ashes 282
The Threat of the Crowd 286
Take a Stand for the Truth 289
Don't Take Yourself Too Seriously..292
Feeling Sorry For Yourself?..295

Are You Spread Too Thin? 297
Value Special Moments 301
Surround Yourself With Beauty... 304
What Kind of Legacy Will You Leave? 308

Epilogue 313

INTRODUCTION

Decision-making is a subject that has intrigued me for many years. I have a file in my office that's as thick as a phone book, full of ideas about decision-making. What you are about to read is an assortment of those ideas... ideas that I've been accumulating most of my adult life. From this file, I've selected those principles that I felt were the best and organized them into categories that will hopefully cover a majority of your life experiences. For these reasons, I feel confident that the concepts I've chosen will help you improve your decision-making abilities. In that process, I'm hoping to also elevate your understanding of what good decision-making is truly all about. I should probably mention that many of these principles were the result of lessons I learned from some of the rotten decisions I've made!

Despite the number of principles I've introduced, this collection is by no means exhaustive. The number of possible decisions you may encounter in your life is magnitudes beyond the quantity to be found in this or any other book. However, I hope that the ones presented will provide good counsel for a surprising percentage of your future decision-making moments. I even feel that these principles will awaken an awareness of certain patterns that are common to most good choices. As you begin to recognize some of these patterns, it's up to you to embrace their teachings. And when you do, you should begin to notice your increasing ability to identify that option, from among your many choices, that provides the most promise.

Thus, if you will make the effort to etch them upon your mind, they will serve as important contributors to an improved quality of all your future decisions. You will likely have gained insights that may result in new respect from those who witness your increased wisdom. After all… it's usually the wise, not necessarily the intellectual, who lives a life everyone envies.

To assist your understanding and recollection of a given precept, an illustration or short story (often taken from my own life) has been provided. I do feel a need to prepare you for my use of some illustrations that may seem somewhat corny or annoyingly obvious. However, after much deliberation, they made the "cut" because they *did provide* a fitting, and easily understood, an example of the concept I'm trying to impress upon you.

The nine sections of the book have been arranged in an order that attempts to organize their sequencing as per my expectations of your need for the advice they provide.

They begin with a chapter entitled, *Sensible Decision Making*. The principles contained within this chapter address fundamental perceptions, beliefs, or attitudes that typically lead to bad decisions. By calling your attention to these harmful tendencies, the unwanted consequences of the decisions they spawn can be avoided.

Insightful Decision Making is a collection of concepts that might best be described as subtle nuances that might be considered *collateral* considerations, often of hidden importance, to the decision being contemplated.

Eliminating Waste is a brief section that contains helpful, as well as interesting, suggestions for creating dependable habits that are aimed at minimizing losses of time and money.

The next three sections become more personal. The first, *Examine Your Shortcomings*, introduces concepts designed to help you deal with your weaknesses by urging you to consider the impact your character flaws can impose on *all* decisions involving your relationships. Hopefully, the suggestions provided by the principles contained within this chapter will motivate you to make a serious effort to address the need to "work" on those areas of your life. The second section, *Personal Improvement* is an about-face from the previous chapter. It is a collection of principles aimed at stressing the extraordinary value of those character qualities that enhance one's character and the decisions that will contribute to that accomplishment. The benefits derived from these two sections should conclude in one's improved ability to successfully deal with people, as well as an enhanced feeling of self-worth. The third section, *Dealing With People*, goes one step further. It contains *special insight* into people. Its principles strive to increase your ability to understand a person's hidden nature by providing an awareness of their concealed characteristics. They point out the necessity of dealing with people in recognition of their true nature and thus assist you in structuring your decisions accordingly. They should prove valuable in dealing with a broad range of people in a variety of circumstances.

Next, you are introduced to principles contained within a section entitled *Success And Goal Seeking*. It addresses the various decisions necessary to successfully seek and realize your goals. As you attempt to reach your goals (at least those that relate to your career or finances) it becomes imperative that you make quality decisions in these areas of your life. A related section, *Business, and Investments* presents sound principles that are constantly being overlooked, particularly by those who haven't realized success in their past management of career decisions or investment choices.

Lastly, I've included a chapter on *Attitude And Habits*. Its principles deal with several interesting and possibly different slants on issues on your habits and attitudes, as well as issues that relate to the quality of life itself. I would be very surprised if the principles introduced in this section didn't prove valuable to you.

I hope my experiences along with the principles they birthed, will help you avoid poor choices and improve the quality of all your decisions with the result being a life well-lived. Here's to good decisions!

ACKNOWLEDGMENTS

First, I want to thank my wife, Janet, for all her time and clear thought that served to enhance the value of this book.

I would like to acknowledge Jo Ann Colton's counsel regarding the world of authors and publishers.

I also wish to thank Lorna and Gene Kissinger for their help and encouragement. Additional thanks to my lifelong friend, Jim McLellan for his insistence that I persist in my efforts to produce a quality product.

My appreciation also goes to Carrie Daniel who helped me select, from among my main ideas, those principles and accompanying illustrations that were worthy of inclusion in this book.

Finally, Barbara Kaptanian provided a wealth of encouragement, grammatical input, and wise counsel on all manner of content considerations.

My thanks to you all.

I. SENSIBLE DECISIONS MAKING

There are countless approaches to making decisions. The ways that you will encounter in this section chronicle courses of action that typically lead to problems.

These concepts will help you avoid decisions that are unlikely to result in good outcomes. Being the product of faulty reasoning, careless indifference, or simple misunderstandings, they hold little potential for serving as worthy guides to properly dealing with life's challenges.

It is the misleading subtleties contained within these kinds of decisions that are typically responsible for distracting your attention away from the heart of the issue and thus render sensible conclusions unlikely.

While far from exhaustive, I believe that the advice to be gained from these eleven principles will protect you from making some of the bad decisions you might otherwise make.

These principles are as follows: Relinquished Decisions, Everybody Loves A Yes-Man, Is Celebrity Endorsement Reliable Advice?, Ready-Made Wisdom, Only A Fool Answers Dares, Check Your Focus, Assumptions Can Be Dangerous, Don't Bet Heavily On The Untried, Tempted To Take A Break, Not Deciding Is To Decide, and Buy Time.

If you are guilty of making decisions after the manner described in these principles, you will find that these concepts contribute to your heightened awareness – an awareness of what not to do – as well as an understanding that there's a price to be paid if you do.

RELINQUISHED DECISIONS

How often have you done something like this when the stakes were much higher?

This decision-making principle is well illustrated by a story that occurred when I was twelve years old. I ignored every concept contained within this principle but, given my age at the time, my foolishness might be somewhat understandable. Such forgiveness, however, should not extend to a mature adult for whom the consequences of irresponsible decision-making often result in big losses and/or big problems.

At the urging of an older "friend" (he was fifteen), I accompanied him on a trip to the hobby store. Once inside, *he decided* that I should buy a model airplane. The same "friend" then decided that he would build it for me. I now realize that one of only three reasons for buying a model plane is to enjoy the act of building it yourself. The other two reasons would be to fly it and/or hang it in your bedroom. Being young naïve, and lacking the necessary courage to confront him, I gave him the model so he could build it for me – the final insult was the fee he charged me for building it! In any case, joy number one was now gone.

But there's more to the story. There was a public park not far from my home. Once my "friend" completed the model, he decided that we should take the model plane up to the top of a ten-meter diving tower situated out in a lake that was within the park and fly it off. That sounded like fun until I began to worry that my little plane might not remain airborne long enough to reach the shore.

Given what I was about to learn about his plan for my plane, making it to shore was not something I needed to have been concerned about. After reaching the top of the diving tower, he reached into his pocket and brought out some matches, and proceeded to light the tail on fire! His bright idea (decision) was to watch the burning plane spiral down into the water. I was demoralized to realize this was to be its first *and last* flight.

Gone now were reasons number two and three for buying a model plane. But it was too late (as the tail of my plane was in flames) to now concern myself with either of those purchase motivations. I watched as my "investment" hit the water – a charred mess, floating lifelessly on the lake below. I was crushed. I had allowed him to decide that I should buy a model airplane. I let him decide that he should build it. I allowed him to decide to fly the plane off the diving tower, and I allowed him to light the tail on fire. I had offered no resistance to any of his decisions.

Sensing my displeasure, he asked me if that wasn't what I wanted to do. How cleverly he reinterpreted decisions that he, not I, had made. When I told him "no" that wasn't what I wanted to do, all he could say was, "Sorry"! He didn't offer to buy me a new model let alone include the building of it as a gesture of apology. His "I'm sorry" did *nothing* to make me feel better.

The lesson to be derived from "Relinquished Decisions" focuses on the habit of allowing someone else to make your decisions for you so that you will have someone to blame, besides yourself, should things not turn out as planned.

I had foolishly dodged any responsibility for the decisions that were made regarding my model airplane. Fortunately, all that lesson cost me was the price of a model airplane, my "friend's" fee for building it, and a crushed spirit.

We are living in a time marked by widespread irresponsibility – an age where blaming others for our problems is the norm. For many, *it's always someone else's fault.*

In the business arena, many people have made investments because of the recommendations of another – often a friend or neighbor not qualified to give such advice. But, the advisor did have one qualification: *He was someone they could blame if the investment went sour!* But then, what other possible good is an advisor whose advice turns sour and costs you money? Maybe you hope he'll give you your money back? Well, you can forget that. *Refunding your loss won't ever enter his mind!*

At best, you'll just get him, "I'm sorry." More likely, he won't return your phone calls.

When needing advice, seek sound advice. Don't be tempted to transfer the responsibility for the decision to the advisor for a decision you can't, or won't make just so you'll have someone to blame should things go wrong. Assume responsibility for making your own decisions. *Never relinquish your decision-making rights.*

EVERYBODY LOVES A "YES" MAN

When you get the "word" from someone like this, why would you bother seeking a second affirmation?

My teen years were spent in a small but comfortable house in a nice part of town. Across the street from our house, however, was a luxury enclave known as the Polo Grounds. As one of the ritziest residential areas in town, it was enclosed by walls and fences. There was some vacant ground, but most of it consisted of many large and magnificent estates. One of the three entrances into that enclave was only one block up the street from my house.

Just inside that entrance was a vacant lot that was yet to be developed. It occupied a couple of acres, and like all vacant lots, it was full of weeds. But it had two trees that happened to be about one hundred yards apart – perfect targets for a little two-hole golf course. Because I attended the same school as one of the kids who lived there, I didn't feel at all uncomfortable going over to hit a few golf balls whenever time permitted.

One day, a guy who introduced himself as Randy came walking by the tree (my first tee) on his way home. Since I was only fifteen at the time, I'd never met Randy who was five or six years older than I was.

Because the golf community is a rather friendly bunch, and since my dad was the state champion, he knew a lot of people, among them, Randy's parents.

It turned out that Randy lived in the mansion next to the vacant lot that had become my golf course. He asked me how I was doing, and we talked for a while. Randy, who also enjoyed golf, wondered how I liked fighting the weeds that were so prevalent on "my" golf course. When I replied that I was doing OK, he said that I was welcome to come over to his house and set up my course on the enormous lawn which surrounded his parent's estate. I couldn't believe his offer. What a super nice guy!

His house and yard were magnificent In fact, I was to later learn that Randy's parents were the owners of the Carey Salt Co.! No wonder they could afford such a palace. I was now being invited to make this into my playground. *Just what I wanted to hear!*

I quickly scouted out the terrain and figured there would still only be two golf holes. The first would start at the entry gate to their property with the first tee being just a few feet from the driveway (right next to a beautiful flower bed). I'd be hitting toward their house to a tree that was about twenty yards to the right of their garage. The second hole's tee was next to that tree with the green being another tree that was growing very near their entryway.

Before moving to this new venue, I had been working on my swing, but I found it a little tough because of the uneven ground and the weeds. Thanks to Randy, I didn't have those problems anymore. I knew this opportunity would prove to be a big advancement in my plans to improve my game. I worked on all the swing mechanics that I had read about. For example, all the pros took divots with their iron shots. So I decided that's what I needed to do. Because I had selected such small areas for my tees, I had to move my hitting area around every once in a while to find fresh grass that hadn't been dug up by my nine iron.

Because this was such great fun, I came often and occasionally at odd times, like Sunday mornings. I remember one Sunday morning when I arrived *early*. I'm sure that it was because I hadn't warmed up yet, but my opening shot off the first tee was a high looping hook that hit their garage door with a surprisingly loud bang. I wasn't sure whether or not I should play out the hole. I wasn't sure if I should even hang around. Better yet, I decided to give my game a rest for a few days.

The next time I showed up, I was about to hit off the first tee when *Mr. and Mrs. Carey drove up.* Mr. Carey stopped the car and rolled the window down and asked, "Would you mind discontinuing play for a few weeks to give us a chance to reseed?" Even though I was young and shamefully insensitive to what I had been doing, I caught *that* message! I was so embarrassed! I felt so little I'll bet I could have crawled into a golf hole. After that, I never again hit another golf ball on Carey's front lawn.

In retrospect, the thought of using the manicured grounds of Carey's estate as my playground should have been something I would never have considered doing. It certainly embarrasses me to recall it now. But, I kept excusing myself. After all, Randy had said that it was alright. Deep down, I wouldn't have wanted to ask Mr. Carey if he minded if I dug up his lawn. I knew what his answer would have been. Understandably, it was a question I never asked. I already had the answer *I sought*... But then, I was just a kid – some continue to favor this "selective" reasoning as an adult.

"Everybody Loves A 'Yes' Man" urges you to consider the valueless nature of the advice that comes from someone who's programmed to tell you only what they think you want to hear. History is full of stories about kings and monarchs who surrounded themselves with "yes men" whose role was to always agree with the king, telling him what he wanted to hear. It was job security for the "yes men", but inept and regrettable governance for the people being ruled by a leader who only listened to what made him feel good.

Corporate executives also have been known to do the same thing. As soothing as yes men can sometimes be, the nature of their one-sided advice can have disastrous consequences. The important question that you need to ask yourself is, "Are you willing to risk failure because you insist upon confining your counsel to those who agree with you and will only tell you what you want to hear?"

Success will prove elusive when your advice comes only from yes men. Make a habit of taking advice from this kind of advisor and failure may be just a short step away.

Usually, the best advice you will ever receive comes from the person who's willing to risk your displeasure by telling you the truth. This is the kind of individual who's not afraid to challenge your plans or ideas. If those plans and ideas can pass the mustard with this type of critic, they're probably sound.

IS CELEBRITY ENDORSEMENT RELIABLE ADVICE?

Celebrities, and those who pay them to endorse their products, may be pulling the wool over your eyes.

People love celebrities. They want to know all about them, get their autographs, and vicariously identify with their fame and success. It is amazing to observe the influence these famous people can have on us. It's not surprising that celebrities have been used to endorse products since the pre-television days of radio broadcasting. The age of television merely served to broaden the use of celebrity endorsements. Decades ago, celebrity endorsements were presented as a testimony to that celebrity's personal use of the product being promoted. More recently, celebrities are often used to endorse products with which they may have little familiarity and probably no expert knowledge.

Please excuse the use of these rather antiquated personalities for my illustrations, but the perfect example from those old days was provided by Mickey Mantle, the famous New York Yankee baseball player of the 1950s and 60s. He endorsed Gillette razors because he was a celebrity, not because he was an expert on shaving. He had no greater qualifications to be granted "expert status" on razors than any other man. When deciding to buy a razor, we needed to remind ourselves that Mickey's claim to fame was baseball, not shaving!

The same could be said for the dry cleaning chain owned by Arnold Palmer. He quite naturally endorsed its services. As rich and successful as Arnie is, one has to wonder how much he worries about his laundry. With all the clothes he endorses, he may not have any dirty clothes that need laundering because he may never wear the same outfit twice!

Consider those big-name celebrity athletes who have been paid to sing the praises of some mid-priced American-made car. You sometimes wonder whether these people ever park their sporty, foreign-made, luxury machines long enough to give themselves a little more time behind the wheel of one of those cars they endorse. It may even be fair to say they may spend no more time driving one of their endorsed products than it took to film the ad.

This is not to say that a given product is unworthy of consideration just because a famous person recommends it, but these examples do explain why it's unwise to base your decision just upon a celebrity's endorsement of a product. Logically, it should be the inherent merits of the product that determine the choice you make. The example of celebrity endorsements was chosen because it so clearly illustrates the lack of a logical connection between the celebrity's knowledge about that which made him famous as opposed to something about which he probably knows little if any more than the average person.

The point is: *we often allow an unqualified advisor to give us advice.* At one time or another, most of us have succumbed to the counsel of someone not qualified to give advice, and despite their lack of adequate credentials, we accept their advice. This happens because many people seem to have opinions about many things; such a non-expert won't usually refrain from expressing his opinion. To the extent you are influenced by their unsolicited advice, you may learn (the hard way) that most of this type of advice, from this kind of adviser, is often devoid of any real value. Such an advisor will often have no more knowledge about the subject (if even as much) as the one they're advising.

Decide you'll accept advice only from those qualified to give it. Who would have argued with those who sought Mickey Mantle's suggestions about buying a baseball glove? But, don't bother to call on Mickey for his counsel on shaving.

When making *important* decisions, seek the guidance of the most qualified expert you can find. For less important matters, decide to surround yourself with *wise* friends and associates who can be counted on to look over your shoulder when you need a second opinion.

READY-MADE WISDOM

At first, it may seem unbelievable to you that anyone would choose this approach to reach a decision. But, after reading this principle, you may realize that you have done so yourself!

This principle addresses those decisions that may require the exposure of some personal problem or embarrassing revelation to your family, friends, neighbors, or close advisors. Just the thought of having to bare your soul to any of these people can prompt you to wish to remove yourself from having to involve *anyone else* in your decision.

To avoid revealing your private affairs, you may be tempted to resort to "impersonal" advice – such as the insights that might be gained from a famous quotation or cliché. It might seem that all you have to do is pick one that seems to apply to your situation and you have spared yourself the anguish of unpleasant disclosures.

There is nothing inherently wrong in studying the recorded thoughts of some renowned intellect. These little bits of "wisdom" or humorous sayings can often enrich your speech and provide clarification to ideas you're trying to communicate.

Nevertheless, they represent a poor substitute for the value contained in making your decisions for yourself. Your own informed decision, one that considers the facts surrounding the situation at hand, has no suitable substitute to be found in a volume of famous quotations. It is foolish to think you can trust some little saying in hopes that it might miraculously provide your answer. After all, the person who originally penned these platitudes knows nothing about you or your circumstance.

"Do something, even if it's wrong" is an example of the ill-advised use of a cliché as an aid to decision-making that comes from these senseless words offered as a solution to being stuck on the horns of a dilemma. When subjected to the light of common sense, most reasonable people would logically conclude that doing nothing is almost always better than doing something wrong.

In the days of the ownership of my construction company, I found myself in need of a day-to-day manager for my company. A well-qualified man was being considered for the job. The decision to hire him finally came to rest upon his request to have the power to hire whomever he deemed fit, or fire whomever he thought wasn't. With some hesitation, I finally agreed to his request and hired him. During several casual conversations with this new manager, I noticed his frequent use of this saying: "You never make a mistake firing someone." That cliché seemed to summarize his feelings about the dispensability of any employee. Because things seemed to be going smoothly, I didn't pay a great deal of attention to the manager's frequent references to that cliché…until that horrible day when I discovered that my manager had just fired my son-in-law! There aren't words to describe what that cliché cost me.

Another young man had just made the devastating decision to divorce his wife. In a subsequent discussion, I was curious as to what thoughts had led him to that decision. He told me that another friend (who had also been divorced) had noted the couple's constant quarreling and had, therefore, advised him to get out of a marriage that was killing him so that he could "Live to fight again another day." In assessing his conclusions, he had hung his hat on the idea of "living to fight again another day."

Drug samplers might justify their initial experiment with the supporting thought that "Everybody's doing it." And with that their decision was made and they started down a very dangerous path.

People at the gaming tables in Las Vegas might excuse their gambling excesses with the justifying statement that "You can't take it with you." The dissipating lifestyle of the inveterate party animal is exemplified by the old dictum, "Eat, drink, and be merry for tomorrow you die" or "you only live once." All manner of misbehavior has been rationalized with an adherence to the saying, "Life's short, let's just have some fun." There is no end to the clichés, and there's virtually no end to the decisional folly of those who make their decisions based upon them.

Because there seems to be a cliché to match every situation, some might regard such a collection as ready-made wisdom. Admittedly, many clichés speak to wise observations. But no one, most particularly a saying, knows your situation as well as you do. Moreover, allowing a clever saying to make your decisions for you is an irresponsible way to face life's challenges – it can even become a habitual way of dealing with all tough decisions.

If you are confronted with a decision and find yourself citing some cliché that supports the choice you favor, reexamine the reasoning behind the decision you're contemplating and make sure this cliché isn't doing your thinking for you!

ONLY FOOLS ACCEPT DARES

A macho mentality can prove very costly!

At one point in my career, I owned several rental properties. Most of these were buildings located in an older but rather classy section of Denver known as Capitol Hill. Some of the buildings needed "facelifts" as their exterior appearances were showing signs of age. One building, in particular, was a magnificent Victorian structure that I felt needed a paint job. I hired some freelance painters to do the work.

After receiving a call saying the job was finished, I decided to visit the property to inspect their job and pay them for the work. When I arrived, I noticed that everything had been painted except the chimneys. These chimneys were very tall as they extended well beyond the eave of the very steeply pitched roof. The eave itself was a full three stories above the ground and the chimney was probably another ten feet above the eave. Their forty-foot rental ladder was leaning against the building ready to perform the job. Wondering why they had not finished, I pointed out the unpainted chimneys. They quickly shot back that the chimneys were too high and they weren't going to paint them. The questioning look I gave them must have communicated "cowards". They all looked at me and rather sarcastically said, "Well, why don't you paint them?"

They were daring me to get up on that ladder and paint the chimneys! Not wanting to look like a coward myself, I retorted, *"Give me that roller!"* I grabbed the roller and the pan of paint and started up the ladder. As I was making my way up, I passed the point where the two sections of the ladder were joined together and realized the ladder had been fully extended to its maximum length. When I finally reached the top of the ladder (forty feet off the ground), the highest rung was at my belt buckle! With my arm outstretched and standing as close to the highest rung as I dared, I was barely able to reach the top of the chimney. As I reached up to start at the top of the chimney and work my way down, I heard a *click, click!* Before I knew what was happening, the two sections of the ladder had separated! *There was no longer anything holding up the section I was standing on!* That section of the ladder, the roller, the paint pan, and I were now all freefalling!

It all occurred so fast that I had no time to contemplate what was happening. On my way down my arm hit the metal balcony railing of the second-floor apartment. I finally struck the ground on a sort of three-point landing. My heels hit the ground first, followed by my rear end, and then my hands which were outstretched behind me. I felt like I had broken my tailbone (although I hadn't) and severely cut my tongue. When I got up my foot and wrist all felt like they were on fire – they were both broken. However, the most lasting damage was to my arm, the one that hit the balcony railing on the way down. When I glanced down at my arm, it looked like some gory anatomy picture!

Later, a neurosurgeon friend of mine, commenting on my mishap, told me that had I not been slowly rotating in the air, I would have landed in a standing position. Given the force of the fall, it would most likely have compressed my spine, paralysis being the outcome. Had I over-rotated and landed on my back, it could have burst my aorta.

In addition to an almost ideal landing position, what also contributed to my still being here was the fact that the chimney was on the north side of the building in the shade, providing a soft lawn for me to land on.

A few weeks later, after I had been treated for all my injuries (two casts and surgery), I returned to the scene of the accident. I noticed that there was another identical chimney on the south side of the building. This one lacked a lawn. The ground between my building and the neighboring building was covered with a concrete walkway. The thing that sent a chill down my spine was the wrought iron picket fence that ran between the buildings and down the center of the walkway. Even if I had survived landing on the concrete walkway, there would have been no way I would have missed being skewered on the iron fence!

Because I didn't want to look like a coward, I answered a dare from a group of men I didn't even know. *What a stupid thing to do!*

Though more appropriately addressed to preteens and teens, even adults sometimes worry they'll be seen as cowards if they're not courageous enough to accept the challenge of a dare.

What takes real courage is to decide that you will make your own independent decision as to what risks you are willing to take and not worry about what others will think of you if you don't accept their challenge.

Never allow yourself to be maneuvered into making a bad or dangerous decision just to answer someone's dare.

CHECK YOUR FOCUS

Though responsible for many poor decisions, politicians find it to be quite useful.

Our family vacation to Hawaii gave us the perfect opportunity to learn to scuba dive. We discovered a bargain scuba school that offered cheap diving lessons. My sons and I decided to enroll in their scuba diving class in hopes of getting our diving certification and enjoying some diving off the coast of Maui.

Carl was our scuba instructor, but he didn't do much instructing. What instruction we did receive was a bit of a joke. The office was a house trailer, which served as the classroom. Instruction was frequently limited to "on-the-job" training. We put on our flippers, mask, tank, regulator, and goggles and awaited his instruction which was, "let's get in the water." Our first "in the water" experience happened to coincide with the low tide. The problem was that we were in knee-to-waist-deep water with coral below that we had to walk on or swim over. The Coral is very uneven and *very* sharp. Walking on it proved to be very difficult as your foot often got wedged between two coral limbs that would cut your legs and ankles. For that reason, we were told to start swimming with our faces in the water. Once again, the shallowness of the water and the exposed coral below caused us problems. Our legs and knees were cut and scraped on the coral which was only a few inches below the surface. Loud complaints from all of the students brought that session to an end.

We were given an instruction booklet on which we would later be tested. Carl's instruction to prepare us for that test consisted of a Saturday meeting in the "classroom" where he supplied *all the answers* to the test questions. We all passed.

There were several exercises we were supposed to perform to prove our diving competence. The final session was a dive into a depth of twenty-five or thirty feet where we practiced various maneuvers. The one I remember best was the buddy breathing technique. This involved becoming familiar with our underwater breathing mechanism, a regulator, which is attached to a hose that leads to the air tank on your back. No worries. You merely put it in your mouth and breath normally. The idea behind buddy breathing is to be able to address an emergency – like someone's air tank going empty. You have a diving partner for just such emergencies. The diver who still has air then takes turns sharing his air (via his regulator) with his "airless" diving partner. Thus, as the regulator is being passed back and forth, each diver takes a big gulp of air and then hands it back to his diving partner. In such an emergency, they are to stay very close to each other and get to the surface as quickly as possible.

As we finally settled on the bottom of the ocean (some thirty feet down), Carl signaled for everyone to practice a few of the techniques that had been talked about in the "classroom." The first was how to recover your regulator should it, for whatever reason, become dislodged from your mouth and end up dangling behind your tank – a tricky recovery technique compounded by one's uneasiness of being without air.

The next exercise was the buddy breathing technique. Unfortunately, I was still thinking about that regulator recovery technique and the panic I'd feel should I ever have to recover my regulator when it came to my turn to engage in the "buddy breathing" and give my regulator to my diving partner. Instead of taking in a big gulp of air, I exhaled! I then calmly took the regulator out of my mouth and handed it to my diving partner! Carl glanced over as my diving partner gave me the "OK" sign (using his thumb and forefinger to make an "O") to make sure everything *was* OK. A return "O" meant that everything was fine. Having forgotten about the OK sign (maybe that was among the things Carl never explained), I didn't realize that my diving partner was asking me if everything was OK. Stupidly, I flashed the "OK" sign back to my partner who then assumed all was well with me and swam away. How could he know that I had just exhaled and desperately needed to take a deep breath of air? I had failed to concentrate on the most important thing – a gulp of air! While I didn't drown, there were a few tense moments.

What had diverted my attention *couldn't compare in importance* to the thing I had ignored – breathing!

In my defense, I'm not alone in misplacing my focus. We are all guilty of this more often than we think. Usually, it only involves a small, unimportant issue, but it can just as easily happen when it is not small, or unimportant!

There are times when our focus is diverted or our emphasis is misplaced as a consequence of the deliberate intentions of another person or group. Many a strategy, whether it relates to personal relationships, games, politics, business, or war, revolves around an effort to divert the opponent's attention by getting them to transfer their focus to an issue of lesser consequence.

Expect your adversaries to attempt to sidetrack your resolve by diverting your attention away from the most important issues to ones of minor significance.

During any negotiation, it's also wise to carefully monitor your own undisciplined or disorganized thoughts. They can become unexpected and unwelcome adversaries that will cause damaging inattentions.

Occasionally, we all need to be reminded to stay on point. Many people, even very intelligent people, entertain failure when they get sidetracked by allowing less important issues to divert their focus away from that which is *most* important.

On any occasion of confrontation or negotiation, decide that you won't allow the opposition to divert your attention away from the key issue. Whether it's politics, business, or war…they will try.

You can be one step ahead of your opponent when you anticipate his probable use of that strategy.

Avoid falling prey to such a strategy by deciding, ahead of time, that you will remain hyper-vigilant regarding the introduction of any distractions, and be determined to force the other party to remain focused on the main issue.

ASSUMPTIONS CAN BE DANGEROUS

This was one assumption that almost cost me my life!

During both my high school and college years, I spent summers working for my dad's small construction company. I vividly remember one on-the-job incident during the summer before I started college.

My assignment was that of a laborer for a roof decking project on a supermarket building. My job was to bring the insulated panels to the men who put them in place on a supporting grid system. These panels would later be covered with a lightweight, cement-like compound on top of which tar and gravel would be applied. These insulating panels were transported from the parking lot below onto the roof with the use of a lativator, a machine that works somewhat like a cog railway. It looks like a ladder with a big gas engine on one end. Cables that connected a simple platform (it had no railings) with the engine enabled the platform to ride up and down the side rails of the "ladder" which served as tracks. The platform would be loaded with the insulation board by a man on the ground while another man on the roof (me) would unload them onto the roof.

After finishing lunch, I walked by the lativator on my way to the temporary stair system which provided the workers access to the roof. Possibly due to the heaviness of my lunch, I was feeling a little lazy and asked Lingam, the lativator operator, to give me a lift up to the rooftop. I put a load of insulated paneling on the platform and then climbed on the rear of the platform for the slow ride to the top of the supermarket's front wall, a vertical height of approximately twenty feet. Neither Lingam nor I, had any reservations about the lativator's ability to handle my extra weight. We both *assumed* that if my weight exceeded its capacity the machine would simply fail to move the platform upward.

When the machine finally reached the top of the building, Lingam applied the brake to allow me to get off the platform. But, the brake didn't hold! The platform began to *freefall* back down the track! The sudden jolt when the platform began to drop launched me into the air like a back dive from a diving board, causing my body to rotate in the air. By the time my arms, shoulders, and head first reached the rungs of the lativator, my body was positioned like a falling arrow with my feet pointing at the sky!

By some miracle, my head missed hitting either of the side rails or any of the rungs of the lativator. Instead, my head, shoulders, and arms passed between the rungs of the lativator. I was now plummeting toward the asphalt parking lot, head first!

Then another miracle occurred. My leg caught on one of the rungs! There I was dangling upside down, twenty feet off the ground, spared only by my leg! I guess you could say that I had a "leg up" on most other victims of ladder accidents.

Both Lingam and I had made *a very dangerous assumption* about the mechanical capabilities and safety aspects of using the lativator as a vehicle for human transport.

A second example of the cost of improper assumptions occurred during my days of converting apartments to condominiums. I purchased two beautiful buildings from an estate being managed by a bank. One of the buildings was a magnificent six-unit apartment building. The other building was a wonderful old Victorian home. The two properties sat side-by-side and backed up to one of Denver's most beautiful parks.

There was one small problem. There was only one driveway connecting both garages to the street. The only place to locate a second driveway was in the courtyard of the apartment building. But that courtyard was a beautifully landscaped garden that added tremendous value to the apartment complex that I hoped to convert and sell as condominiums. A second driveway would ruin the courtyard. The *only* acceptable solution to the problem was one shared driveway.

Since the Victorian house was not a part of my grand plan, I decided to put it up for sale. It wasn't more than a week later that I received a call from a man who wanted to buy it. He had prepared a contract for the purchase of the house and wanted to bring it by my office. I explained that I was very short on time that afternoon as I had another appointment. I suggested that we meet the next day. He was very insistent that I meet with him that same day. I told him that there was one problem that he needed to know about. I then explained the driveway situation and gave him my reasons for not wanting to add a second driveway. He was disappointed, but I finally got him to understand that it was my way or he needed to look for another property. He finally said that he understood but was still insistent that he bring the contract by that afternoon. He told me that it would only take a minute since it was a very straightforward offer that met the price and terms I had advertised. He came by with the signed contract as he had promised. I looked at the terms of his offer and found them satisfactory. I signed the contract and left for my other appointment.

That night, I sat down to read the contract again. I came across a sentence that reads: "The existing driveway that now exists between the two properties shall be for the exclusive use of the Victorian house." *How could this have happened?* After our telephone conversation, I *assumed* that he had not only understood my explanation about the driveway but also believed that he was making his offer in acknowledgment of my requirements regarding a shared driveway. It now became apparent to me that he had no intention of agreeing to the idea of a shared driveway. His strategy rested upon the hope that my need to rush off for my appointment would only allow time for a hasty examination of the contract. Because that little sentence was buried in the small print, he hoped I'd overlook it and sign the contract without challenging his demands that the driveway is for his sole use.

I was livid. Though it was late, I quickly picked up the phone and called the man. I told him that I was now aware of the reason for all the rush. He didn't want me to take the time to read the contract and notice the clause he had inserted about the driveway. I also informed him that this wasn't the way I conducted business. He responded that I should have read the contract before signing it. I retorted that I had thought we had an understanding of the driveway before he came to my office. His reply made me want to jump through the phone. He said that our phone conversation was not legal, but the contract was. He informed me that I had made a mistake and that we all have to pay for our mistakes. He then compared my actions to those of a person caught running a red light and said that we all pay for running red lights when we're caught.

I had incorrectly *assumed* that he was agreeing to respect my wishes regarding a single driveway. I now realized he had understood my position regarding the driveway all along. Unraveling that mess created by my erroneous assumption cost me time, money, and a great deal of aggravation.

"It's Dangerous to Assume" warns of choosing to travel down a path of expectations that are based upon nothing more than assumptions. Faulty assumptions can cause all kinds of problems. Do not fail to verify as factual that which you *assume* to be fact. Decide to dispense with assumptive conclusions and start basing your decisions on hard facts.

Don't assume that which is not in evidence. Decide that you will take the necessary pains to make sure that you're not allowing assumptions to dictate your decisions. Check things out.

Don't assume that something unknown, or untried, is safe when you haven't, or can't, check out its reliability. And don't assume someone agrees with you if they haven't directly said so.

Don't assume the honesty of someone you don't know.

Don't assume that an important promise will necessarily be honored. Over time, something may have changed, or his memory of what was said may differ from yours. Don't assume!

DON'T BET HEAVILY ON THE UNTRIED

Many get it backward. They are cautious even about the proven, yet often place their full confidence in the unproven.

To an eight-year-old boy, comic books are a big deal. My favorites were the ones that featured my hero, Superman. Noting my obsession with the man of steel, my grandmother, a good woman, and a competent seamstress made me a Superman costume and cape. Wow! Was I ever the big deal? Once I donned the suit, things changed. I could feel those muscles rippling under my rather loose-fitting Superman suit. It's amazing to realize the invincible feelings that accompany such a symbol of power. It was my good fortune that an opportunity to demonstrate those powers came along rather quickly. It happened one day when my mother was planning to go shopping. But when it began to rain, she decided to cancel her plans. Feeling sorry for her, I offered Superman's help. Quickly, but secretly, I changed into my Superman suit. My confidence now boosted, I reasoned that a quick run around the block would stop the rain. Fortunately, it never occurred to me that a more logical course of action might have been to fly around in the clouds and mess with them somehow. As I returned from my "power run," it stopped raining! What else would you expect? My mother complimented me on my hidden powers and went shopping. Buoyed by this demonstration of my potential, future days would find me strutting around in the front yard for all interested passersby to observe… Superman! There was only one small problem. My mother insisted that I wear shoes. As we all know, *Superman didn't wear shoes!* It sadly turned out that it was, "wear the shoes or don't go out." Mighty though I was, I didn't argue. As I was parading around in our front yard in my Superman suit – shoes and all – some teenage bullies in the neighborhood came walking by. They couldn't resist, "Hey, Soop! What's with the shoes?" Humiliated,

I began to plan the next proof of my extraordinary talents. I decided it was time to fly! There was a twenty-foot-tall tree in our backyard which I figured would be a perfect launch pad. Once again, stepping into the "phone booth," I emerged in my Superman suit ready to fly around for a while. I started climbing the tree and as I neared the top, about fifteen feet off the ground, I stepped on a dead, undersized limb that broke off even under the weight of my scrawny body. I came crashing down through the limbs of the tree, bounced off a fence, and landed in a bush. Miraculously unhurt, I crawled out of the bush. I was very disappointed that I had not been able to test my flying skills, but was relieved to find that I hadn't torn my Superman suit. Since I wasn't hurt, I decided not to tell my mother about the incident. She might have attempted to abort my next test flight – even worse, she might have burned my Superman suit! Think what that would have cost planet earth! Many a corporation has sadly succumbed to the charm of a new CEO who has assembled a great resume and glowing reputation as being the "perfect hatchet man" to solve the corporation's problems and lead them back to profitability. Many of these "gunslingers" quickly change the company's landscape. New (untried) ideas are promoted to levels of unreasoned reverence as the new management team is increasingly seen as the supreme problem solver. Changes occur so rapidly that it's not long before veterans of the enterprise can no longer recognize it. New divisions are acquired or started, and old ones are sold off, or simply shut down. Wholesale layoffs occur and new "friends of the boss" are hired to replace the old. At the heart of many of these intricate plans lie complicated, radical, and untried ideas. Should his new "program" not work as planned, the company may find itself in a position of no return. As promising as it all sounded, having bet the "farm" on this new leader and his fresh "vision" may prove to have been a fatally risky venture. When the Board of Directors finally realizes their error in granting such complete control to an untried person and his untried ideas, they would probably give anything just to return to their pre-hatchet-man days. Maybe they should have taken a page out of the successful politician's "playbook" that sends out "trial balloons" to gauge the public's potential reaction to decisions he's contemplating. Many corporations wisely test market an idea or product before ever investing in a full-blown commitment.

Just as it's unwise to attempt to fly out of the top of a tree in an untried Superman suit (far better than the maiden flight from the top of a footstool), it's wise to approach new ideas, unknown people, or unfamiliar things with a degree of caution. *Decide that you will never risk the farm by placing your total faith in the unproven!*

TEMPTED TO TAKE A BREAK?

This concept speaks to a decision that's almost always emotionally influenced. Such moments cry out for sound reasoning.

After spending ten years as a stockbroker, I became discouraged and disillusioned with the stock market and decided to leave the business.

In the years immediately following my career in the securities business, my attention turned to small businesses. Intrigued by a class I had taken during my MBA studies on how to own and operate a small business, I decided to look into the idea of owning my own business.

Early on, it dawned on me that glamour businesses sold at very high price-to-earnings ratios. In other words, you were paying a premium for the glamour. The best values were to be found in businesses that weren't glamorous. After much searching, the best value I was able to find existed in a small, specialty laundry – of all things, a diaper service!

As I contemplated becoming the owner of this very unglamorous business, I could almost hear the jokes ringing in my ears. To say the least, it was not the kind of involvement that one would announce at the country club.

Despite all my misgivings, it did make money – and I could afford to buy it. After reassurance from some friends who didn't laugh at the idea, I decided to buy the business. One comforting aspect was that all the accounting records provided for my investigation confirmed that it was a money-making enterprise.

After we closed on the purchase of the business, I learned that Joe, a very prolific guy (he had ten kids), would often have them come in and fold the laundered diapers or perform other work at the laundry for which they received no compensation! Because he didn't pay them, no salaries for the functions they performed were listed on the expense a statement he provided for my due diligence. This was the same expense statement that led to my decision to buy the business.

I was forced to put an extra person or two on the payroll to make up for this unexpected labor need. There was also a need for an office manager since Joe's wife had performed that duty while Joe filled the slot of "washman" and part-time route driver. I decided to take on the role of office manager and hire someone to fill the position of washman – another key position for which no expense had appeared on Joe's expense statement.

Because of its link to the accounting system, the job of the washman was a very important position To know how much to bill each customer, you had to *hand count* each bag of dirty diapers received from the clients, *diaper by diaper.* As you might imagine, it turned out to be a very difficult job to fill! Once the requirements of the position were described to a prospective washman, he (for some reason) lost interest. Fortunately, I eventually found someone willing to take on this role.

One afternoon as I was about to leave for the day, the new washman didn't show up for work. Since all the washing was done at night, I had to find someone to do the job…that night! If the diapers were not washed that same night, the delivery could not go out the next day. Even when the delivery driver was just a little late, the telephones would ring off the wall. If an entire delivery was missed, I'd likely suffer the loss of a sizeable percentage of my clients, or worse, it could put me out of business. To my extreme disappointment, I couldn't find a replacement washman for that night. I realized I was it!

I turned on the washers and started counting. The hours went by about as slowly as any ever have. To "entertain" myself, I decided to figure out (in my head) how much profit my little business was making. Since I couldn't take the time away from the machines to use a pencil and paper, it took quite a while, figuring in my head, for me to arrive at the bottom-line results. But when I finally did, I was devastated. I wasn't making *any* money! How could I have misjudged this situation so totally?

After a few moments of reflection, I realized that it wouldn't take a CPA to identify the source of my problems. The strain of the additional salaries rather snuck up on me. But it was obvious that I now needed to cover the additional expenses that resulted from the loss of Joe's family's services. It was apparent that the business couldn't operate without these employees, and at that moment, I couldn't see any way to pay for them and remain profitable. I felt that I was doomed!

For the first time, I noticed that the birds were chirping outside. I looked at the clock. It was five a.m., but I still had three or four hours of washing yet to do. I was exhausted and discouraged. The "revelation" of my unprofitable status only added to my incredible fatigue. I didn't know what to do. I only knew that I didn't want to continue doing what I was doing. I couldn't recall a time when I had wanted to walk away from a situation more than I did from that one!

I just wanted to turn off the lights and the machines, go home and crawl into bed. I just stood there, wanting to cry.

If the business was going to fail, why worry about the wash or the routes? The urge to just walk away was enormous. Nevertheless, I realized to take a break at that moment and walking away would likely close the door on any hope of a solution. I had not finished the wash. If I took a break then, some routes would not receive their deliveries. To irresponsibly pick this particular time to indulge my needs might irreparably damage the business. In just a few hours, the phone would start to ring with complaining mothers on the line worried about their delivery. Things would begin to pile up at the plant with increased pressure on the whole operation being the result. I realized that choosing this particular moment to take off for my much-needed break would be to stage my return for a time that would make the current mess look like a picnic! If there was any hope for a recovery, taking a break now would probably end that hope. It was the worst thing I could do.

Let's face it, things happen! And, some events are so upsetting that all you can think about is getting away from it all for a while. It's in times like these that you are most vulnerable to making a poor decision. *Be very careful in picking the time to take a break.*

Walking away at the peak of difficulties is usually the worst time to take a break. When you finally do come back, you may be returning to an even bigger mess than the one you just left!

It is then that you will wish that you hadn't left the situation for later. It is just this kind of predicament that leads to a break that becomes permanent. (Taking a semester off marks the end of a college degree for many students.)

At such times, you need to remind yourself that all pursuits, goals, and dreams encounter "bumps in the road." You can't treat yourself to a break every time a challenge presents itself. Allow this principle to serve as your encouragement to avoid rash actions that you will almost certainly regret later. Best to *tough it out!*

Fortunately, I reluctantly decided to stay, tough it out, and finish the wash. That decision was one of the best I made at the diaper service.

Decide that you will wait until the hard part is behind you before you ever consider taking a break. Take your break when the situation you'll return to is something you know you can handle – something you may even look forward to.

NOT DECIDING IS TO DECIDE

A **gory example, but it makes the point.**
In today's gory movies that are filled with sex and violence, I remember one particularly unsavory scene from the film *Mad Max* starring Mel Gibson. The hero (Mel) has subdued the villain and handcuffed his ankle to a time bomb. He hands the scoundrel a hacksaw and sets the timer for ten minutes. He then tells the man that it'll take ten minutes to cut off the handcuffs, but only five minutes to saw off his foot.

The villain is left with that "painful" choice of losing his life or his foot. He has no time to set up a pro/con balance sheet – nor can he waste *any time* procrastinating. He's either got to start sawing (immediately!) or he can sit back and try to "relax." In the latter scenario, that might be rather hard to do since he knows he's not going to enjoy the bang he'll get out of that decision.

Distasteful as this story is, few could better serve as an illustration of a decision that must be made immediately. You are being *forced* to choose between two clearly defined alternatives. If you choose to act, you must do so before the "door of opportunity" closes. But it's also important for you to understand that there are consequences to be faced for not deciding at all.

Granted, few will ever face a decision between two such horrific choices. Nevertheless, the most difficult decisions will usually involve the challenge of accepting a choice between the lesser of two evils – like the mischievous kid having to choose between two distasteful punishments.

When time is really short, good decisions are difficult to make. You have no time to waste weighing the benefits versus the sacrifices or risks. The true issue here is whether you'd rather make no choice and thus allowing your indecision to make the choice for you, or whether you'd prefer to remain in control and retain the power to choose. The point is to make you aware that *by not choosing, you are choosing!*

The idea that "not to choose is to choose" applies equally to decisions that are not burdened by pressures of urgency. Despite the absence of time pressures, most decisions do have some sort of time frame within which a decision must be made. This can apply to matters as simple and relatively unimportant as events that have ticketing deadlines; or it can apply to much more serious matters such as tax protest deadlines, enrollment deadlines, investment decisions, personal issues, etc.

When the time does allow, be sure to gather facts, weigh the pros and cons, and anticipate outcomes. When time is short, do as much fact-gathering as possible, then make a tentative decision. Sleep on it and allow your awakening impressions to help you make your decision. The insights provided by your subconscious will often prove to be more valuable than hours of agonizing analysis.

The fear of making a mistake often causes people to put off making a decision. Don't get into the habit of sidestepping decisions. The more decisions you elude, the easier it becomes to dodge the next one.

To avoid making a mistake, you may elect not to make a decision.

But in not making a decision you are *making* a decision. While you may make some mistakes, always a*void the non decisions.*

MAKE A DECISION.

BUY TIME!

There are times when a decision you're comfortable with cannot be reached in the time allotted.

Unfortunately, many assume that they are bound by a timeline within which a decision must be made. They go ahead and make a decision, often not the quality of the decision they might have made if they had the benefit of more time. Unfortunately, there are times when there are no other alternatives. If the deadline can't be extended, they are better off making a decision rather than not. This was the essence of the principle presented in "Not Deciding Is To Decide."

However, there are great merits in trying to buy a little extra time when you are being pressed to decide on an issue wherein many unanswered questions remain.

Sometimes buying time refers to that situation where the solution you've determined to be the best needs more time to be implemented. Such was the case during my dark days at the diaper laundry. I needed to figure out a way to buy the time necessary to research a viable solution. A principle introduced earlier, Tempted To Take A Break, summarized my experiences at the diaper laundry. After that bad night (the night when I first realized I wasn't making any money) I went over the figures many times and continued to come to the same conclusion. As things were then structured, *I wasn't ever going to make any money!* Worse, I couldn't see any solution.

As I was sitting at my desk agonizing over my situation, I happened to notice that day's stack of mail. On top, was a copy of the month's National Association of Diaper Services newsletter. As I looked through it, I noticed an article that described the business success of Ernest Parks, the owner of the nation's most profitable diaper laundry.

After reading the article, I was determined to meet Mr. Parks and see what advice he might offer me. However, with all the various roles I was trying to fulfill at the laundry, there wasn't any way I could leave the laundry long enough to take a trip to Atlanta, the location of Mr. Parks' business. I decided to buy some time by hiring a woman who would assume my responsibilities at the business. In the financial position I was in, it was a somewhat risky undertaking since I would undergo the expense of the trip plus the cost of her salary for what was a shot in the dark. Buying time in this way would increase my losses if my visit with Mr. Parks proved unproductive, but my alternate decision would be to shut the business down. This was a risk I knew I had to take!

Fortunately, the trip paid off handsomely. He advised me to reduce my deliveries to once per week from my current program of two deliveries per week. This resulted in huge savings in the area of my delivery expenses. But that change would require twice as many diapers. I had to find a way to afford to double my inventory (which was one of the reasons I had never considered that option before). But Mr. Parks wasn't daunted. He called the manufacturer (he was probably their best customer) and convinced them to ship the extra diapers I needed on credit terms. It saved my business!

A year later, I sold the business for 67 percent more than I originally paid for it.

Whenever a problem surfaces for which the only solutions that immediately come to mind make you uncomfortable, *buy some time!*

But, don't make a practice of buying time just to delay making a decision you know you'll have to make. Buying Time is to be used when you're convinced that the availability of more time will result in a more acceptable solution to your problem than the one that now exists. Under such circumstances, buying time is not procrastination, nor is it deciding not to decide.

II. INSIGHTFUL DECISION MAKING

New ways of looking at things can often bring surprising results.
When all the "big solutions" have been tried with no resulting success, many won't continue to persevere. The few, small steps that could be taken are frequently discarded because they're viewed as having little chance of contributing to an answer.

However, the promise of many solutions lies in how their viewed. A small twist in the interpretation of their application may introduce a solution that works. Even partial solutions can start the process of recovery. Moreover, the accumulation of a series of small solutions can often prove sufficient to resolve a really big problem. If you are willing to keep trying, these "unlikely" solutions," might just start to turn things around.

First, Seek A Small Victory promises that a disproportionate boost is often realized from having achieved minor success. Reassess Your Resources advises you to look more closely at the available assets you may have previously dismissed or overlooked. The value of Backward Steps Can Produce Progress is the suggestion that an existing disaster be stripped back to a sound base rather than pouring good money (and effort) after bad in trying to make that mess work.

An infrequently considered aspect of decision-making, Filter Your Decisions, points out the all-important need to run from any temptation to yield to decisions that might involve a compromise of your principles or somehow lead to the damage of your reputation.

Decisions Don't Exist In Isolation reminds you of the need to look ahead to avoid unwanted "peripheral" consequences of the decision you are about to make.

An Unusual Crystal Ball and Jump The Fence each contribute unique insights into the likely conclusion of events currently in process.

SEEK A SMALL VICTORY

Because people in need of a solution to a big problem are usually looking for a big solution, this principle may be initially overlooked.

There was a time in my life when I played a lot of golf. Late spring, summer, and early fall were times filled with numerous opportunities to test your skill against other golfers in tournaments that occurred around the state where I lived.

My favorite, and probably everyone's favorite, was the Broadmoor Invitational held every July at the Broadmoor Hotel in Colorado Springs, Colorado. Everything about the weeklong event was great. The hotel was a magical place, as was the area around it. There was so much to do and see. Many of those invited were out-of-state people who arranged their summer travel plans around this event. There was always that good feeling of reuniting with old friends. For others, it was those things, but of greater importance to them was the tournament itself. Because it was rated as one of the half-dozen biggest amateur golf events in the country, it drew some of the great names in amateur golf.

The thirty-two players with the lowest scores in the eighteen-hole qualifying round made up the championship flight. Five days of matches determined the tournament champion. One's first-round opponent was determined by a formula that used their qualifying score as a method of ranking the players. My first-round opponent, Jim, was a highly regarded amateur from Kansas. As I write this, he has become a well-respected instructor to the pros on the PGA tour.

On the day of our match, I wasn't playing poorly, but I wasn't playing great either. Because of a few errors on my part, as well as some good play on Jim's part, I found myself standing on the fifteenth tee three holes down with only four holes left to play. To have any chance at victory, I realized I could only afford to tie one hole while winning each of the other three holes. As improbable as that was, it would only gain me a tie that would force the match into extra holes. To be sure, it presented a problem that seemed almost insurmountable. But I couldn't be thinking like that and have any hope of winning.

I remember standing on that fifteenth tee thinking, "Something needs to happen…*quick!*" There were few solutions available: Jim screws up and bogeys three of the last four holes, I make at least three birdies on the last four holes, or some combination thereof. Since Jim had played well all day, I'd be kidding myself to count on him to start making mistakes now. Victory, if there was to be one, was up to me. What stood in the way of that victory, however, was an enormous challenge.

I decided to break the problem into smaller parts and seek a small victory by narrowing my focus to just making a birdie on the fifteenth hole – something I had done before, so…why not now? I thought to myself, "If I can birdie this hole, my confidence would get a real shot in the arm. It might also create a little concern in Jim's mind about the certainty of his victory. I had to birdie that hole." *This would be my small victory.*

Given the difficulty of the fifteenth hole, I chose to further reduce my focus by concentrating on each shot. As I pictured each shot properly executed, rather than feeling fear, I somehow found myself feeling positive.

Believe it or not, I birdied that fifteenth hole! But, despite my good fortune, my problems were far from over. I still couldn't allow myself to think about the uphill battle that yet faced me. As we stood on the tee of this par three sixteenth hole, I had earned the honor to hit first under my birdie on the previous hole. As I prepared to hit my tee shot, I once again shifted my total focus to just hitting it close to the flagstick. I had to *believe* that I *would* get it close. With my confidence beginning to flow, I hit the iron shot to within three feet of the hole! Witnessing that shot may have had some effect on Jim's tee shot, which ended twenty feet from the hole. He missed his birdie try, but I made my three-foot birdie putt! I was now only one hole down, and I could smell victory – could that possibility now be occurring to him?

But there were still two holes left to play and I was still one down. As I stood on the seventeenth tee, I thought I detected a change in his mood. Maybe the same circumstances that had begun to lift my spirits were now deflating Jim's. While I felt that he might not be able to muster a birdie, I was certain that he would at least par the hole. I knew I needed to make another birdie.

The seventeenth hole was a par five that was reachable in two shots if you hit a good drive. Again, I had to place this drive in a position where I could reach the green with my next shot. It ended on the right side of the fairway, the perfect place to approach the green. Jim, however, hit him in the left rough. He couldn't reach the green from the rough and had to settle for a par. I reached the green in two shots and two-putted for my birdie to square up the match!

I had continued to set small goals for myself – goals I believed I could achieve. With the accomplishment of each small goal, a minor victory was achieved and my confidence grew along with my belief in eventual success. The reverse of that psychology was working on Jim.

We tied the eighteenth with pars to send the match into extra holes. By this time, the mental advantage was mine. Having lost a lead he had held the entire match, Jim was now clearly at a disadvantage.

On the nineteenth hole, I hit my drive down the center of the fairway. But, surprisingly, Jim hit his drive into the trees to the right side of the fairway, a position from which he couldn't save his par. It was virtually Jim's first mistake in the entire round. My par on the hole beat his bogey, and I won the match! Later, I ran into Jim in the locker room. He congratulated me and said, "You were beaten, but somehow you didn't know it."

It was a very satisfying success that was the result of the accumulation of several small victories. As I mentally reviewed the last four holes of the match, I realized that each of these small victories had a disproportionately greater impact on the outcome than just hitting a good shot or even winning a hole. And so it is…small victories *can solve* major problems.

When you are down and out and there appears to be no solution to your predicament, failure looms. This may be the time to look for something capable of moving you out of the doldrums, *such as a small victory.*

Remarkably, a minor victory can boost your confidence and alter your entire attitude. Moreover, it will temporarily take your mind off the "big" problem, and possibly pave the way for a major victory by breaking the problem into smaller, more manageable pieces.

Decide that you will believe in the value of a small victory as well as in the possibility of its occurrence. Once achieved, things will begin to feel different to you. The obstacles that remain should now start to seem vulnerable to your now emboldened efforts to overcome them.

No matter how deep the hole you are in, it isn't over UNTIL you believe you are defeated and stop trying!

REASSESS YOUR RESOURCES

Ingenuity is available to everyone but it's something that's relied upon by only a few.

James Bond described himself as a "licensed troubleshooter." In light of the exploits of the person we saw in the movies, this was a rather classic understatement. His frequent life-threatening encounters made him, if nothing else, the quintessential problem solver.

The thing that made his solutions to problems so impressive and entertaining was that he often seemed to be on the short end of the balance of power. Because his enemies usually appeared to have the upper hand, the likelihood, of injury or death was ever present. To make matters worse, there was seldom anyone else around to come to his aid. Despite these serious disadvantages, he was not without certain weapons or "tools."

In the movie, *From Russia with Love*, Bond was issued some "tools" that his superiors believed Bond would find useful in his expected confrontations with Russian spies as well as the unexpected encounter with a paid killer from Specter, the international crime syndicate. These tools were tucked away in a briefcase that Bond was instructed to keep close at hand. Early on, the viewer is introduced to the briefcase and the tools inside – a tear gas canister, a rifle that comes disassembled, a sheath of gold coins, and a small dagger. They watch as Bond is given a demonstration of how one of the implements, the tear gas canister, is to be properly deployed.

This foreshadowing sets the stage for Bond's likely need for all these things. The suspense begins to build as the obvious limitations of the contents of Bond's briefcase are not lost on the audience. They understand that should Bond find himself in danger, they're probably his only defense, inadequate as they appeared to be. Greater comfort would certainly be gained if a bazooka and the marines were a part of his arsenal.

Thus begins the anxious anticipation of the events to come – in what kinds of danger will Bond find himself? How will he use this curious collection of things that are concealed inside his briefcase?

Predictably, trouble does arrive, but all ends well as the "tools" he was issued turn out to be all he needed. He was a proven master at making do with what was readily available and was never daunted by his lack of more potent weaponry. Though mere fiction, people like James Bond provide us with two valuable insights into decision-making and problem-solving.

First, many problems go unsolved because the problem seems too big. Feeling overwhelmed by the immensity of the problem and the seeming hopelessness of the situation, their brains shut down. All too often, no serious attempt at solving the problem is ever made.

Second, we often *overlook the potential solutions* we do have because the implementation of the solution seems impotent. We heavily discount whatever assets are at hand as being capable of providing a solution. By failing to appreciate their value, we refuse to consider their use, never bothering to even open the briefcase or lift the lid of the toolbox. When we discount the usefulness of our assets, we also abandon any hope of solving the problem. Those who have encountered seemingly unsolvable problems but, refused to give up, decided to find a solution by making use of the available asses. Success was the frequent reward.

There are inspiring examples that fortify this principle. When I was just a boy, I knew a man who was in the lawn sprinkler business. He faced crippling financial losses because his huge inventory of metal pipe had been rendered obsolete by the introduction of plastic pipe. Never one to be easily disheartened, he recouped his investment and also realized a nice profit by selling the *playground equipment* that he made out of his metal pipe!

Another man was traveling along a very deserted back road and came to an open gate that accessed a large ranch property. He drove through the open gate only to find that same gate closed upon his return. To his horror, it was not only closed but had been secured with a very thick wire, the ends of which had been twisted together. He had no tools and the wire wouldn't yield to his efforts to untwist it with his bare hands. In true James Bond fashion, he found two flat rocks and placed one on each side of the twisted wire. Holding them together with his hands he was easily able to untwist the wire and open the gate to freedom. Each of these two men solved their problems by making use of the only resources available to them.

This approach won't solve every problem you encounter, but you need to adopt the attitude of the batter who unfailingly tries to outrun the ground ball that seems like a sure out. Sometimes he's the beneficiary of an error on the part of an overconfident outfielder!

Because you've now been introduced to an overlooked tool chest filled with unexploited resources (things readily available to you), you will be rewarded with a greater number of answers to problems that, up to now, have thwarted your efforts to find a solution.

As your ingenuity improves, it will be frustrating to look back and recall all the problems you could have solved had you thought about reassessing your resources.

This isn't about finding answers to problems where implements for a solution exist – it's about problems for which all means of a solution seem to be lacking. This concept urges you to look more creatively at the assets that *are* **at your disposal.**

However insufficient or insignificant your available tools of the solution may seem, *you must decide that everything necessary to solve your problem is already available.*

Eventually, you will increasingly believe in the value of this concept as you watch your expanded imagination solve problems and meet needs that, formerly, would have caused you to walk away in despair. One day, when you're in a bind, you may even find yourself looking forward to an opportunity to test your newfound skills of ingenuity!

BACKWARD STEPS CAN PRODUCE PROGRESS

It may seem illogical, but you may be surprised by the results.

How do you decide which course of action to take when you find yourself needing to readdress an issue you thought you'd already resolved? It's that uncomfortable position of knowing you've failed to do things "right" the first time and now need to take a step backward before any forward progress can resume. But maybe you've already committed more (financially and otherwise) than you had intended. Do you continue to try to make the mess you've created work? Or do you feel it's best just to give up and walk away? Before you do either of those things, why not consider an investment in a backward step?

I have experienced several painful, flawed beginnings – times when I was facing a situation that didn't go as planned. These were the moments when I was forced to consider some unpleasant options. For me, one of those came at a crucial time in the beginning stages of an important project – the building of my own home.

For many years, I had wanted to build a very special house in the mountains. After the plans were complete and the decision was made to begin, I spent months gathering old beams and timbers from demolished warehouses for use as the exposed, structural elements of the house.

After the completion of the excavation and foundation work, the framing (using those old beams) began. The garage was the first area to be tackled, and it seemed to be relatively free of any complexities. Assuming there would be few questions or problems, we left the carpenters with the plan and departed for a two-week vacation. When we returned, the garage ceiling had been framed using a variety of different-sized beams taken from the enormous inventory of old timbers we had sitting around the lot. Thinking they would all be covered up with sheetrock from the underside, the carpenters just used whatever beams were most handy.

Something did not seem right to me about what was happening. I felt that I had not presented a clear enough picture of the look I wanted. I spent the rest of that day and much of the night wondering what to do next. I finally realized that the look I wanted was a stillborn dream given the beginning I had just witnessed.

The next day, I arrived at the job site and asked them to tear out what they had taken two weeks to build during my ill-timed absence. I told them I would pay them for both the tear-out and the rebuild. I explained that I wanted the beams, which were to provide the support for a bedroom above, to all be of the same size and to extend two feet beyond the outside wall to achieve an old-world look to that façade of the building. Rather than expressing anger or resentment, the carpenters' (these were true carpenters, not framers) the whole attitude toward the project changed. From that day forward, our old beams and timbers were to play a major role in the look of the finished home since our plan featured all open-beam ceilings.

That process was, to begin with, a careful examination of each beam to properly inventory them. The carpenters also numbered, marked, and identified each beam as to where it would be used.

A new mood, a striving for excellence, permeated their approach to their work and the look of this house. Furthermore, they decided that rather than butt-end the beams against each other, they would notch all of the beams at their connection points to create evidence of the craftsmanship that none of us would have thought worth doing had we not taken that first backward step.

Since that time, my other projects have benefitted from my attempts to "get it right" the first time. Nevertheless, for an endless variety of reasons, mistakes do occur. But the knowledge gained from my experience in constructing our house has led me to *never* hesitate to tear out that which has been incorrectly built or rewrite the report that fails to measure up. Nonetheless, you will sometimes be called upon to stomach seemingly wasted effort as the dictates of excellence demand a backward step is taken, but it's just the price you'll sometimes pay to achieve excellence. As painful as that has often been, it was a rare occasion when I've ever regretted taking that step. I sincerely believe that if it's worth doing, it's worth doing right!

However, doing something right doesn't always mean that it has to be done with excellence. Not all pursuits are worth the time and cost that excellence demands. These would be tasks the mere completion of which is all that's required (the letter will still get delivered even if the stamp is placed askew on the envelope). The road to excellence is never an easy one to walk; don't put yourself through that hardship when it's not called for.

Nevertheless, the road herein described is the *only* one to follow when you are striving to achieve something really important to you, something that only a conclusion of excellence will prove completely satisfying.

Until a project is finished, mistakes can, and often do occur. Left unattended, they can easily torpedo your pursuit of quality. Worse, the impact of mistakes tends to compound and, in the process, often endanger the success of the entire project.

For all undertakings that are important to you, seriously consider taking a backward step to correct those mistakes before they infect the whole project, even if that means dismantling all that you've done. Whenever the current status offends the excellence you had hoped to achieve, start the corrections before you've had time to change your mind.

If the project was worth undertaking in the first place, then the backward step, *when required*, will be worth its cost in time and money. Think of it as a step toward forward progress.

FILTER YOUR DECISIONS

You may get away with neglecting, even mistreating, some things. But the subject of this principle isn't one of them!

During the first summer of my marriage to Janet, we decided to take a family vacation in Mexico. It was to be the first trip out of the country for her three daughters.

We were all very excited about the upcoming adventure and bought a car to take on the trip. This would enable us to enjoy the scenery on the way down as well as have transportation once we got there. Our journey down took us through Tucson where we stayed one night in a beautiful hotel that had a big pool. Our first night in Mexico was in the old town of Alamos – a quaint, fascinating place of old but restored haciendas.

In the middle of the fourth day, we arrived in Puerto Vallarta and pulled into the garage of the villa I had owned for several years. We stayed for a month and had a great time.

When it was finally time to return home, we decided to go in a different direction and experience some new scenery. This time we chose a route that would take us up through the middle of the country. We stayed one night in Zacatecas at a beautiful hotel that had been fashioned from an old bull ring. We left Zacatecas the next morning. Soon, we started getting into some very isolated areas. The formerly vegetated landscape turned into desert and towns turned into villages which became increasingly smaller and ever more removed from one another.

Noticing these changes, I began to think about the gas gauge. When I saw it drop to half of a tank, I began keeping an eye out for a gas station. We finally came upon a sign that announced a gas station seventy kilometers ahead. That seemed acceptable since seventy kilometers was only forty-two miles and represented less than two gallons of gas. Our half tank should provide more than enough fuel to get us to that station. I continued to push on.

As I watched the odometer, I noticed that we were close to having driven the seventy kilometers from the place where we saw the sign announcing the next gas station – but no gas station. We drove for another thirty minutes, *well past* the seventy-kilometer mark but still no gas station! I wasn't sure what to do. I knew there wasn't a station behind us within the range of our now exhausted gas supply. But I didn't have any idea of how far it was to the next station ahead – if there ever was one! I kept telling myself that there must be another station – but how much further was it? It seemed that we didn't have any other option but to drive on. All the while, I watched the gas gauge needle continue to drop. As far ahead as I could see, there was no sign of a station or, for that matter, any signs of life.

I began to get this awful feeling. What if we run out? What will I do then? It's just me and four women. Do I dare leave them and go for gas alone, or do I take them all with me and leave the car? I couldn't imagine a choice I'd feel good about, nor could imagine a good outcome! What a mess. I was feeling stupid, guilty, and very nervous!

It wasn't long after those thoughts that I noticed the gas warning light come on! Out of the corner of my eye, I saw my wife staring at it too. Not wanting to alert the girls as to the trouble we were in, neither of us said a word. What a sickening feeling!

We drove another ten miles when suddenly we came upon a house. Its front door was standing wide open which enabled me to see some tables and chairs inside. It was one of those roadside homes/restaurants that one frequently sees in small Mexican villages. I'd never felt so relieved! I went inside and asked if they might have some gas. The guy motioned for me to come around to the back of the building. There, sitting in the shade, was a big forty-gallon oil drum. He took the lid off and there was something in there that looked like dark ale. I asked him if it was gas and he said, "Si, Si." What if it wasn't and the engine became gummed up or something? But then, what choice did we have?

He put a plastic tube into the vat, sucked some "gas" to his lips creating a siphon, and proceeded to fill a five-gallon bucket with the "gas." He went around to our car and pulled out a gauze-like screen and placed it over the mouth of the pipe that led to our gas tank. It was soon apparent why he used that filter. When he had emptied the five-gallon bucket into our gas tank, the disgusting crud that covered that filter was enough to turn your stomach. We were so relieved when the car started and continued to run. Though it was getting dark, we headed straight for the U.S. border and McDonald's for dinner. In the darkness, our drive through the deserted wasteland of northern Mexico prompted us to appreciate the safety of our car and reflect on the miracle of the existence of that little store, in the middle of nowhere.

After dinner, we continued our journey. Soon, silence fell within the car. My thoughts about our earlier adventure continued to occupy my mind. I began to realize that once we had settled into the safety of that little house/restaurant, running out of gas would still have represented an inconvenience but no longer much of a threat. But the store owner's conscientious filter of the gas was another matter. His unfiltered gas could have caused us far greater problems than running out of fuel. We might have driven ways down the road only to have the car succumb to his crud-contaminated gas. What would we have done with a car whose engine no longer worked, stranded on a very lonely highway… in the dark? We would have been in *really big trouble.*

In pondering this "filter thing," it occurred to me that filters were very important in a variety of uses, some that are not mechanical–like our minds! Engines aren't the most valuable things that can be harmed by the lack of a filter.

In the world we live in today, there is a great need for mental filters – one that will screen our decisions and reject any immoral or unethical elements that would influence a pending choice or our thinking in general. The character-altering attitudes brought about by exposure to moral and ethical poisons can compromise our reasoning, and thus the quality of our decisions. Just as crud contaminates the gas and fouls the engine, contaminated thoughts can alter our speech and actions. The stain of unethical or immoral conduct can contaminate our reputation and foul up our life.

Begin building character by ruling out *any decision* that involves a relaxation of worthy moral or ethical standards. Don't ever compromise those standards or in any manner "grease the way" to arrive at a conclusion you *know* is wrong. Any decision that calls for such a concession is a bad one! This can be avoided by screening all your choices through a moral and ethical filter.

Building a character of quality and depth is not easy to do, but it is worth the effort and sacrifices that may be involved. You will be greatly rewarded by the good feelings you'll have about yourself and the respect you'll gain from others.

By faithfully adhering to this principle, one day you'll have constructed a monument to your character – a reputation that all can see – *one that can't be bought.*

DECISIONS DON'T EXIST IN ISOLATION

We often fail to realize the full consequence of pulling out that bottom domino from the tall stack of dominos.

In the early '80s, I purchased a drywall company. It was the largest in the Rocky Mountain region with 300 plus employees. The former owner, Don, was friends with all the big builders and virtually all of them were clients of the drywall company. Don had created a simple operating system that took the guesswork out of the picture. Each separate operation was priced by the sheet of drywall. All we had to do was accurately count the sheets of drywall that would be needed to complete any given house and we would be guaranteed the gross profit margin. The only way for us to get in trouble was to suffer a downturn in the economy which might cause our volume to drop to a point where our normal profit margin on that reduced volume wouldn't yield enough to cover our overhead.

Unfortunately, a recession that began a year and a half after I bought the business started to affect our volume. If our volume continued to shrink, we would be facing losses unless we could quickly cut our overhead or find some way to rebuild that volume.

As a way to boost our volume, we decided to enter the arena of commercial work (offices and retail structures versus housing). This was an arena that had always been the domain of union contractors. However, we felt we had one big advantage over union contractors: we were a nonunion shop and thus not bound by the exorbitant benefits packages and high wages being paid to union workers. Fortunately, all our workers were paid on a piecemeal basis (a by-the-sheet compensation arrangement) wherein they could virtually write their paycheck depending on how hard they wanted to work. As a result of our payment policy, we never experienced any discontent from our workers.

We bid on a large hotel complex and were awarded the job. Things went smoothly for a while. But, one day the IRS contacted us saying they were going to audit our company's tax returns and needed all relevant information for the three most recent years of operation.

We weren't very far into that audit process when another company I owned also received notice from the IRS that it was going to be audited for the three most recent years of its operations. Not long after that, we were contacted by the labor department as well as their wage and hour division. They wanted to review our pay practices.

All of these government investigations forced us to hire attorneys to represent us in defense against these threats.

I wasn't very worried about the wage and hour people since, to the best of my knowledge, we didn't have any disgruntled employees. Our employees were their bosses and could work as many or as few hours as they wanted. Because we didn't compensate our employees on a per-hour basis, there was no increased pay for overtime work. All the employees knew that.

Irrespective of the compensation agreement we had made with our employees, the wage and hour people decided to make an issue of our nonpayment of overtime pay rates for all hours worked beyond eight hours per day. The government wasn't successful in finding any complaints from the existing employees regarding our treatment of this overtime issue. To make their case against us, they sought former employees and urged them to file a complaint against us suggesting they might receive back pay for the overtime hours they had worked.

As if all this wasn't trouble enough, I received another notice from the IRS saying that they were going to audit my income tax returns going back three years.

It took two years to finally complete all the tax audits and conclude the wage and hour department investigations. We were only fined $5,000 by the wage and hour department for our "supposed" abuses of the overtime pay-rate rules. We were not charged any additional income taxes as a result of any of the audits conducted by the IRS. However, we did receive a bill from our attorneys for $250,000!

One day, Don (the former owner of the drywall company), received a call from an old friend of his. This friend had just left his position with the Colorado Justice Department. The friend told Don that he had not called Don before because of his obvious conflicting connections with the Justice Department. Now that he had severed his ties there he called Don to show him copies of all the records the Justice Department had on my drywall company saying, "I thought you'd be interested in seeing this."

He produced a large stack of documents relative to the company with a "sticky note" attached to the top sheet. The "sticky note" had a message written on its top half saying, "Sorry, but we can't get anything on these people." The recipient of the note answered that message on the bottom half of that same "sticky note" with the words, "Aw, shucks." That response had been written and signed by the United States senator from the State of Colorado! I know this to be true because I saw the stack of documents as well as the two messages on that "sticky note."

The events of the previous two years were now all making sense. It's dismaying to realize the government has this kind of power and chooses to use it in this way. Our decision to enter the commercial arena was not an isolated decision. *There were consequences* to our decision. Little did we know how severe they would be.

Few decisions stand in isolation. After making one decision, you may soon find yourself needing to make another just to answer the unanticipated consequences brought about by your first decision. Seek to minimize those consequences by attempting to foresee these "aftershocks" before they hit you like an avalanche.

Before making any important decision, ask yourself this question: "Given the possible consequences I can reasonably anticipate, would a few *unanticipated* consequences cause me to rethink things and possibly decide differently?"

AN UNUSUAL CRYSTAL BALL

Unlike crystal balls, this concept makes sense. After you've tested it, you may forever dispense with all other forecasting devices.

There seems to be no end to funny golf stories. It's a game that brings out all the extremes of emotion, both good and bad, stripping bare our character for all to see. One particularly funny, *and true*, story is worth retelling. The unbelievable bit of theatrics happened on the eighteenth tee of a prestigious country club. The focus of this story was a very colorful man named Sid, who was playing as the guest of one of the members. It seems that Sid was rumored to have made some of his money defrauding people with phony investment schemes. His "walking around money" was usually supplied by suckers who foolishly gambled with him on the golf course. Sid consistently won because he had a phony handicap.

This was a big money game with all the bets riding on the last hole. When it was Sid's turn to hit his tee shot on this par five hole, he stood over the ball facing a carry of more than two hundred yards over a lake to reach the fairway. His first drive didn't make it! He slammed his club into the ground and kicked his golf bag. After somewhat composing himself, he reached into his bag for another ball. It also went into the lake! This time he threw his driver into the lake! Still fuming, he picked up his whole bag and threw it into the lake, clubs and all! About this time, his caddy couldn't control himself any longer and roared with laughter. That did it! Sid ran over, picked up the kid, and threw him into the lake!

Anyone experienced with the gut-wrenching emotions of golf would quickly understand Sid's feelings. More particularly, anyone who was acquainted with Sid (his temper widely documented) would have been able to predict the eruption of fireworks that would naturally follow these misfortunes. Even without knowing Sid, the sequence of events just witnessed would have told almost anyone of the inadvisability of laughing at the enactment of Sid's final frustration. The caddy *should have been able to predict* Sid's response to his laughter and muffled it!

Observing and analyzing a series of events and their logical consequences will find usefulness in any number of areas of life. You will often find that it can provide a fairly reliable prediction of coming events. This concept posits the predictability of the outcome of a series of related events once the beginning event has occurred. Each ensuing event will measurably add to the accuracy of your expectations. To help you better understand this principle, consider the workings of a conveyor belt. Many manufacturing plants utilize conveyor belts to eliminate the need to hand-carry objects involved in the manufacturing process from one workstation to the next. When the process is complete, the finished item falls off the end of the belt into the "bucket" where it is inspected, packaged, and shipped. As an item reaches the end of the belt, the next forward movement of the belt drops that item into the bucket. The item that was next in line has now moved to the end of the belt as all other items on the belt have each moved one notch closer to the end. Once in the bucket, the process for that item has ended.

The principle of the conveyor belt becomes a means to better decision-making by helping you anticipate the events that are yet to happen, by closely observing those that have already occurred. When things are many steps away from the "end of the belt," time remains to allow you to sidestep the progression of the sequence and thus avoid the anticipated, but undesired, outcome. You will increasingly gain insights as to the conclusion of such a sequence. Obviously, the nearer you are to the "end of the belt," the more apparent the outcome and the fewer time and options you have to alter your situation. Continuing with the analogy, once that "something" has dropped into the bucket, no further options remain.

In actuality, like railroad tracks, we are all being carried along on two separate conveyor belts. The first (we'll call the macro) is one that everyone travels. It represents your position as a nameless member of society, traveling along a conveyor belt that's involved with issues on a grand scale – government policy, the economy, war, natural disasters, etc. These are all things over which you have little, or no control. But, your lack of control doesn't mean that there's no value in what can be understood from that first belt's movements. The second belt, or the micro belt, is the one that speaks to the sequence of events peculiar to your personal life. The information gleaned from this belt, in combination with the insights from the first conveyor belt, provides a valuable understanding of the probable course of future events by supplying information that has become useful for successful decision-making.

Your ability to understand the portent behind the movements of these two belts should result in a level of sagacity uncommon to most people. Should the coming sequence of events now being revealed to you by movements on either of these belts pose unacceptable threats, you must decide to do whatever is necessary to protect yourself from the coming events you've foreseen. At all costs, avoid the continued forward movement of the belt while you are still on it! Somehow, you've got to get off that belt! This is particularly true when that belt is about to crank forward for that last, fatal time – that time when "things" drop into the bucket and the "game" is over! The movie, *The Sound of Music,* addressed this very concept. The Von Trapp family made a tough decision to get off the belt while the time to do so remained.

The conveyor belt principle should prove to be quite valuable in assisting you in understanding the relationship of various events and their meaning in terms of their likelihood of impacting future happenings.

Pay close attention to the sequences unfolding before you, then, relate them to the sequences that have already taken place. By contemplating the meanings behind all these events, you will have greatly increased your chances of determining "what's next."

These steps provide the foundation for arriving at a sound plan of action that's capable of making a reasonable assessment of the likely path and progression of future happenings.

This principle will not only help give meaning to the events you've been monitoring but will also enable you to confidently act in time to avoid the "bucket" – that place of finality where you're backed into a corner and further choices don't exist!

JUMP THE FENCE

We tend to edit our mental picture of the future to make it look the way we want it to look. In the process, we make our decisions accordingly. This often results in poor choices. There's a better way!

With some of the decisions were faced with making, the stakes are very high. When several alternate possibilities exist, deciding which to pursue can prove to be agonizingly difficult.

Such was the case for me when, several years ago, I became enamored with a quaint and beautiful beach town in southern California. Several vacations there only served to enhance my enthusiasm for the place. And, why not? It had fantastic weather, great restaurants, gorgeous scenery, magnificent homes, and beautiful beaches. On each trip there, I sampled a different golf course and dined at new restaurants.

On one trip, I spent some time looking at houses. Before I knew what was happening, the realtor had prepared a purchase contract for me to sign. I was inches from being the proud owner of a California residence. Previously, all I had been able to focus on was the weather, the scenery, and the romance of it all (and, just maybe, an escape from the pressures of life in Colorado). I thought this was what I wanted.

Before the finalization of the purchase, I suddenly had this strange feeling come over me. It was as if I had already moved there – mentally and emotionally – I had moved there. I had "jumped the fence." My focus and reality had switched from Colorado to southern California. It was as if I was no longer a Coloradoan. Suddenly, my home in Colorado seemed far away as I was now living, in my mind, as a Californian. Everything felt different! I was experiencing life as if I were now living in California has decided to buy that house and move there. I was tasting life on the other side of the "fence" without having finalized that decision.

It wasn't surprising that I began to have thoughts that had *never* entered my mind before. The first of those was an *astounding* question that I began asking myself: *What was it that I found so attractive about this place?* Given my previous romanticized version of it, what would cause me to now have such a thought? Because I had mentally "jumped the fence" from being a Coloradoan to being a Californian, I began, for the first time, to visualize what my life might feel like living there in southern California. It all seemed so real.

Before this moment, I had been unable to make a truly rational decision. Everything was so glamorized by the dream that all I could see was the fairy tale. Only when I had "jumped the fence" could I understand what my life would be like actually living there. I began to realize that no place was all good, or all bad. No matter where you live, there's more to life than just those things you'll encounter on a few brief visits. It was unfortunate that I had been unable to make this mental "jump" before I had gone so far. Sure, the place was beautiful, but it was usually too cool for patio dinners in the winter and I heard that summer mornings were often foggy. I didn't know anyone there, nor was I sure how I'd make a living. The traffic in southern California was another thing – it's notoriously bad because it's so overcrowded! This casted doubts on my choice of golf courses since the one I had picked presented a longer commute than I had planned. In short, I was now seeing it as it was – a nice place, but not perfect. Ironically, I found myself missing Colorado! I was now able to appreciate the benefits of Jumping The Fence as a decision-making tool. By mentally moving *into the reality* of the first possible decision and then to another, I was able to *"live"* the feelings that I would experience under each of my options and taste them as if I had made that decision.

My struggles over the decision to move from my home in Colorado to California were very effectively resolved by the principle of "Jump the Fence." It was that struggle that inadvertently led to the birth of this principle. I've come to realize the beauty of its wisdom. I now feel certain that it has worthwhile applications to a wide variety of decisions people routinely struggle with.

Marriage is such a decision. How do you know what lies ahead after the wedding? Excitement about the wedding and fantasies of the honeymoon capture most peoples' thoughts and attention.

The bride thinks of the beauty of the ceremony. All her friends and family will be there. She'll look the most beautiful she's ever looked. The spot picked for the wedding has been given very special attention. An expensive photographer is hired to record the whole experience and provide them with a lifetime of pleasant memories. The groom is more likely to focus on the honeymoon, a dream vacation to a romantic getaway at some expensive resort. For some couples, the joy of being married goes downhill from there.

Many victims of marriages that end in divorce admit that something didn't seem right from the beginning. What if each of the partners of the failed marriage had, before the wedding, "jumped the fence" to imagine what life together, *after the honeymoon,* might be like?

They should extend their mental journey beyond the wedding and the honeymoon to the dingy basement apartment or the back bedroom in one of their parent's homes as their new abode. With no money in the bank and bills to pay, they both need to work. Their romantic dates now being few could bring the fantasy to a screeching halt.

If their commitment can withstand the *reality* of their life together *after the honeymoon,* the odds of that marriage's success dramatically improve. It's best to attempt to imagine that life…*before* the wedding!

To successfully project yourself into the decision-already-made posture requires intense concentration. **This will enable you to envision life, as it would be, should you choose the option you're now considering. It can all be accomplished without having to make a decision. It's like a test ride or tryout with a money-back guarantee.**

"Jumping the Fence" can help provide valuable insights into a broad range of issues such as marriage, a new job, or a career change.

III. ELIMINATING WASTE

Time is an asset that's available to everyone. How you use that asset dictates the effectiveness of your efforts. To waste time is to suffer unnecessary inconveniences, unwanted difficulties, and even failures.

The incorporation of timesaving procedures, which hopefully become habits, should significantly reduce lost time and your level of aggravation in dealing with life. Fortunately, attention to methods aimed at improved efficiency and effectiveness can significantly contribute to your success.

This is not to suggest that everything you undertake must be tightly controlled by a concern for the efficiency of your thoughts and movements. Many occasions call for just taking time to enjoy the specialness and beauties of the moment by stopping to smell the roses. But when a task doesn't offer many prospects for enjoying the process, getting it done in the most efficient manner possible is the way to go.

Ever-growing technological advances make most hand-performed recordkeeping obsolete and have thus removed some of the burden presented by former meticulous bookkeeping and organizational systems.

What has not been removed, however, is the waste and inefficiency caused by occasions when the technology can't help you – times when you're out of touch with your computer – like laying in bed. As wonderful as it is, technology has not made us completely immune to the aggravating habit of forgetting things: important ideas, instructions, appointments, etc. Or maybe you are guilty of frequently misplacing things – a great contributor to the loss of valuable time.

First Things First, Misplaced Items Waste Time And Cost Money, and A Costly Memory Lapse may prove surprisingly helpful as they will save you time and reduce waste. Which, in turn, equates to saving money.

FIRST THINGS FIRST

You are about to read a story that describes a lose, lose way to celebrate a victory!

Roy, and his two partners, owned a business that they had all agreed to sell. They had a buyer for their business, a publicly owned investment trust. All parties to the transaction had agreed to a formula that would determine the price to be paid for the business based on an earnings report submitted by the sellers. The only thing that stood in the way of the final closing (and cash-in-hand) was the seller's submission of their business's most recent profit statement. Roy and his partners had high hopes that the profits would be sufficient to justify the price they were asking. If the earnings fell below the estimates, everyone had previously agreed that either the price would be lowered or the sellers would have the option of postponing the closing in anticipation of better results in the next quarter. None of this caused Roy any concerns since the Investment Trust was committed to buying, and Roy and his partners were committed to selling.

In anticipation of the closing of the sale of his business, Roy began to make plans for his future. His first item of business was to free himself from his contentious wife. Temporarily lacking the funds from the sale of his business, he mortgaged his house to finalize his divorce settlement. He had his dream car, a sleek Porsche, all but parked in his garage. His next move involved a trip to a tropical resort to pick out a lot for his new dream home (this was my resort project and was the beginning of my friendship with Roy). Before it was time to return home, he had placed a deposit on a lot and had looked at some boats. He had met a wonderful woman with whom he had discussed a life together. Everything was falling in place for Roy!

As luck would have it, however, the earnings didn't come in as hoped. To sell at this time was to realize much less for the business. Roy wanted to go ahead with the deal, but the majority partner preferred to wait for better results. So, the sale was delayed. Regrettably, future quarters' results weren't even as good as the initial profit report – the same one the majority partner had previously decided not to act upon since it couldn't justify the price they wanted for the business.

Time passed, and along came October 2008. The stock market crashed and the prospects for the sale of the business crashed with it.

A year later, the business's revenues had fallen 25 percent and the net profits had suffered even more adversely. As a result, Roy's salary was reduced which placed an almost unmanageable strain on him. Some of the things he had committed to when he thought his business was going to be sold, as well as the burden of the giant mortgage he had placed against his home, were putting him in a world of financial pain. Roy got things out of order. Granted, it looked like the sale of his business was a sure thing, but how much better it would have been had the money been in hand *first!*

While it's easy to be critical of Roy, we all get things out of order. Sometimes it's the simplest of things, like vacuuming the floor before dusting the tabletops or dusting the tabletops before removing the cobwebs from the ceiling. Sometimes it's washing the car as the storm clouds are building, or more costly when we complete a step in a construction process that will be ruined by the step we take next. And who isn't occasionally guilty of prematurely revealing the contents of their dream (plan) to someone who will play a part in that dream only to have the whole thing unravel the very next day, necessitating an awkward explanation and the embarrassment that wasn't necessary.

If you are involved in a business negotiation, many separate steps are often necessary for a successful conclusion. Putting these steps in their proper order is usually very important since getting them out of order may result in tipping your hand prematurely or having to backtrack. It might cause the loss of your opponent's respect for you. Worse yet, it may lead to a lower price than you'd hoped to receive or a higher price than you'd hoped to pay. Worst of all, the negotiations could fall apart altogether.

Most people fight the temptation to enjoy the fruits of their labor before their "ship" has come in. But while it's still out to sea, rushing the celebration of its arrival presents two problems.

First, the push necessary to cross the finish line often depends upon the incentive provided by the "carrot" that waits. To remove (or eat) that carrot prematurely is to remove the very reason, maybe the only reason, for continuing to fight the battles necessary for victory. But, even if the hoped-for success does materialize, its occurrence becomes anticlimactic when you've already jumped the gun by prematurely enjoying the prize.

Second, to treat yourself to the spoils of victory, before the fact, is to face the most unpleasant of all situations should that triumph never occur.

When things are not coming together as fast as you'd anticipated, *decide that you won't allow your impatience to cause you to get things out of order*. No matter the perceived certainty of overcoming the snags to completing the deal, this is not the time to start sampling the "expected" profits.

MISPLACED ITEMS WASTE TIME, COST MONEY

Like the TV series *Airport*, nearly everyone who frequently travels by plane has a tale or two about their mishaps at the airport. The mere telling of my story upsets me all over again!

My own "airport experience" began with a vacation splurge on a cruise up the Inland Passage of Alaska. My wife and I needed to fly to Seattle where we would board the cruise ship. We thought it would be great fun to take a very early flight the day before boarding the cruise ship and have a full day of sightseeing in Seattle.

When we arrived at the airport, because of a very early flight, the sun had yet to come up. We decided to speed things up and use the curbside check-in service. There was a line, but we decided it would be quicker than going inside. As the sun started to rise, we watched the check-in process come to a halt as the airline's employees spent twenty minutes trying to rig a canopy over their desks to keep the blinding, low-angle sun out of their eyes. Thirty or forty minutes had passed by the time we reached the counter – only to be told that they could not check us in due to the "type" of the ticket we had. Realizing we were now running very low on time, we hurried inside to the regular check-in counter. Additional precious minutes passed as we waited in the long line that had been building during the wasted period at the outside check-in counter. Once they finally checked us in, we rushed to the security clearance area.

When the document reviewer looked at our ticket, she directed us to the "special" security section (we later realized the last-minute booking of our flight was the reason our ticket had been flagged). Knowing this would delay us more, I made the mistake of politely informing them of our time crunch and asked if they would mind hurrying the process along as much as possible. That was my first mistake.

The man examining me noticeably, and deliberately, began slowing everything down – way down! I renewed my request for urgency, telling him that we were about to miss our plane. That was my second mistake. He gruffly scolded me for "ignoring" the warnings to show up one and a half hours early. I explained that we had observed that rule, but we had been held up at the curbside check-in. He told me that was not his problem. I reminded him that all I had requested was for him to go through his procedures as fast as possible. He bristled and said, "Don't tell me what to do." I then suggested that it wasn't his job to keep people from catching their flights. That was my third mistake. Not like my "attitude," he called another of his coworkers over to make sure I wouldn't cause them any trouble. The three of us started arguing, and *all TSA's efforts* to provide my security clearance ceased. We missed the plane!

When we finally arrived at the gate, the agent was refreshingly sympathetic and began searching for the next available flight to Seattle. Unfortunately, this wasn't until 2:00 p.m. With a feeling of sadness, we booked that flight. We calculated that this would not get us into Seattle in time to do any sightseeing. So, when an announcement was made that we could give up our seats on that flight for tickets on one that would leave two hours later in exchange for two vouchers for travel anywhere in the U.S., we decided to delay our departure for a second time. The agent was also nice enough to give us vouchers for a meal, albeit a fast-food one. So, we consoled ourselves with the gift of the trip vouchers and rationalized a "quiet" day at the airport.

A couple of months later, we decided to take advantage of the trip vouchers. After hours of searching for the vouchers, *we finally had to conclude that we had somehow lost them!*

Why had I treated those vouchers with such careless disregard as to have misplaced them? I should have taken the time to put them in a spot that would have related to our travels – maybe with my passport? But I didn't, and they were gone.

From that time forward, I've made a concerted effort to have a place for everything and everything in its place. As I now put things in the same location from which they came, the taxing of my memory has been greatly lessened. But more importantly, I now save a lot of time that was formerly wasted searching for misplaced items.

Studies have calculated that a surprising amount of our life is spent waiting at red lights. But most of us waste as much time searching for a misplaced item as we do waiting for those red lights to turn green. Unfortunately, there isn't much we can do about red lights. However, wasting time looking for misplaced items can be avoided. By observing this simple principle, a great deal of time will be saved and unnecessary losses can be avoided.

For things you fear misplacing, *don't trust your memory.* **When a new item is introduced into your home or office, form a habit of** *immediately* **making a place for it – even if that place is an envelope, box, or drawer where all such things go. At least, you will be able to find the item in question after just a brief search.**

After using it, put it back in that envelope, box, or drawer. If you've created a special place for something, *always* **return it to that designated location.** *A few other approaches work as well!*

A COSTLY MEMORY LAPSE

I felt my stomach tighten and my face turn pale when I realized what I had forgotten to do!

My business frequently takes me to Mexico. After several trips, I begin to slide into a routine about such things as packing, transportation to and from the airports, and immigration documentation. As a matter of great importance, I always keep my passport in my briefcase – a briefcase I never fail to take with me on each trip to Mexico. Fortunately, that simple act has always worked. I've never been turned away at the check-in counter for want of my passport.

Although my wife, Janet, doesn't always accompany me to Mexico when she does she needs a passport as well. Because we never travel separately, we decided to put her passport in my briefcase.

A business meeting in Mexico altered our normal, joint travel arrangements. I went ahead without my wife to get this meeting out of the way. She was to join me a day later.

Before leaving, I was in my car when the upcoming trip to Mexico began to occupy my thoughts. Suddenly, the subject of her passport popped into my mind. I realized that I needed to make sure to retrieve her passport from my briefcase and give it back to her for our upcoming rendezvous.

Because I was driving and didn't have anything to write on, I made a "mental" note so as not to forget about her passport. *I never thought about it again!*

She arrived at the airport and discovered she had no passport! It was still in my briefcase…in Mexico.

Why didn't I pull the car over to look for something to write on? Why didn't I do *something* to remind myself to give her the passport? Since that unfortunate experience, I have decided that I would develop the habit of acting upon thoughts like the one I had in the car by immediately doing *something* that would ensure that the item, or issue, isn't forgotten.

I've adopted the useful habit of leaving a visual reminder where I'll be sure to see it. This memory jogger can be *anything* that doesn't belong where I put it. Later, when I see this object, it instantly brings to mind whatever it was that I didn't want to forget.

When it's late at night and I'm too lazy to go up to my office and write something down, I might leave the toothpaste tube lying over my wristwatch. Or throw something, a book or magazine, on the floor that's in the path of my route into my office. The next morning, when I see the toothpaste, the magazine, or whatever, I don't wonder why it's there. This little exercise *has never failed* to remind me of the thing I was afraid of forgetting! Give it a try.

IV. EXAMINE YOUR SHORTCOMINGS

Take a look at your life. How do you think others see you? How would you describe yourself?

Your thoughts, statements, and actions define you in the eyes of others.

This may not be how you see yourself, or how you'd like them to view you.

If this concerns you, these principles should be of value.

In this section, the beginning four principles deal with character flaws you should strive to eliminate. They start by asking: Do You Twist The Truth? This principle aims at people who see nothing wrong with bending the truth to get what they want. Control Your Anger illustrates the needless costs that are often the result of losing your temper. Unbridled Greed provides an insight into the ugliness of greed and the unanticipated results that sometimes accompany it. Seeking The Easy Way Out speaks to those who habitually choose to side-step hard work. This principle promotes the value of a good work ethic and applauds the occasional need for plain old hard work.

Does your life seem to be in a state of never-ending crises? Are you guilty of constantly putting things off until later? Procrastination Causes Problems quickly exposes the ways of the procrastinator and provides reasons for changing those habits and the methods involved in doing so.

Do people sometimes dismiss you? Maybe it's because they watch you repeat the same mistakes over and over. Repeating The Same Mistake is a principle that will bring this blind spot to your attention.

When acquaintances see you coming, do they cross over to the other side of the street? If so, possibly it's because you are often perceived as a long-winded, self-focused person. The principle, Do You Bore People? should open your eyes!

Believing that you are immune to the adverse consequences that haunt everyone else's bad decisions is to deceive yourself. I'm Bulletproof addresses this and argues its potential destructiveness.

DO YOU TWIST THE TRUTH?

Can you say that you've never done anything like this?

Forgive my frequent use of stories from my childhood, but they contain the unusual value in that they so clearly reveal unmasked motives. A young child has no inhibitions about reaching for the biggest piece of cake. Adults, however, often attempt to disguise their motives. An adult might seek to mask his greed by voicing the rationalization that all the rest of the cake eaters are on diets and should only want small pieces.

Therefore, it would seem that the best way to illustrate certain of these shortcomings would be to select illustrations whose point isn't clouded by an adult's self-protective rationalizations.

Thus, another story is taken from my childhood days. This event occurred when I was about eleven years old. Our family of four lived in a two-bedroom house. I shared a bedroom with my younger brother. All things considered, he and I got along pretty well. If there ever was a problem between us, it would probably have been my fault – such as the time that I was playing with one of his toys when he was somewhere else in the house.

I don't remember what kind of a toy it was, but somehow I broke it! Before he had a chance to come back into the room, I pushed the two pieces of the toy back together. Without glue, it wouldn't hold together, but my goal wasn't to fix his toy – just to mask its condition. I even went one step further. Rather than ever taking the blame for breaking it, I decided to make it look like he had broken it. So, I cleverly balanced his pieced-together toy on the very edge of the top of the dresser. I knew that when he opened a drawer, the vibration would knock the toy off the top of the dresser. When it hit the floor, it would be certain to break into two pieces again.

When he finally reentered the room, I nervously waited for him to pull one of the drawers open. I wondered if he'd notice his toy, inappropriately sitting near the edge of the top of the dresser, and realize what I'd done. Somehow, that didn't happen. He went over to the dresser to get something out of one of the drawers. Just as I had figured, the vibration from his actions caused the toy to fall to the floor and fly into two pieces.

His response was one I could never have anticipated. He yelled, "You dirty rat!" Now, how did a kid, only seven years old, figure that out? But, figure it out, he did. He said, "You broke my toy!" My ruse wasn't as well disguised as I had thought. Naturally, I rationalized that while I had broken his toy and even schemed to allow him to think he broke it, I had never claimed not to have broken his toy. But, wait a minute, *what we're talking about here was deception. What I had done was dishonest!*

As an adult, a total about-face from the previous story taught me a huge lesson in the value of honesty. This incident occurred when I was involved in a real estate project in Mexico. My right-hand man, Oscar, was invaluable to me and so his needs were important. One day, Oscar asked if I knew anyone who might want to loan him $20,000 to finish building his house. He told me of a longstanding Mexican tradition that when a man gets married, he's supposed to provide his wife with a home. So, it was important to Oscar to get his house finished and fulfill his obligation to his new wife. I felt that he probably hoped that I would loan him the money, but I was reluctant due to do so because of the association we had, and the problems that could potentially arise if something went wrong. I decided that I would try to find someone else to make him that loan and turn the situation into an arm's length transaction. A good friend of mine said he was willing to make the loan after I told him of Oscar's character and the reason for his need. The house was finally finished and the loan was repaid.

One day, this same friend informed me that he would like to come to Mexico and see my project. He said, "By the way, while I'm down there I'd like to see Oscar's home." Right then, I knew that he probably thought that I was the true recipient of the money and believed that I had been too embarrassed to tell him that I was the one who was really in need of the loan. Since we were contemplating other business deals together, I think he wanted to see if I had been honest with him.

Fortunately, I was able, with a totally clear conscience, to tell him that Oscar would be happy to show him around his home and point out what his money had accomplished. When my friend returned from his trip, somehow I felt that a new level of friendship and trust had emerged from his experience of seeing Oscar's house and knowing that everything had been *exactly* as I had told him.

There isn't an area of life where honesty isn't of huge importance. It's important to the health and depth of a marriage, friendship, business relationship, and every other kind of relationship. Those who hold the truth in disrespect will be disappointed to learn that there will hardly be enough occasions of truthfulness to offset just one of their lies.

You need to be aware that lies take many forms. The first involves saying that you didn't when you did. Or say you did when you didn't. You have it but claim you don't. You don't have it but claim you do. These all represent untruths being told about basic facts – *they are bald-faced lies!* The second, as seen in my story about the broken toy, is an example of dishonesty by deception. A third area of dishonesty is found in half-truths, exaggerations, alterations of the truth, and the omission of important facts – all subtle forms of dishonesty employed with the intent of misleading someone to believe that which isn't true.

A clever liar makes use of true statements, cleverly crafted, to cause someone to arrive at false conclusions. The liar can throw the other person off balance by starting with a true statement but then withholds important or contradictory facts. The believability of the liar's first statement (the true one) primes the other person to believe all that follows. The liar is thus able to lead the other person to believe something that's not true.

As reprehensible as lying is, developing a reputation for honesty is not an easy thing to do. One of the surest ways to develop a reputation of honesty is to make it a habit to *never bend, distort, or alter the truth,* even when you think the other person can't check up on your story. It's funny how these stories that "can't be checked out" somehow come to light anyway. Should your audience discover the discrepancy between your story and the revealed truth, they will always wonder about the truthfulness of your future statements because you will never be able to convince anyone that the lie you told was *the only one* you've ever told.

The value of honesty can't be overestimated. Having won someone's trust is the highest form of respect. It feels so good to know that you are trusted. That trust doesn't come easily…and tragically, it can be quickly destroyed with just one lie. Once an instance of your untruthfulness surfaces, the level of trust you once enjoyed may never again be quite the same.

This even extends to seemingly unimportant issues – such as a promise to call someone at a pre-appointed time, but then not make that call. If you don't intend to do it, don't make the promise.

The worrisome problem for truth-tellers exists in the price truth sometimes extracts. But don't despair. In the end, the price for being truthful will always prove to have been worth it.

Decide, no matter the price, that you will not yield to the temptation to lie, deceive, tell half-truths, or withhold information that would contradict the perception you're promoting. Whatever you hope to gain will, in the end, turn out to be a hollow accomplishment.

CONTROL YOUR ANGER

This is not a story that I relish telling, but its lessons are worth my embarrassment.

Years ago, I made my living investing in properties, projects of various kinds, and ideas that seemed to hold some promise of financial reward. Not all of these worked out! One, in particular, was a golf-training device that I envisioned as the answer to a golfer's slice.

It was a rather ingenious device that didn't touch the ball, the club, or the golfer. It was all mental – but it worked! Having tried it over an extended period on my golf swing as well as the swings of several other golfers who had "incurable" slices, I truly believed that I had come up with the better mousetrap.

I decided to make a prototype and found a guy who could make my device out of fiberglass. I was shocked by how handsome the final product turned out to be. Additionally, as a result of the many hours we worked together on creating the device, we also discovered another use for the device. It was a tremendous aid in the improvement of the golfer's putting.

Once the manufacture of the prototype had been completed, I spent some intense time writing a little pamphlet describing its uses. This included a guide to its value, both for the slice-prevention aspects of its design as well as its potential in helping one improve their putting skills.

Each year the PGA organizes a "show" in Florida for club pros and golf instructors. A few of the PGA tour players would come but the event primarily attracted club professionals.

I booked a flight to Florida and upon my arrival, the first thing I did was rush out to the practice tee with my training device and a box of pamphlets. I decided to attempt to secure an "informal" endorsement from as many of these professionals as I could regarding the value (or lack thereof) of my device. One by one, they came to the practice tee to warm up for their round of golf that day. I politely asked each one if they would mind taking just a minute to try my device and comment about its effectiveness. In the span of two or three hours, I had succeeded in convincing thirty of these golf professionals to try it out. Of these thirty men, one said he didn't like it and two more said they didn't understand it.

But twenty-seven pros not only liked it, but they were also very encouraging about its prospects for success as a golf teaching aid! One of those twenty-seven, by the way, was the most famous teaching professional of the day, Bob Toski, who asked me to send him one to use in his training school!

I packed up my stuff and headed to the tents that had been set up for the golf equipment manufacturers, hoping to find a "corporate sponsor/ manufacturer" for my training device. The first tent I entered was Wilson Bros. After a rather brief conversation, I was told that Wilson wouldn't be able to fit my training device within their product line.

I went to the next tent, Spaulding, another big name in golf equipment manufacturing circles. Same answer. MacGregor also said the same. Finally, there was only one tent left. It was a small company that made golf tees and divot fixers. They were intrigued and asked if I'd allow them to take my device back to their company headquarters. What did I stand to lose? I left them with my device and headed for the airport.

Two weeks later, my device arrived in the mail along with a "Dear John" letter that tactfully explained their lack of interest.

I put my device on the workbench in my garage and forgot about it. Over the next months, "things" were somehow piled on top of it. When I discovered what was happening, I pulled my invention out from under all the junk that had been tossed on top of it (rather disrespectfully I might add) and threw my "better mousetrap" into the trash barrel.

For tax purposes, I wrote off the cost of its development, as well as the expenses of my trip to Florida, against my income for that year. Sometime later I was notified of the IRS's intention to audit my tax return for that year. There was something about this examiner that told me he was new on the job. The first question out of his mouth was concerning the write-off of my losses on my golf training device. My accountant and I calmly explained that it was a legitimate loss and that no potential for recovering that loss existed. The examiner wasn't convinced. He continued to suggest that the deduction be disallowed. It was apparent to my accountant, and me, that he felt a great need to avoid returning to his office empty-handed. So, we calmly asked him why he was taking this posture to which he lamely said, "How do I know that you won't resurrect this idea someday and profit from it?" I explained that I would certainly declare any income that might result from such a miracle.

He said that he guessed that he could live with that and moved on to other areas of my tax return. When no other improprieties appeared, he realized he was going to have to return to his office and face the disappointment, or disgust, of his supervisor. There was a long silence that was finally broken when he said, "Let's talk about that training device again." If there was ever any doubt in my mind about the fairness of these audits, that did it for me. It was apparent to everyone in the room that the legitimacy of the deduction wasn't the real issue. This man was faced with meeting some sort of quota! (I should have just agreed to pay the tax, approximately $5,000, on the tax deduction he wanted to disallow, **but** *the whole thing incensed me.*)

It was at that moment that I lost it and did something I'd never done before (and certainly not since). I threw my pencil across the room! The IRS agent didn't say a word. He calmly put his papers in his briefcase, closed it, and walked out without saying another word. We knew that I had just committed a very costly error!

Weeks later we received the IRS's response to the agent's visit. His supervisor looked at the tax return in question and told the agent, "You are barking up the wrong tree. Forget about this golf device deduction. We can get him on a much more important point. This man (meaning me) has too many real estate transactions to qualify for capital gains treatment of his income from his real estate activities. Disallow the capital gains tax rate on his real estate dealings and charge him the ordinary rates!"

After calculating the impact of this ruling, my accountant hit me with a knockout punch. He had concluded that I would owe an additional $100,000 in income taxes for that year! He offered to help me go to court and fight them, but victory certainly wasn't a sure thing. Moreover, the costs of such a fight might easily represent a large part of what we'd be fighting to save since the court would not award us our attorney fees even if we prevailed against the IRS. We decided to pay them, but I didn't happen to have an extra $100,000 just lying around. Fortunately for me, I happened to explain my plight to an old stockbroker friend from my days in the stock and bond business. He told me about a very special private placement (a natural gas drilling project) that was a guarantee to yield the needed profits necessary to take care of my tax obligation that resulted from the IRS's audit. This was such a good deal that even the partners of his stock and bond firm were getting involved! The only trouble was the "entry fee" for this investment was $170,000!

I went to my bank, explained everything to them, and convinced them to loan me $270,000 (the cost of the investment plus the $100,000 owed to the IRS). About eighteen months later, I received a notice from the company that was responsible for the natural gas project suggesting that I put more money in or sell my investment back to them. One of my closest friends was a petroleum engineer. I asked him to look at the specifics of the gas wells' prospects as provided by the gas company as part of their disclosures. My friend suggested not investing more money and that I should sell what I had back to them. I was stunned when he advised, "Gary, my calculations indicate that the $19,000 they are willing to offer you for your investment is more than it's worth. Take it!" This represented a $151,000 loss to me! Some quick arithmetic revealed that my pencil-throwing tantrum had just cost me $251,000!

Displays of temper, telling someone off, and talking when silence is the wiser course all speak to a lack of self-control. They are the by-products of the misguided notion that life should be fair and that there's some profit or at least a twisted satisfaction in putting someone in their place.

Such losses of self-control carry ugly consequences that can extend beyond your most pessimistic imagination.

Don't ever make that mistake. It's *never* worth it.

UNBRIDLED GREED

After you read this story, you may find yourself cheering about the outcome.

In the early days of the development of Wall Street, big money interests were dotting the landscape with newly erected skyscrapers. As a ground for development was being assembled to make way for these spectacular new structures, small houses were being torn down. A true story that I encountered years ago was about one such assemblage.

This incredible story came from an old book written about the early days of Wall Street. I found the book in the underground section of the public library that housed old out-of-print books. I have not been able to find the story again, so some of the details are from my best recollections of what I had read all those years ago. Being fairly certain about the main points of the story, I'm comfortable with the value it provides as an ideal illustration of the basics of this principle.

A very wealthy group of investors/developers had targeted a particular block in lower Manhattan for a large office building project. Their plans had to remain very secretive since word of those plans would create a forest fire of greed on the part of the people whose houses the group sought to acquire.

After much time, effort, and haggling, all that remained to complete their assemblage was one little house. For the most part, things had gone well for them as the majority of the properties had been acquired at the group's target price or close to it, that is, all but *this* house.

The owner of the house got wind of the group's intentions or somehow figured it out. The price he had been offered suddenly seemed (to him) grossly insufficient; he wanted more, much more!

He quickly realized that he held the trump card relative to the completion of the group's plans. Already in receipt of a reasonable offer for his house, he boldly contacted the group and defiantly rejected their offer. He informed them that the selling price for his property would be double what they had previously offered him! He made it clear to them that he knew of their plans and the key role his home played in the accomplishment of those plans.

A bit took aback, the group deliberated for a short time but realized they had no other choice. They quickly agreed to his demand. A few days passed while the contracts were being prepared. When the group's attorneys brought the contracts to the homeowner to secure his signature on this last piece of their puzzle, they came to the cold realization that the homeowner was just getting warmed up.

The little homeowner had, once again, reconsidered their most recent offer. Emboldened by his property's obvious strategic value to the buyers, he focused his newfound powers on strong-arming them into agreeing to yet another increase. If they failed to agree, he made it clear that he'd hold up their entire project. Predictably, he again doubled the previously agreed-upon price! Angered, the attorneys reported the results of their meeting to the group. Though incensed by what was happening, the group was forced to acknowledge the leverage this property owner had and rationalized that the premium being requested still represented only a small increase in their overall land acquisition cost. They reluctantly agreed to pay the homeowner's latest demand.

The contract was signed and the attorneys began preparing the closing documents. Preliminary to the closing, a document containing certain legal issues relating to the closing needed signatures from both the buyers and the seller. This document was taken to the seller for his signature. By this time, he was buoyed by his previous shrewdness and refused to sign unless the price was enriched by another 50 percent of the last agreed-upon price! His never-ending demands were beginning to become a big hurdle for these otherwise levelheaded businessmen. Nevertheless, cooler heads prevailed and the group honored the homeowner's latest demand.

The day of the closing finally arrived, and the group's representatives, attorneys, and the homeowner were finally at the closing table. The documents were all prepared, ready for signatures and the final closing of the transaction. When the pen was handed to the homeowner to sign the documents, his greed overcame any sense of honor, or even common sense, as he positioned himself for a goal-line stand. He demanded yet another 25 percent for his final signature. Already, the price being offered to him was many times the building's worth – an amount that would have made him a rich man. The group retired to another room to discuss this latest price increase. After some time in deliberation, they returned to the closing room. What happened next made Wall Street history.

They told the little homeowner he could keep his house – they were going to build around it! His house was renamed "Spite House."

The little homeowner went from rags to riches and back to rags. His monumental greed couldn't resist one last turn of the nut. It turned out to be one turn too many. He had stripped the threads. Lost forever was the windfall of a lifetime – he was determined to get the very last drop!

Expecting to receive the true worth of what you own is not the same as greed which leads to the unrelenting pursuit of more, just to satisfy that insatiable "need" for more.

Unbridled Greed testifies to that irrepressible need to squeeze the "last drop" out of everything. Such a pursuit is often fueled by the awareness of another's vulnerability. But, those guilty of this shouldn't be surprised when, at the very first opportunity, the exploited party seeks to "square accounts" with them.

When you have already been offered all that the object is worth, yet you are tempted to continue to push for more, recall the times when you've stripped the threads by attempting to get that one last turn of the wrench.

You have no reason to expect that your methods will go undetected. The word about you will get around. If you find yourself in the grip of greed, you can expect your future negotiations to be an uphill battle – that's if people will even want to do business with you.

SEEKING THE EASY WAY OUT

After countless disappointing results, I've developed a healthy skepticism about always seeking shortcuts!

When I was about twelve years old, my dad decided to spend a Saturday afternoon remodeling a rental property he had purchased. He asked me and my younger brother to help him clean an upstairs bath and adjoining bedroom. A wall had been taken out and the debris from that demolition had to be hauled out of the building.

When we arrived at the property, our dad took us upstairs and showed us the areas he wanted to be cleaned. He walked over to the window and pointed at a pile of trash out by the fence near the garage. He wanted us to put the debris in buckets and carry those buckets downstairs to the pile of trash in the backyard. When all the trash had been removed, we were to sweep up the area. Dad left us with a couple of buckets, a shovel, and two brooms. We were told that he would be downstairs working on some plastering which would take him most of the afternoon. He assured us that we would have plenty of time to accomplish our assignment.

At twelve years old, I was not only the oldest but felt I was also the wiser brother. So, I took it upon myself to examine the project we'd been assigned. I was particularly focused on the stairs and the distance we'd have to travel from the back door to the trash pile. It seemed like a long way particularly when weighed down by those heavy buckets. Considering the only available manpower was my eight-year-old brother, I could see this was going to be a lot of work, and I'd be doing most of it!

Seeking ways to put off starting, I walked over to the window one more time. Noticing a rope clothesline in the backyard, it hit me. Why not use that rope and figure out some way to attach one end to the garage and the other to a place on the wall near the window. If we could accomplish that, all we would then need would be a way to get a bucket to ride down the rope. I figured the time it would take to rig up this little pulley system was well worth the time we'd save hauling the trash down in buckets.

I don't mean to accuse anyone, but my brother wasn't much help. I'd be outside trying to attach the rope to the garage but before I was able to secure it, he'd lose his grip and drop the rope out the window. I was amazed at how rapidly the two hours went by before we finally got the rope "properly" attached at both ends!

If we thought that part was hard, we hadn't seen anything until we tried getting the bucket attached to the rope in a manner that would allow it to slide download.

We were still working on that problem when my dad came upstairs to say that it was time to leave! We had yet to get the pulley system working and had not succeeded in getting as much as one bucket of debris hauled down to the trash pile outside!

I can still remember the look on my dad's face when he viewed the same mess he had left us with four hours previous. To say that he was a little unhappy isn't accurate. I, of course, informed him that my brother kept dropping the rope. How was I supposed to get this thing working without competent help? My poor little brother; just stood there looking up at my dad with this pitiful expression. As for me, I didn't look forward to the ride home. I never could understand why he failed to appreciate my ingenuity. Had he waited just a little while longer, I would have had that place all cleaned up, and he would have realized that, because of my shrewdness, not one bucket had to be hand-carried outside.

True to the kind of man he was, he wasn't all that upset with *me* (he had already figured out who was behind the failed scheme). His only reprimand was stated in terms of the disappointment that he felt in me for having sought to take the easy way out. He then told us that all the trash that was upstairs in those two rooms would not have taken more than ten bucket trips – probably little more than half of an hour of hauling. The two rooms could have been swept clean in another half an hour – a one-hour job in all. Instead, we accomplished nothing and it took four hours to do so.

This principle also contains a very valuable corollary that speaks to misguided schemes to "get ahead" the *easy way*. What's referenced here are the underhanded means by which some less-than-honorable people seek to gain fame and fortune.

A few quick examples should set the tone for *the decisions you should make r*egarding your conduct in these kinds of situations.

As a young boy, you don't try to gain that baseball cap you admire by extorting some smaller kid with threats of a beating if he doesn't "gift" his cap to you. You don't get your college degree by paying someone to take your tests for you or by plagiarizing others' writings and submitting them under your authorship for course credits. You don't get the promotion at work by torpedoing your fellow workers. You don't fatten your paycheck by padding your hours. You don't kiss up grandma on her deathbed in hopes of beating your brothers and sisters out of their share of the inheritance. You don't win at golf by teeing it up in the rough. You don't gain recognition by taking credit for the work someone else did. Decide that whatever you accomplish, however little that might be, will be a set of achievements that you can feel *totally* good about. Those are the only ones that will end up mattering!

Make sure that the effort exerted on your "time-saving" idea is worth the time and trouble that its implementation will require. Beware, of the unanticipated "things" that can easily thwart your plans. Getting your idea up and running can take considerably longer than you might imagine – longer than just carrying the buckets!

But let's get down to the really important aspects of this principle:

You need to make a firm decision that whatever achievements you may someday claim won't have come from conducting your affairs dishonorably. The shady tactics and sleight-of-hand that are often the tools of choice for those committed to "Seeking the Easy Way Out" will not bring honor to your name.

There are no worthwhile benefits to be realized as these kinds of achievements won't deliver the satisfactions you sought.

PROCRASTINATION CAUSES PROBLEMS

The results of having procrastinated seldom turn out this well.

Events from our college days are often the source of interesting memories – some good, some bad, and some that couldn't happen anywhere else. The latter would describe one such memory of mine. It all began when I enrolled in an accounting class – a required course. The lessons I learned from my experiences in that class caused me to conclude that I'd be better off outsourcing all of my future bookkeeping needs. Bookkeeping was not turning out to be one of my "A" skills.

In particular, one memory of that class will always remain – my experiences with the "practice setting." A major portion of my grade was wrapped up in the completion and correctness of that practice set. For one entire semester, we were all required to properly keep a full set of books, which involved hundreds of entries. Most students began working on the assignment almost immediately and worked on it steadily throughout the semester. I was not properly motivated; besides, a lot of other more interesting things had captured my attention.

Needless to say, I put off the beginning and when I did begin, I didn't work on it consistently. In the last couple of weeks of the semester, I spent some very late evenings trying to get that practice set finished. Upon completion, there was a "grand total" at the bottom of the last page. If that number was correct, your work had been conducted properly.

Upon completing my practice set, I checked my grand total with one of the smarter students in the class. We were miles apart! Because I decided to wait until the last minute to begin, I was forced to depend upon a flurry of activity to finish. Therefore, I had no time left with which to find my error(s). But I couldn't afford to flunk the class since it was a degree requirement. So, I did something which I feel embarrassed to admit. I erased my grand total number and inserted my smart classmate's number instead. I was nervous about being discovered, flunked, or even being called in front of the dean for cheating. But, if not to turn it in, or left the incorrect total, I would be sure to flunk. So, I couldn't see that I had much to lose and turned in the "altered" practice set.

About a week later, the professor called me and wanted me to meet him privately. That invitation about *stopped* my heart! On the day of the meeting, I sat down with the professor who proceeded to tell me that he had some bad news for me. I thought, *"I'm in trouble now!"*

Believe it or not, he had put my practice set in the back window of his car and as he was driving down the freeway with his windows down, *it blew out the window!* He told me how sorry he was and that though he couldn't give me an "A" because he hadn't been able to review my work, *he was willing to give me a "B" for the class.* To say I was relieved was a gross understatement. But, two regrets lingered. First, I wished I had allotted the time necessary for the production of a quality job. Second, I regretted that I hadn't turned my flawed practice set in, *unaltered.*

One realization persisted…*procrastination does cause problems.* Only a miracle (that I didn't deserve) saved me from some very unwelcome consequences.

There are choices about ways to go about the pursuit of a destination. There was a choice made by that smart classmate who applied a consistent effort and steadily progressed toward the goal. This stands in bold contrast to my approach (the approach of all spurt workers).

The "spurt worker" approach gives them a temporary feeling of freedom from the drudgery of being chained to a task. But even before beginning the task, these feelings of freedom are increasingly disturbed by a growing awareness of the assignment's looming deadline.

But that was college; all that was at stake was a grade! What about later when an investment, a job, or even a career is on the line? It might be argued that no harm has been done if the job gets completed. But running out of time creates problems – the mere task of finishing may be in jeopardy. As a result, the production of any *quality* becomes an unlikely accomplishment. You may be doomed to the production of a mediocre product. The harsh realities of today's competitive world make it difficult to hold your own if all you do is turn in mediocre performances. How do you even keep your job, let alone ever advance?

The answer is a *"steady approach."* It is something *you can consistently do*, even on days when you don't feel like it. Deciding to adopt this methodical approach of steady progress will get the job done, along with the greatest assurance of creating a quality product.

This involves the division of the task into equal time segments. For this approach to work, three conditions are required:

First, the total time you allot should only amount to eighty percent of the total time you have. That extra twenty percent can be used to handle unexpected problems, or infuse an extra touch of quality.

Second, remain disciplined! *Don't ever miss a segment.* A missed session is an immediate alarm that you've fallen behind, and beginning a pattern that, if continued, will dictate the failure of the project.

Third, if you miss a day, vow to *immediately* make up that missed session no later than the *very next day.* This means that you either stay up late that night to complete it or double up the next day! The imposition of this unwelcome burden should prompt you to stick to the schedule.

This principle isn't addressing procrastination over projects that may or may not be undertaken. It deals solely with putting off a project that you must complete. When faced with a deadline, *decide you will commit to a schedule of steady, consistent effort…* effort that not only ensures completion within the time allotted but also ensures the additional time necessary for the production of excellence. Admittedly, the idea of the steady effort certainly isn't new, but it's still the system of choice – its benefits have been proven.

People who apply a steady effort get into a "zone." This "zone" protects them from procrastination as they experience increased satisfaction in watching the results of their consistent effort steadily advance them ever closer to the finish line. They will even arrive at a point where they will gain satisfaction just from the process itself *which is the <u>secret</u> of mastering any discipline.*

REPEATING THE SAME MISTAKE

The first time may earn you a little sympathy; whereas, the second time may bring ridicule and laughter.

After I finally learned to swim, I began to enjoy diving. I wasn't very good and never progressed very far, so it wasn't something I took seriously. Nonetheless, finding swimming somewhat boring, I spent most of my time at the pool on the diving board.

The University of Denver had a nice indoor pool in their field house that had both one and three-meter boards. I used to go there fairly often and was fortunate that the timing of my visits frequently enabled me to watch wonderful maneuvers performed by a diver named Jim. He was a great diver, so smooth. At the end of each dive (they were all beautifully executed) he would enter the water with his body exactly straight up and down, cutting the water like a knife. Barely a ripple resulted as he disappeared under the surface of the water. He was my hero.

One night while I was there practicing my very limited repertoire of dives, my hero, along with some other "advisers," suggested I try a front double-front flip from the high board. I had never tried such a dive before, but I was encouraged by my hero and those other advisors to give it a try. I was more than a little timid. After all, I had no idea how to perform the dive! When I admitted this to them, they all said, "It's easy. All you have to do is leave the board with your hands in the air and your head and quickly bring them down to your knees as you tuck your upper body into your folded legs and roll forward. When you've spun around twice, you'll feel when to open up, and you'll end your dive entering the water feet first."

As easy as that sounded, I was very aware of the increased difficulty of completing a front flip versus a back flip. In the case of the backflip, the direction of your body's rotation gives you a view of the water well before you enter it. Unlike a backflip, the direction of your rotation for a front flip prevents any view of the water until it's too late to make any "course corrections," for under or over-rotation. You have no idea where you are until the very last second. Mention of that concern gained this response: "Like we said, as you're spinning, you'll get the *feel*. When the time *seems right*, open up from your tucked position."

Encouraged by these pearls of divine wisdom, I confidently climbed the ladder to the three-meter board (that's roughly ten feet). I wasted no time. I bounced a couple of times and then…airborne. Hands in the air. Hands to the knees. Tuck and roll. So far, so good. I must admit that I was surprised at how fast I was spinning. In addition to the speed of my spin, I was also in a free fall from over fifteen feet in the air. As I was spinning, I was aware of the water then the ceiling, then the water, and then the ceiling, and … it seemed like it was time to open up. So, I did. But…I had over-rotated! Instead of a "front two", I had performed a front two and a quarter. Splat! A miserable belly flop! Though thus described, it was not my belly that felt the misery. My head hit first which caused my eyes to feel as if they were connected to some sort of spring. It seemed as if they had moved to the back of my head and then sprung back. To say the least, it was exquisite pain. For what seemed like an eternity, I just lay there in the water, helplessly floating like a lily pad. There was more than a little embarrassment as I finally made my way out of the water. Everyone at the poolside had witnessed my foolish display.

I slinked away into a corner and sat against the wall – embarrassed, hurt, and discouraged. To the rescue came my three advisers to offer their condolences. The conversation soon turned to the subject of fear – or maybe I should say the avoidance of fear. Their advice was that I would build up a deep dread of ever trying such a dive again, unless…I immediately got up on that diving board and tried again! Whoa. I wasn't sure I wanted to hear that advice. All the unpleasantness of that first attempt was still fresh in my mind. I didn't respond immediately. What was the hurry? Maybe the pool would close while I was still thinking.

But then, for some reason, I began to recall statements I had heard about getting thrown off a horse. "If you get thrown off, get back on immediately or you'll forever fear riding again." Resigned, I slowly got up and climbed the stairs to the three-meter level, and walked out to the end of the board. Not wanting to think about what I was about to do, I immediately began bouncing. As before, bounce, bounce then airborne; then, hands in the air, hands to the knees, tuck and roll; water, ceiling, water, ceiling – open up. *Splat!* **An exact repeat!**

Like before, it felt like my eyes had been pushed to the back of my head! I again lay there in agony, floating with my face in the water. I was too embarrassed to emerge. They say that from a height, water can become like concrete. I fully agree! I now understood why you never read of the survival of one of those Golden Gate Bridge suicide jumpers!

After a while, I slowly climbed out of the pool and went straight into the locker room where a mirror revealed two huge shiners!

The Japanese have a word for what I should have done, *Kaizen*. I read an article about its application in the workings of an assembly line. A perfectly functioning assembly line would be subjected to deliberately imposed, excessive speeds of operation. As the speed continued to increase, the assembly line would finally break down. They would take it apart and find out which part couldn't withstand the pressure and *redesign it*, then run the assembly line again. This time they would run it even faster and it would break down again. Once more, they searched for the failed part, *redesigned it,* and started again – and so on. This is an ingenious approach to seeking continuous improvement which was quite unlike my approach to perfecting my diving attempts.

I had neither consulted my advisers about what I did wrong nor made any decision regarding some form of corrective maneuver *before trying again!* How foolish I was to expect different results when I had made *no effort to alter anything* from my previous failed attempt.

When something doesn't work the first time, take the time to examine what went wrong and make the necessary corrections before trying again.

First-effort failures are excusable. If you'll analyze what went wrong, you shouldn't need to prepare an excuse for a second failure.

DO YOU BORE PEOPLE?

Read this story and you'll be able to taste my embarrassment.

As mentioned in a previous principle, mid-July marked the time of a very special golf tournament held annually in Colorado Springs, Colorado. This tournament always included a wonderful cocktail party held after the qualifying rounds on the evening before the first-round matches were to begin. It was at this party that the match pairings for the first round of elimination were announced. Most conversations centered around one's qualifying round and the identity of their first-round opponent.

A man I knew fairly well came up to me and asked how I had played. Believing my qualifying round was particularly spellbinding, I proceeded to tell him what I shot, including detail about a few of the highlights. Because he seemed so engrossed in my story, I began to expand on the quantity of detail that I felt would aid in his appreciation of my experience, even including some shot-by-shot analysis of my round. And so it went for roughly fifteen minutes. Once my story ended, he complimented me on my exciting round. Then, we parted company to mingle with some of the other guests.

After an hour of food and other conversations, I bumped into this same man again. Astoundingly, he asked, "How did you do today?" I was stunned. I couldn't believe it! I couldn't decide who should feel more embarrassed, him or me.

I had just spent fifteen minutes telling him, in great detail, not only what I had shot, but how I shot it! I didn't have any idea how to respond to his question. As I contemplated how boring I must have been, and how foolish I must have looked, I wanted to crawl into a hole. In stark contrast to my earlier verbosity, I was totally at a loss for words!

One thing for sure: he had not been listening to me…*at all*. Rather, he was merely politely waiting for me to shut up. Yet, he had seemed so interested in my story. I would never have guessed how eager he was for me to finish my story and quit talking. I learned from this that even our best friends, including family, frequently aren't interested in all the detail we may be so intent on providing. Most people have less interest in you, your dreams, and your problems than you might think.

The respect you hope to establish with others might be best enhanced if you don't err in assuming they have a greater interest in you, or in the details of your life than they do. Don't bore them with too much talk. The details from your life ought to be shared by invitation only.

Everyone is more interested in themselves, and their story than they are in you or your story. Thus, by paying particular attention to this truth, your future interactions with others will greatly improve.

Do not assume that just because you talked, the other person was listening! Many decisions are made based on the assumption that your requests, instructions, or warnings have been heard and absorbed. If you overlook a person's lack of response and assume their quiet assent to your statements and requests, you may have missed their total inattention. Your belief that you were heard may be in serious error. Unfortunately, if you assume that you were heard and you proceed with your decisions, decisions that were based upon *having been heard,* how flawed might these decisions be if you weren't heard? Don't count on any of those decisions turning out as planned!

First, realize that the details of your life are less important to others than they are to you. As has been said, "You have one mouth, but two ears." In keeping with that ratio, it's wise to listen twice as much as you talk. When you do talk, make it mostly about them.

Second, before making an important decision that requires another's involvement, confirm that they have heard and understood all that you intended for them to hear and understand.

An important plan or decision that's based upon the cooperation of another person, or persons, can only be successful if that other party, the one that's supposedly agreeing with you, has heard and understood you.

I'M BULLETPROOF

Life is a precious gift. It was not meant to be risked for a cheap, momentary thrill!

I've read several stories about the hazards facing climbers who attempt to conquer famous peaks, like Mt. Everest. Almost everyone who attempts such a challenge has some hair-raising tales to relate. Story after story graphically describes the stark realities of such temptations of fate. As I read about their adventures, I find myself vicariously sharing their experiences, almost breaking into a sweat myself. The tales of their battles and suffering make me wonder how anyone could ever voluntarily take such a risk and willingly undergo torture and discomfort.

To successfully reach the summit of Mt. Everest, the king of all mountain climbing challenges, you must first begin your journey at a base camp that is at an altitude of 17,000 feet! As you look up from there, you see the summit of Everest towering another 12,000 above you!

Even at the elevation of the base camp, the body stops acclimating. Breathing becomes one of the major challenges. Because less oxygen is reaching the body's cells for their rejuvenation, the body begins to slowly deteriorate. You move slower, get weaker, and mentally begin to shut down.

The cold is another factor – the severe, unimaginable cold. With wind chill, the temperature can easily drop to forty degrees below zero or more. Tearing eyes will freeze shut, and any task requiring a gloveless hand will expose that hand to frostbite in just minutes.

The wind is another hazard that will, almost without exception, greet every expedition at some point along the ascent or descent. Its presence will plague, endanger, or even halt the journey. These winds can reach hurricane force and may last days. They are so powerful, they can rip tents into mere shreds of fabric, rendering them useless as shelter.

Avalanches are a danger to be reckoned with on virtually any assault on the summit. It's nothing for a storm to dump three or four feet of snow on the side of the mountain. As the sun comes out, that blanket of snow can become very unstable. Getting caught can either bury a person or sweep them over the edge of a precipice to their death.

It's not uncommon for climbers to suffer injuries. When injured that person requires the help and attention of the entire climbing team. If they have advanced too far above the base camp for rescue attempts from below to be effective, their objective to reach the summit must be put on hold or sacrificed all together. They are forced to shift their attention to the injured climber whose life is now dependent upon their efforts to return him to the safety of the base camp below.

As climbers successfully near the top, their physical condition is virtually at its lowest level. A single step can be agonizingly difficult. Heart rates may be almost double normal levels and breathing becomes so difficult that each step may need to be accommodated by five minutes of rest. Time quickly passes with little progress to show for the agonizing effort. Determination to reach the top has spelled death to more than one climber who exhausted his final resources in that attempt, leaving nothing in the way of energy to make his way down the mountain. Until he can reach the safety of the base camp, there is nothing that will restore his exhausted strength. His only hope of making it back down the mountain lies in not having drained all his energy on the way up.

Add all these risks together and it's easy to believe that *one out of every four* climbers who attempt to reach the summit of Mt. Everest dies trying! Even those who do live through the ordeal often lose fingers and/ or toes to the ravages of frostbite.

What you just read about the dangers of attempting to conquer Mt. Everest serves as *the classic example of a decision where all must go well to qualify as a good decision.* Granted, some people value a successful assault on Mt. Everest as being worth some fingers and toes. But, for all others who challenge that mountain, a deep-seated belief in their invincibility to the dangers is the only explanation for their willingness to so eagerly assume such risks. They are convinced that such problems only happen to others.

Granted, God has gifted us all with free will. Thus, you can engage in whatever manner of risk you choose. Maybe you are knowingly deciding to risk injury or loss under the risks you entertain. The important point is to realize the difference between being aware of the risks, as opposed to believing that you are immune to them. This principle addresses those who fall into the latter category – those who believe they're bulletproof.

Such an attitude isn't confined just to physical risks. It can often surface in other areas of life. One such area would be our relationships. The success of our bond with others can be much more dependent upon *our* treatment of others than we might want to acknowledge. Thus, statements or actions emanating from an invincible, bulletproof self-image can be responsible for saying or doing things that can damage, even ruin, a friendship. Unexplainably, people who believe they are indomitable seem to feel that they can say or do anything without any adverse consequences to their relationships with those they love or value as friends. But, a belated "I'm sorry" seldom heals all the wounds. Your mistreatment of them may be forgiven, but don't count on it being forgotten. For this reason, the damage to the bond may be beyond repair.

Thus, pay particular attention to the dangers of assuming that you can say or do anything to another person and still retain their admiration and respect for you. You are not bulletproof, nor are you impervious to the consequences of your wounding of others. Their reaction to your abuse of them will likely result in a changed opinion of you.

There are yet other ways in which this bulletproof attitude can place you on a path of problems and misery. As an example, *much* must go smoothly if you expect to experience a positive outcome from a marriage to a person who has a history of alcohol or drug abuse. Nevertheless, those who believe they are immune to the problems experienced by everyone else, routinely assume all will turn out well because they're confident they will have a positive influence on their addicted mate.

What they forget is that people with drug and alcohol problems are people for whom the pressures of life have a way of overcoming their ability to face challenges. Drugs and alcohol provide them with a way of escape. The sober mate may eventually be forced to live with the constant fear that, at any time, one of those pressures will raise its ugly head and lead to a downward spiral of their vulnerable mate's ability to cope!

Another example of the dangers of courting a bulletproof self-concept lies in deciding to risk money on a venture whose success *depends* upon the stability of interest rates, a favorable business climate, and smooth sailing for all the other pieces of their investment puzzle. Believing these bad things won't happen to them, they confidently push forward. Because all of these issues lie beyond their control, they will have made a bad investment should any of these conditions go against them – losses being the unwanted result.

Decisions made with the expectation of a total absence of problems are seldom good ones. All of this should seem obvious. Yet, virtually everyone is occasionally guilty of making a decision whose success depends upon everything going as planned...*without a hitch.*

If you think you're bulletproof and make decisions expecting everything to go as planned, you are ignoring the reality of problems. Misfortune has the nasty habit of descending upon people, particularly those who don't believe it will ever visit them. Don't be fooled. There are few such undertakings of any consequence that will escape without problems of some kind!

Don't make any decision based on the expectation of a problem-free experience. **If the decision you are contemplating is only a good one if all goes well, don't take the risk. Instead, make decisions that you feel can withstand some problems and pressures – then, prepare, in advance, for those problems.**

V. PERSONAL IMPROVEMENT

This section on Personal Improvement is designed to inspire you to invest in who and what you are. The intended goal is to make you more productive, more successful, and a more likable person.

The first of these principles, Become A Positive Person, urges you to look at life through rose-colored glasses. The second concept would encourage you to Invest In Others. Acts of selflessness are usually rewarded as both you and the recipient benefit. The next principle, Traits Of The Successful And Great, highlights behavioral characteristics that may possess surprising power to enhance your chances for success. Guard Your Mind warns of the unseen harm that comes from exposing your mind to wrong thoughts and images. Do The Right Thing promises rewards for resisting the urge to act in disregard for the rightful interests of others in seeking to maximize your outcome. As is true of all the principles in this section on Personal Improvement, Protect Your Reputation discusses habits and virtues worth cultivating – traits that will pave the way for gaining the admiration of others.

BECOME A POSITIVE PERSON

These are refreshing people to be around. Take a page out of their book.

Life is full of troubles. Sometimes those troubles can virtually overwhelm a person. The number and variety of antidotes to this problem are many. Some, of course, resort to alcohol or drugs. Others seek an escape through a diversionary activity. But many seek the company of a positive person – someone who sees the glass half-full all the time. Such people have a way of maximizing the good and minimizing the bad – maybe even seeing the good in the bad.

Such a person is my grandson, Josh, who displayed a classic positive attitude regarding a little mishap that occurred after a Thanksgiving meal. Being only ten years old at the time, he was all too eager to join in the adult activity and help clear the table. He pitched right in by hauling the dirty dishes to the kitchen. In this case, the dirty dishes were his mother's best china. One of his trips to the kitchen was particularly memorable. Loaded down with china plates, he was on his way when he encountered the threshold at the doorway into the kitchen. It was the transition piece between the carpeted area of the dining room and the tile floor in the kitchen. Not being able to see over the stack of plates, Josh tripped over the threshold. He and all the china plates came crashing down onto the tile floor. Quickly assessing the damage, Josh picked up the one china plate that had survived the crash and proudly held it up saying, "Look, this one didn't break!"

In another example, a friend of mine, Jim, was just getting his start on his career in the stock and bond business. He loved the business and spent a great deal of time and effort working on the development of his career. One day his draft notice arrived in the mail. Knowing Jim's dreams, it would be hard to imagine that he would have been thrilled by this event. Nevertheless, he reported for duty at the scheduled time and served his two years on active duty. As the end of the two years began to approach, Jim dreamed of his return to his career and eagerly anticipated resuming life as he had left it. Not more than a week before his release, he was notified that he had been reassigned for another two-year term of duty! It's impossible to know the disappointment Jim must have felt at that moment, but he later told me that on that same day, he made up his mind that he was going to become the best soldier they had.

We all admire the positive person, but how do you become one? To state the obvious, you must think positively. You must also think big and think excitingly. That means your focus must be on your successes and victories. Vince Lombardi, the famous coach of the Green Bay Packers, recognized the importance of not allowing his players to focus on their mistakes or weaknesses. He made sure his team entered the field brimming with confidence. To accomplish this, Lombardi limited the viewing of pre-game films to only those that featured the team's previously successful running plays.

Another aid to becoming a positive person is to avoid self-pity by identifying at least three positive things that might arise from your situation. All situations must be consistently viewed to find something positive on which to focus your attention.

The final point naturally follows the other two. The morose whiner wins no one's sympathy. Moreover, his attitudes are particularly destructive to his chances of ever developing a positive outlook.

Tony Robbins was just such a positive person. He has become a nationally recognized motivational speaker – a favorite of some of the largest corporations. In addition to his motivational speeches, Tony became famous through the success of his "Fire Walk" seminars. The principles that Tony wrote and spoke about were dramatically demonstrated in this spectacular display of mind control and positive thinking. A group would gather for one of his much sought-after motivational speeches and he would begin to build their confidence in themselves. He talked of concentration and mental imaging – everything positive. At the end of an hour or so, Tony would lead volunteers to a specially prepared area behind the podium from which he had just addressed the seminar attendees. This specially prepared area was right out of the Arabian night. It was a twelve-foot-long bed of red-hot coals. As the volunteers came up onto the stage, Tony would look at their faces and assess the look in their eyes. He would decide who would take the fire walk and who was not ready to try it.

Those who passed Tony's critical eye were allowed, one by one, to remove their shoes and socks and *slowly* walk across the bed of red-hot coals barefoot! *None* of those who performed the fire walk had so much as a blister on their foot! Tony had successfully transferred his positive thought process to all of these fire walkers.

This phenomenal demonstration should remove even the slightest doubts that attitudes can be changed. Whether it's an attitude of fear, a lack of self-confidence, or a constant state of negativity, you can change it.

Everyone loves a positive person. Like rays of sunshine, they are known for their smiling faces, always looking for the positives in any situation. They expect to succeed. To be in the company of such a person is life-giving.

As encouragers, they can instill a sense of hope and confidence in others, helping them tackle that which they had previously feared.

A person whose glass is half full, no matter the circumstances, is destined to pull out victories from tough challenges much more often than those whose glass is always half empty. Absent a positive attitude, it's an uphill battle.

No matter how dismal the prospects of a good outcome might seem to most of us, positive thinkers make a concerted effort to find the good in all situations…and focus on it. The message is clear: decide you'll become that positive person!

INVEST IN OTHERS

You don't have to be in the spotlight to feel respected or good about yourself. This story should convince you of that!

Although born without health problems, Helen contracted either meningitis or scarlet fever at the age of nineteen months and was rendered both deaf and blind by the disease. Helen was not only deaf and blind, but she also had a severe speech impediment.

Nevertheless, she was forced to deal with life as one who lacks the normal senses that enable a person to understand anything of themselves, others, or their surroundings. These terrible conditions became the very foundation of her incredible story.

Things began to change for Helen when a nurse/tutor, Anne Sullivan, came into her life. Anne, who at one time fought blindness (which was surgically corrected), became Helen's tutor and constant companion. The beginning days of their relationship were not easy as Helen was difficult to manage as she was prone to violent moods of anger and frustration.

Anne began their journey of discovery by writing letters of the alphabet on Helen's palm. At first, Helen didn't understand what Anne was doing. One day as they were out in the garden, Anne ran some water over Helen's hand as she spelled out w-a-t-e-r on the palm of her other hand. Helen got the idea and immediately wanted to know what the word was for the ground beneath her. She reached down and touched the dirt to demonstrate her question to Anne. Before the end of that day, Helen had learned and memorized thirty words!

Through Anne's instruction, Helen began to learn the alphabet and then words as she fought to slowly understand this very unfriendly place into which she had been born. She learned English both manually and through the benefit of raised print (Braille) for the blind.

Benefiting from Anne's tireless tutoring, Helen made up her mind that she would one day attend college. She entered Radcliffe College in the year 1900 and graduated cum laude in 1904. She would later receive honorary doctoral degrees from six different universities, among them Harvard University. After graduation, Helen went on to become an author, lecturer, and social activist. Her writing career stretched over some fifty years, with her most popular book being *The Story of My Life*, which was printed in fifty languages! During her lifetime, she published countless other works and won awards too numerous to count.

Later in her life, Radcliffe College dedicated the Helen Keller garden to her achievements and named a fountain within the garden after her lifelong tutor and companion, Anne Sullivan. The film, "The Miracle Worker," was the recipient of two Oscars which were awarded to the two actresses who played the roles of Helen and Anne in the movie. Helen became acquainted with, and even became friends with many of the leading personalities of her day. Included in the list were John F. Kennedy, William James, and Mark Twain – the latter two each wrote highly complimentary things about Helen and her achievements. In 1965, just a few years before her death at age eighty-eight, Helen was elected to the Women's Hall of Fame at the New York World's Fair.

Helen Keller was remarkable. Not many can ever hope to achieve the things she accomplished. For starters, not many of us are struggling with being deaf and blind. What we can all aspire to is the life and achievements of Anne Sullivan. Without Anne, Helen would most likely have remained an unknown, unheralded victim of her physical disabilities. Through Anne's efforts, a miracle unfolded. While not nearly as famous as Helen Keller, Anne, nevertheless, achieved a monumental accomplishment in transforming this pitiful little girl into a woman recognized, honored, and admired the world over. Consider what she took on! At the outset, Helen was a child filled with rage – one who couldn't understand or be understood. There were no known means of communicating with her. Anne persisted in her efforts to reach Helen and bring her into contact with the rest of the world. She patiently and ingeniously figured out ways to teach Helen to read and write. Was it necessary for Anne's sense of purpose and satisfaction to be in the limelight and receive accolades for her accomplishments with Helen? No, she was content to remain in the background. She accurately understood her role, and unwaveringly committed herself to it.

There are a lot of *potential* Anne Sullivans. These are people who could be influential or inspirational in another's life but have failed to make the necessary commitment. They never take the first step. Fortunately, there's also the Anne Sullivans who have committed to someone in need. Though they may remain unnoticed or are soon to be forgotten, *they become the reason* for someone else's notoriety.

Their success may have had its beginning in merely taking an interest in another person. Thus, the message here is to decide that you will always attempt to show an interest in others. Even though that won't likely lead you to an Anne Sullivan outcome, it's certainly the secret to being well-liked.

Most of us are not destined to be wildly successful or world-famous. Just because those things might not be in your future, doesn't mean that being successful and famous is the only way to live a life that's meaningful and worthwhile.

Decide that you will look for opportunities to take at least a page out of Anne Sullivan's book by investing in the life of another, or others. **Deep satisfaction awaits anyone willing to be someone's teacher, coach, or tutor. This doesn't need to be a career position. If you are willing to give part of yourself to another and accept the challenges that present themselves, you will find it to be a very rewarding experience.**

At a minimum, *decide that you will make it a habit to always take an interest in others,* **being an encouragement to anyone whose life you can enthusiastically impact with sincere words or gestures of inspiration and encouragement.**

TRAITS OF THE SUCCESSFUL AND GREAT

What is it that causes some people to be admired? Why are they the ones everyone wants to hang around with? What's the the secret of their magnetism?

There are many habits and traits exhibited by people who have earned the label of greatness that are worth emulating. Many who are searching for the secret to being admired and respected are looking for *the* answer that will unlock the door to that hallowed realm. It's more complicated than that, which is the reason that those who have been recipients of that label are as rare as they are. However, some identifiable characteristics will greatly enhance your efforts to become admired and respected.

The man who smiles a lot is a man who is easy to like. He projects a non-threatening demeanor, exudes friendliness, and doesn't often wear the frown of a negative attitude. While some might argue that such a man doesn't present an authority figure, the truth is that a greater number of difficult situations and conflicts are resolved by such a man than one who takes every opportunity to display his authoritarian self-image and demonstrate his toughness.

Those who are admired and respected have, over the long haul, learned the value of circumspection. Even deserved and appropriately delivered reprimands are sometimes ill-received. So, when you slander or berate another, it will never be greeted with a warm response. Little is to be gained in doing so, but much can be lost.

You can know a lot about a person by the way they treat those who can do nothing for them. Generosity is a trait that's a joy to witness in action. The biographies of many great people expose their practice of these admirable qualities. Of all those qualities, the one that seems to most capture the admiring public's attention is of generosity. The sports announcers covering the Masters' tournament made a special point of calling attention to Phil Michelson's generosity, saying that he left a tip for the locker room attendants, which they guessed was an amount that would exceed the "tips" of all the other contestants combined. Frank Sinatra, by any account, was a controversial figure. But no matter his detractors, everyone (including them) would have to admit that he was a very generous man. Once when Sinatra was emerging from a cab in front of a restaurant, he tipped the doorman one hundred dollars. As he was about to walk through the door into the restaurant, he turned to ask the doorman when the last time was that anyone had been that generous with him. The doorman answered that the last time he had received a tip that size was the occasion of Sinatra's previous visit to the restaurant!

People who wish to be known for their success or greatness often assume that they must be perceived as super competent and inhumanly self-sufficient. They will never let you see a chink in their armor. With them, everything is always under control. If for some reason you are strangely unaware of their many accomplishments, they are quick to tell you all about them and in great detail. In fact, in a conversation with them of any length, they may tell you of the same achievements more than once!

In contrast, how refreshing it is to be in the company of someone who truly is successful and deserving of a label of greatness when that person feels no need to inform you of their stature or accomplishments. Secure in who they are, they are seldom guilty of boasting about themselves or what they've done. Their humility is disarmingly attractive. Many who are successful and great often have a very difficult time understanding that fact. Because they fear you might not be aware of who and what they are, they feel an irresistible urge to inform you.

During President Reagan's stay in the hospital upon the occasion of his attempted assassination, he spilled his bedpan. Though it was in the middle of the night, he could have easily called for assistance and allowed someone else the task of the demeaning cleanup. Instead, he got down on his hands and knees and cleaned up the mess himself.

Make a decision to consciously attempt to make a smile a part of your wardrobe. As strange as it may sound, wearing a smile can change your entire personality.

Decide to think twice before ever engaging in ill-advised actions such as gossip, slander, or degrading insults.

Decide that you will become known for your generosity; it will truly pay you dividends that may exceed all that you ever give away.

There is something very attractive about a humble person. Others are particularly impressed by someone who they later discover had something to brag about but didn't. Your reputation with others rises when they learn about your accomplishments from someone other than you. It fails when you finally assume they will never know about your abilities and success unless you tell them – so, you make the *mistake* of telling them.

Decide that you will put an end to your pride and arrogance. As my grandmother used to tell me: "If you are any good, others will blow your horn for you."

GUARD YOUR MIND

This concept contains some very significant applications most of us seldom if ever, think about.

I spent my college days as a student at the University of Houston. As a member of the golf team, I spent a lot of time at the golf course. One weekday I was working on putting on the practice green, which was located near the clubhouse and the main entrance to the golf course. It was a rather unimpressive entry in so much as it was only reachable by driving through the parking lot of a shopping center.

I remember it was midmorning on what was starting to be a very quiet day at the course. As I was standing on the practice green, I heard a loud backfire. Minutes later I heard a siren. The siren kept getting closer and closer until I realized that it was right outside the entrance to the golf course in the parking lot of the shopping center. I hurried over to see what was going on.

Parked up against the fence was an older, dark-colored car. A police cruiser had pulled up near the old car. I remembered seeing that car parked there when I drove in earlier. Maybe I noticed it because it was well away from any of the other cars. There were plenty of empty spaces in the lot. There wasn't another car parked within fifty yards of this car. I didn't draw any conclusions when I drove in, but now those curiosities came to mind.

I walked out into the parking lot in the direction of the side of the car. When I was ten to fifteen feet away, I saw that the back door of the car was slightly open. There was blood dripping from the bottom of the doorway down onto the pavement! I couldn't see into the car without getting closer. But something told me that I might be sorry if I looked into the side window. I circled to the back of the car and peered through the rear window. Inside was a man slumped into the backseat with a shotgun in his lap! It was easy to see what had happened. I knew right then my curiosity had ended! I did not want to view the scene inside the car. I walked away without saying a word to the policeman or even glancing over at the car. Wisely, I believe, I had protected my mind from an image I would never have forgotten.

Years later, I was wrapping some food in aluminum foil to be put into the refrigerator. When I first started pulling the foil out of the box, I noticed how smooth, unmarked, and pristine the foil appeared. Within seconds, I had created dozens of marks, or small folds, in the foil. No matter what I might have done to smooth them out or attempt to remove those marks, they were there to stay.

As I was standing there, the memory of the suicide at the golf course came to my mind. I realized that I had spared myself the memory of that gruesome incident – one that otherwise would have been with me for the rest of my life. I didn't want to know what his head or face must have looked like. I didn't want that image burned into my memory.

Some events, sights, or memories create marks on the aluminum foil of your mind. The aftermath of horrible auto accidents is often a scene that involves people who are cut, bleeding, and maybe screaming in pain. This is an image that is impossible to forget. The ravages of war cause some of the most brutal maimings of a human body imaginable. When one soldier has to carry a fellow soldier to safety after his leg has been blown off, that merciful soldier is exposed to an event and sight that he'll never forget. Witnesses to these events will never be able to wipe out those extremely disturbing images from their minds.

Viewing pornographic images represents another form of mind-corrosive exposure. It creates deep marks on the aluminum foil of your mind, and *they are not eradicable.* Lives have been ruined by the effects of habitually viewing pornography. What often starts as a lustful curiosity often ends in tragedy. Marriages are ruined and careers are sometimes destroyed as lives rot under the harmful effects of pornographic addictions.

People are often careless when it comes to protecting their minds from images that will be permanently etched into their memory. Don't make that mistake!

Like drug addiction, there are no "safe" doses for viewing pornography, excessive violence, or crude humor. In the privacy of your home, Cable TV and the internet have made these temptations far too easy for even a casual channel surfer to "innocently" view.

However, you must remember: *there is no such thing as innocent viewing!* Thus, you must decide that you will do yourself a favor of inestimable value. Make a covenant with your eyes to avoid viewing anything that will create permanent marks on the aluminum foil of your mind – things that you might one day wish weren't there!

DO THE RIGHT THING

There are often unexpected rewards!

From the moment I first visited Chacala, Mexico, and the surrounding area, I was intrigued by the idea of owning a fruit orchard. Oscar, my right-hand man in Mexico, and I toured several orchards. Some of them weren't of any interest, but those that were of interest were all priced at about $ 4,000 per acre. This was at least twice what I felt I could afford to pay for an orchard. But, because I couldn't shake the dream of owning an orchard, Oscar and I continued to tour orchard properties.

Over the next three to four years, prices continued to rise and our orchard visits became fewer and fewer. I eventually stopped looking.

One day, a man approached Oscar with the prospect of buying his orchard. His son had been involved in a car accident and had totaled the other guy's new car. Because they didn't have insurance, he was stuck with the repair bill. He had concluded that his only solution to the problem was to sell his orchard. He had sixty-two acres and only wanted $45,000 or *$725 per acre*! Oscar immediately told him we would buy it.

At first, I was thrilled. But as I began to think about it, I couldn't escape the nagging thought that this orchard was the man's only asset. Once he sold it, he'd never be able to replace it. Moreover, he was losing it for the most tragic of reasons, not to mention that his land was worth a lot more than he was asking for it!

The next day, I made the painful decision to pass up the opportunity. I told Oscar of my feelings and asked him to tell the orchard owner that he should seek to solve his problem in some other way. I also suggested that Oscar tell him that his orchard was worth many times what he was asking and that he should hold on to it.

While it was difficult to let this fantastic opportunity slip through my fingers, I began to realize that a clear conscience was worth the pain of the loss of that opportunity. I decided that letting this opportunity slide was the right thing to do. By the time Oscar was able to arrange a meeting with the orchard owner to pass along my message, my pain was largely just an unpleasant memory *and my conscience was clear!*

When Oscar finally met with the orchard owner, he listened intently to Oscar's message. He then told Oscar that he truly appreciated our sentiments, but if Oscar was unwilling to buy the orchard at the price offered, he said he would walk out the door and sell his orchard to the first person who would pay him that same price.

At this point, Oscar told him, "We'll buy it." It's easy to postpone your good intentions until the next opportunity comes along, but we had done the right thing. It paid off: a good price and a clear conscious.

Any unwillingness to face the immediate and painful prospects of making the decision you know you should make almost always forfeits the best long-term outcome. In seeking to avoid the short-term pain that may be involved in doing what's right, you are choosing to live with something you knew was wrong, something that could haunt you for a very long time. There is a pain in apologizing to someone you've wronged or offended. But it is the right thing to do. Putting off such a call is the easier way to go. But as time passes, the apology becomes harder and harder to make, and any good the apology might have accomplished lessens. At some point, your apology to the offended party may no longer matter – the passing of time has allowed the rift between you to become a permanent chasm.

This concept even applies to something of seemingly minor importance – like calling a penalty stroke on yourself amid a golf tournament. The pain of the loss stroke is immediate. The damage done by "letting it slide" may continue to haunt you, even years later.

The classic example of letting something slide is the upcoming marriage that one of the partners knows is a mistake and should be called off. Try as he or she might, one can't continue to blame the "wedding jitters" for the things he/she is feeling. Down deep, he/she knows this marriage isn't going to work, but to call it off at the midnight hour – the families, the guests, the wedding gifts, and the embarrassment – it's unthinkable! So, he/she goes forward with the wedding – to his/her subsequent deep regrets and probable future divorce!

The pain of making a difficult (but correct) decision usually lasts but a short time **and whatever short-term damage is done in making such a decision will usually heal itself. The payoff might not be financial but it's real and can be more valuable than any monetary outcome. Knowing you've done the right thing is therapy, in and of itself.**

The damage and pain resulting from the decision you failed to make may be magnitudes greater than the hurt you sought to avoid. It could lead to regrets you can never resolve.

PROTECT YOUR REPUTATION

The younger you are the less you care about it. The older you are the less you can do to change it.!

Your reputation may be one of the most valuable things you own. Even though the payoff may be years in coming, it's worth the effort to build a good one. If you already have a good one, it's worth protecting. Because…once damaged, it's difficult to repair. The shock waves from a reputation-damaging incident can last long and radiate farther than you might ever imagine.

Fortunately, our thoughts are something we can keep private. But our thoughts sometimes become decisions, which then turn into statements or actions. And it is our statements and actions that finally shape our reputation for better, or worse!

A rather simple analogy might help you more fully grasp the importance your reputation plays in your life. Imagine a large picture window. Think of that picture window as representing your life, your self-concept, and what others think of you. When looking through this window, they see you and what you are. They are viewing your reputation.

In your hand, you hold a rock. Think of the rock as symbolizing some personal indiscretion. Should you commit some act of indiscretion, it's like throwing that rock through the picture window. Even though all the pieces of the window may be carefully gathered and meticulously fitted and glued together, the "cobweb" appearance of the window won't go away. Every time someone looks through it, their view is marred by all the cracks caused by the "rock" of your indiscretion. They serve as a constant reminder of your fall from the fraternity of the respected.

And so it is with a damaged reputation. Attempting to shore up your reputation might be compared to attempting to embellish that picture window with a four-inch border of tile or stained glass squares. Prior to the event of the rock meeting the window, such a border might have enhanced the beauty to be enjoyed by looking out the window –framing a view of you and your reputation as it were. In keeping with our analogy, this border might represent reputation-building gestures, such as acts of humility, generosity with your money or your time, some form of self-sacrifice, etc. But, once the rock is thrown through the window, anyone looking through that window will automatically focus on the ugly cracks which quickly divert any notice or appreciation of the embellished border. The person looking at the window may even wonder why anyone would go to the trouble and expense to encase such an ugly window with such an artistic border.

There is a true story of a *highly respected* financial advisor and money manager, a pillar in his community, who was beginning to acquire a reputation as a very savvy investor. A brilliant investment strategy that he had devised had built his reputation in financial circles as a financial genius. His clients were willing to supply testimonials of the wealth he had created for them.

As his success grew, he began attracting more and more people to invest in his money market fund. To launch himself into the big leagues of money management, he offered an inducement of a guaranteed 20 percent annual return to attract the really big money. This strategy caught the attention of some very big "players." He soon became the subject of dinner party conversations. So, it wasn't long before he had attracted some of the wealthiest people in town as prospective clients.

As you might expect, many asked to be shown his methods and to see his books before making any commitment. He refused to say that his secrets were all he had to sell. He explained that once people saw how he did it, they wouldn't need him anymore. If that wasn't a satisfactory answer, he was happy to have them invest their money elsewhere. This should have sounded a loud alarm in their minds, but because all of his older clients had nothing but glowing things to say, most went ahead with the investment rather than persist in knowing more about his methods!

Of course, the more money that came into his fund, *the more 20 percent returns he owed.* Few money managers have ever lived who have been able to consistently produce a return of 20 percent year after year! Yet, that was what he had promised.

The eventual wreckage was widespread. Losses for his clients were staggering and this financial wizard went to jail for what now would be universally recognized as a Ponzi scheme!

Tiger Woods, once a national icon with a wholesome image, now suffers the enormous consequences of his indiscretions. His golf accomplishments may always be coupled with, or overshadowed by, his philandering. There isn't any place Tiger can go where his past baggage doesn't travel with him. He'll live the rest of his life plagued by the universal awareness of his debauchery.

Rich or poor; young or old; famous or the man on the street; the well-educated or the uneducated – all benefit greatly from a good reputation. Conversely, all suffer under the weight of a bad one – even presidents!

Think of the colossal blunder former President Richard Nixon made when he went along with the Watergate break-in scheme. Following his resignation as President of the United States, I watched the hollow gesture of his wave salute as he left Washington DC to climb the steps of the plane that would take him back to California, leaving the White House, and his presidency forever! What greater price could he have paid than this universal humiliation?

Former President Clinton threw away his reputation and suffered immense embarrassment in front of the whole nation, in fact, in front of the entire world! He may be better remembered for his dalliances with Monica Lewinsky than for any of his accomplishments as President of the United States.

What are the chances that either of these former presidents can ever hope to erase people's memories or repair the damage to their reputations those blunders created?

Most start life with a relatively neutral reputation. During your life, you will create your reputation. Along the way, you will face situations or temptations that have the potential to ruin it.

Realize that *temptations* are the possible beginnings of something you'll have to live down! Should you yield to those temptations, no matter the extent of your efforts to keep the lid on your indiscretions, you should count on their eventual discovery. As for that group born into fame, wealth, or royalty, their lives are already in the limelight. They should never think their mistakes won't make a front-page!

If up to now you have avoided all those things that cause reputational damage, it's time to participate in things that can positively contribute to a good reputation. This is the creation of that beautiful stained glass border around your picture window. It speaks of personal sacrifice, doing things that benefit others, and attitudes of humility.

Decide now as to the kind of reputation you would like to leave behind and direct your thoughts, statements, and actions accordingly.

VI. DEALING WITH PEOPLE

There are three different levels of interaction with others: business, social, and friendship. While the eleven principles included in this section can't claim to cover all aspects of this subject, the truths to be found in some of these principles do serve as reminders of frequently overlooked facets of understanding people and dealing with their character traits.

The first five of these principles apply largely to business relationships: It May Be Legal, But Is It Right?, Protect Your Interests, There Are Givers…And Takers, Investigate Any Potential Associate and Guard Against The Inside Job.

One principle, Beware The Charmer, deals with both business and friendship relationships.

The last five principles apply to business, friendships, and social involvements: Is He Your Friend?, He's Your Competitor…Don't Forget It, Identify The Dominator, Don't Burn Bridges, and Trade Viewpoints.

Some of the concepts contained within these decision-making aids may feel familiar; yet, you might be pleasantly surprised by your exposure to the nuances that can provide fresh insights and subtle understandings (helpful understandings) that may not have occurred to you previously.

IT MAY BE LEGAL, BUT IS IT RIGHT?

Is this a sign of the times, or have people always been this way?

Saturday mornings are busy times at the bakery. It's always crowded.

I remember walking in and waiting for my turn to be called. Since there were about six people in line ahead of me, I lost myself in a study of the goodies in the display cases. A few more people walked in after me and took their places at the back of the store. After patiently waiting about ten minutes, the customers ahead of me had made their selections and paid their bills. I stepped to the counter to tell the clerk what I wanted when I heard this voice call out, "Number forty-two." Some guy from the rear of the shop came forward and laid this little stub, numbered forty-two, on the counter. I looked at him and said, "Gee, I guess I forgot to take a number but I was ahead of you. I had already been here ten minutes when you walked in."

He answered, "Maybe so, but according to their rules, I have the right to be served next…sorry." So, without any hint of guilt, shame, or embarrassment he went about the business of placing his pastry order. All I could do then was run over to the number machine and take a number. But I had moved to the back of the line which, in the meantime, had become longer!

Now, I can't fault this man because he did nothing wrong. He was just observing the rules. However, I have been in a situation like this where I was the one holding the "number" and a woman who had come in before I did had forgotten to take one. I gave her my place in line.

I had hoped this man's sense of fair play would have dictated a similar concession to me. After all, the cost to him (if there even was a cost) was that mere two-minute delay while he waited for my order to be filled. The cost to me, however, was to be relegated to the back of a now long line to wait for another ten to fifteen minutes for my turn to come up again – all because I had failed to take a number.

No matter whose side you'd take, it's obvious that many people operate based on what's legal, not necessarily based on what's right or fair. It's amazing how different these two can sometimes be.

The countless number of bizarre (frivolous) lawsuits being filed today highlight people's warped sense of fairness. When it comes to money, many people, even some whom I had regarded as friends, are capable of the unbelievable…and they are all quite comfortable with the posture they've adopted because of the "legality" of it all.

Make no mistake: if you are dealing with a person who is willing to press his "legal" rights over a small matter in the bakery store, *watch out* when some real money is involved. You will have your hands full dealing with him!

It is a large mistake to ever make a decision or commitment based upon an assumption of the honest and ethical inclinations of someone you don't know very well. Unfortunately, this principle sometimes applies to people whom you do know.

Don't make decisions where the benefits you are hoping to receive depend upon the other person doing what's right, or fair. All too often they will only feel bound by what's legal. **You cannot count on them to do what's right. Consider yourself lucky if they're even bound by what's legal.**

No matter the conduct of others, *decide that you'll forget about what you could "legally" get away with and do what is right,* **you'll seldom regret it.**

PROTECT YOUR OWN INTERESTS

You, and others you know, may reject this concept but to do so is to deny the realities of human nature.

My wife and I were spending a lazy day lying on a beach in Mexico with nothing to do but listen to the waves, read a book, and ward off the beach vendors.

After several annoying interruptions by the unrelenting vendors, one came by with an article that I liked. I asked him how much he wanted for it and he quickly answered, "Thirty dollars." It wasn't worth that much to me. So, I thanked him for his trouble but told him that the most I would pay were twelve. Typical of all beach vendors, he was not easily discouraged. He said, "Amigo, this is fine quality. You would be a lucky man if I sell you this for twenty-six." I repeated my twelve-dollar offer. He countered at twenty- four, but I stuck with my offer of twelve. He finally said, "This is your lucky day, amigo. I will sell to you for eighteen dollars!" I said, "Sorry, my best offer is still twelve."

He countered, "Sixteen." I replied, "Forget it." He said, "OK – twelve." After paying him and watching him walk away, I began to feel guilty. The more I thought about it, the worse I felt. I asked myself, *"What kind of jerk beats up a poor beach vendor? After all, he's only trying to make a living"*.

A few days later, despite some feelings of guilt whenever I thought about the incident, I had finally put the beach vendor out of my mind. Until…we were in the village roaming through the various gift shops when I spotted the *same article* that I had purchased from that beach vendor sitting on a shelf in one of the gift shops. I couldn't resist looking at the price tag. Would you believe…eight dollars? What made his price seem even higher was the fact that those gift shop operators pay enormous rents. Their markups have to be extremely high in order to cover their overhead. What must the actual wholesale price of that article have been? Even at twelve dollars, he made out just fine. In fact, in his position of having no overhead, he could purchase his entire inventory from that gift shop (at their *retail* price) and easily make 50 percent of his money! All he had to do was find more suckers like me. Somehow, I no longer felt guilty.

Some people say that they subscribe to a negotiating philosophy of "win-win" as the guiding principle of their negotiations. A cursory examination of this philosophy might lead one to favor it as the proper approach. But human nature being what it is, given half a chance, people are prone to take every advantage they can.

Such was the contention of John Nash, a Nobel prize recipient whose theories were the subject of the movie, *A Beautiful Mind*. The movie pointed out that his award was the result of his theory regarding a nation's behavior in international economic negotiations. It stated that nations could predictably be expected to always act in their own best interest. Thus, according to Nash, people are self-preservationists. What may start as a commitment to a philosophy of "win-win," often ends up anything but?

If this is true, can one ever expect a "win-win" philosophy to prevail? You might anticipate a negotiation with a good friend to be a pleasant "win-win" experience. Yet, we've all heard of the tragic cases where best friends have become bitter enemies over business deals – deals that were conceived with the very expectation of a "win-win" outcome. With the possible exception of negotiations over the distribution of the assets from the estate of a deceased relative, you might insist that a "win-win" outcome should be expected in negotiations involving a *close* family member. However, many victims of family battles can knowingly speak of other subjects, or areas of negotiation, wherein close family members also failed to achieve satisfactory outcomes from their "win-win" attempts. It seems that even the bonds of familial closeness don't prevent lawsuits that pit children against their father, mother, or each other!

In marriage, the supposedly closest of all human relationships, countless negotiations are conducted under conditions that could never be described as "win-win."

The "win-win" approach may find you making compromises you're not particularly comfortable making. These compromises, supposedly an aid to a successful negotiation, often turn out to be one-sided. Your opponent may have little interest in compromise, giving little more than lip service to a "win-win" result.

While a ruthless approach to your negotiations is not recommended, an attitude of self-protection is!

Forget "win-win" and look out for your own best interests! **Don't worry; despite altruistic statements made to the contrary, the other person will quite naturally be looking out for theirs. That beach vendor was not about to sell that item to me for less than his cost!**

THERE ARE GIVERS...AND TAKERS

This taker surprised me, but true of all takers, he behaved predictably.

Years ago, I was involved in a real estate project that at one point in its development needed an infusion of cash. Since I was not in favor of bringing a partner into my project, I decided to find a lender who would loan me the money I needed for the completion of the infrastructure for the project.

For various reasons, my project didn't fit within normal banking guidelines. However, there are several financial institutions that either make loans directly or are in the business of searching for organizations that provide financing that falls outside the requirements of standard commercial banks.

A friend of mine, Chuck, was aware of a financial institution that he thought would welcome a loan application from a project such as mine. He introduced me to a friend of his named Al who represented this institution, which I'll refer to as ABC Financial. Though ABC didn't make loans, they were an example of an institution that worked with borrowers to find sources of financing needed by the borrower. Since I knew Chuck, and both Chuck and Al had good reputations in the community, I decided to engage in initial discussions with ABC Financial.

A brief introductory meeting with some of ABC's staff allowed me to present my project and explain its needs. That meeting resulted in a positive response to my project. They urged me to continue to pursue their help in identifying the source of the funds I needed.

However, they informed me that before they could begin, I had to wire transfer $7,500 to their bank account in Philadelphia. They explained that this was to pay for the cost of the research that would be needed to create a presentation convincing enough to interest a lender.

I later realized that much of that, if not all, probably went to Al as a commission for his role in getting me to sign up with ABC.

I told them that I wouldn't make any payment without receiving, in writing, the terms and conditions of the proposed loan. They immediately sent their letter of "interest," which stated that they were pleased to advise me of their acceptance of my application. They outlined the terms of the three-year loan which would include an interest rate of seven percent, plus an origination fee of three percent. This translated to an up-front fee of $150,000. Over the three-year life of the loan, I would be paying a total of $1,200,000 in interest and fees. If all went well with their detailed research of my project, they would issue what they called a term sheet. Coincident with that issuance, I would be required to pay a $15,000 loan fee. This was in addition to the $7,500 I had already paid. I would also be obligated to pay all travel expenses of their appraiser's site visit to my project. It all seemed very expensive. Yet, I needed the money and since I felt good about both Chuck and Al, I decided to move forward

The first step in this in-depth investigation process required that I provide ABC's research committee with all the relevant information about myself and my project (past, present, and future). While this process was going on, I was contacted by a woman who had been assigned the duty of appraising and physically inspecting my project. I bought plane tickets for both of us, secured a hotel room for her, and paid for her transportation and meals.

When that process was finally concluded, I received a call telling me that the term sheet had been issued and it was now time to pay the last $15,000. I informed them of my concerns with proceeding. I had no evidence that a loan would be forthcoming and the very reason I was seeking a loan was my current lack of money. I stated that their current request was dear money to me and that I needed assurances that there would be a loan available to me after this process. ABC informed me that they already had a lender for the project in hand, so I sent in the last $15,000.

After a few days had passed, I received a call from John who was ABC's person in charge of making the actual contacts with the lenders. He announced that he had a letter of intent from a lender. I asked him what the terms of the loan were, and he answered that it would be a three-year loan with *eight points* of loan fees. This would amount to a total of $400,000 in loan fees *which were in addition to the fees I would be paying ABC!* I was scared to death to hear what interest rate was being proposed. I should have been sitting down when he told me the rate for the first year would be 12 percent, the second year 15 percent, and a whopping 18 percent in the third year. Over the three-year term of the loan, I would be paying $2,650,000 just in fees and interest! This stood in sharp contrast to the $1,200,000 in total fees and interest I had been promised when I sent them the first $7,500. I was crushed and incredibly angry.

I called John to ask what happened to the terms I had been quoted when they so hotly pursued me for all their loan fees. He said that the market had changed. Baloney! The time between their initial quote and this report was too short for such a gigantic change to have occurred. He then reassured me that this loan offer was just their first shot at it. I should relax and give him a little time to get responses from all the other lenders that had been given my folder. I remember hanging up thinking, *I'll bet this will be the only loan offer they'll ever present to me.*

My hunch was right. No other loan offers ever surfaced. I am now certain they knew what the terms of this loan proposal were (terms they knew I could never afford nor accept) when they were pressing me to pay the final $15,000 loan fee. They had used this "promise" of a loan to convince me to go ahead and pay them their final loan fee before revealing this loan's onerous terms. I felt they knew that once the terms were revealed to me, I wouldn't send in that last payment of $15,000. They judged correctly. There was no way I could not afford to go forward with the loan – the fees and interest would capsize me.

I called Chuck and informed him of the terms of the loan I had been offered. He remarked that this wasn't a loan, it was confiscation.

I immediately called Al and told him I wanted to meet with him to discuss the situation.

At that meeting, I reiterated the loan terms that I'd been promised versus those that were now being offered. I voiced my belief that they knew that the only lender they had was quoting terms that were well beyond what they had led me to believe would be available. They were fully aware that I could *never* agree to terms such as these! I also told him I was certain they knew the terms and conditions of this loan offer when they told me they already had a lender who was interested in making a loan proposal to me but didn't disclose them to me for fear I wouldn't send them that last $15,000 loan fee!

Despite their obvious awareness of the great disparity between the loan pricing that had originally enticed me and this outrageous proposal, they continued to lead me to believe they would be able to secure a loan under the terms and conditions originally quoted.

Given their deception, I wanted Al to approach the president of the company and request a refund of at least $15,000. As I was making this request of Al, who up to that point had been maintaining eye contact with me, he slowly looked down and without raising his head said, "That would be awkward." Despite ten more minutes of reiterating my beliefs and making strong assertions that Al was damaging his reputation by doing business with people like this, Al refused my request to seek the return of any of my money. I felt certain that he had received a commission from my payment of the loan application fee, but even when confronted with my conclusions, he made no offer to seek a refund of my $15,000 or even return any of the commission he had unjustly received. Al was a taker. In retrospect, I'm sure he was aware of the truth of my allegations.

It might seem that my assumptions about what went on were exaggerated guesses that were the result of my deep disappointment about the loss of the money I had paid as well as the dashed dreams of getting the loan under the terms and conditions that were so appealing. Had I just jumped to some wrong conclusions?

All doubt about the accuracy of my suspicions, however, was removed when Chuck sent me an article that had appeared in the *Wall Street Journal*. It read:

"The Federal Bureau of Investigation and securities regulators in California and Pennsylvania are probing a Philadelphia-based loan broker over allegations that more than 100 prospective borrowers lost millions of dollars through a practice in which the firm collected upfront fees for real estate development financing but didn't find any funding."

The article also mentioned that the financial institution had been named as a defendant in six civil lawsuits in California that alleged an "advance fee scheme" which collected nonrefundable fees from would-be borrowers with "no intention of providing the financing."

Subsequent conversations with two other *legitimate lenders* confirmed the dishonest and illegal nature of ABC's dealings. They both claimed that they had learned that the executives of ABC were part of the Russian mafia and that authorities were trying to shut them down!

It makes you wonder about Al. At worst, he knew what he was doing and was one of them. At best, he's a purebred taker and, as such, wasn't anyone I should have been doing business within the first place.

Most people are either givers or takers. When two givers do business together, neither of them will certainly come away injured.

When doing business with a taker, it's seldom a fifty-fifty proposition. They are always self-serving. Their objective is to see how much they can squeeze out of you in a negotiation.

Before engaging in serious dealings with someone, determine which type they are. If they're a taker, despite what you give, your gesture will not be reciprocated. Be forewarned, you cannot expect them to willingly give you anything.

INVESTIGATE ANY POTENTIAL ASSOCIATE

Some people first present themselves in disguise. Only later does the mask come off.

A longtime friend, Richard, and I share a love for Mexico. He is an ex-banker who is now spending his time identifying lenders who will finance land and home purchases in Mexico.

Approximately eight years ago, I became involved in a development project in Mexico. Richard reacted enthusiastically to my new venture and not long after that came to my home with a new acquaintance of his to announce their intentions to join hands in a mortgage/finance company that would specialize in loans in Mexico, something they thought might be helpful to me.

Richard seemed quite impressed with his new partner, Aaron. For some reason, I had exactly the opposite reaction. A month or two later, they once again came to my house to further discuss the availability of Mexican mortgages with me. During that meeting, Aaron said some things that further added to my suspicions about him. When Richard informed me that he intended to go into partnership with Aaron to buy a piece of development ground, I felt obligated to warn him about my doubts and fears regarding Aaron – particularly as a would-be partner.

Richard assured me that he saw no reason to distrust Aaron, but thanked me for my concern. Explaining that he needed some of Aaron's experience and contacts, Richard proceeded to consummate the partnership with Aaron. A short time later, they bought the piece of land and arranged for some large loans to assist in the development of their new project.

One day Richard called in a state of shock. Aaron had helped himself to the large balance that was sitting in their joint bank account! Richard was devastated! Richard was now in a very tight spot. The money that

Aaron had taken represented funds they had *borrowed* to advance their project. Several serious concerns began to haunt Richard: What would the lender think? Would they also blame him? What should he do?

Not knowing any of the answers, Richard decided to confront Aaron regarding the missing funds before telling the lender. But Aaron was nowhere to be found. Richard began to check into Aaron's background.

He discovered a trail of similar misdeeds. Aaron was a career crook! One day Richard informed me that he had finally tracked Aaron down. The exchange between them left Richard feeling physically threatened. Richard confided that this unsavory aspect of Aaron's persona was a part of the checkered past that his background investigations of Aaron had revealed.

A short while later, Aaron came boldly calling on Richard to notify him that he would not go away quietly. Richard realized the lengthy amount of time a court trial in Mexico might take during which everything would be tied up – not to mention the uncertainty of the outcome. Adding the threat of physical harm from Aaron, Richard decided he wasn't willing to take these risks and agreed to pay a "severance fee" to Aaron. Months passed, and Aaron finally accepted a payoff in the tens of thousands to "go away." Aaron's parting gesture was the theft of all the computers and electronic equipment they had in their shared office!

You can never afford to relax your standards regarding your selection of a potential business associate. Don't compromise this principle by collaborating with a person of questionable character or unethical conduct…for any length of time, for any reason.

Insist on knowing everything you can about the reputation of those you are contemplating conducting any in-depth business with, ***particularly*** **someone you'd ever consider for a partner.**

You will then have restricted your business dealings to persons of ***known good character*** **who have** ***reputations worth protecting.***

GUARD AGAINST THE INSIDE JOB

Some things can cause you to lose your faith in people.

At one point in my business career, I had the bright idea of buying businesses and finding some young, ambitious man to run them. I planned to offer him a salary that wouldn't break the bank but give him the option of buying half the business, at my original cost, five years down the road. If he made the business successful, we'd both have a good deal.

I found Tony, the brother of one of my friends. I described my plan and he was all for it. All we needed was a business.

Another friend of mine told me about a manufacturing facility that had gone out of business. The assets of that business were being auctioned off by the SBA. Tony and I had some long discussions and all was well; he was eager to proceed should we be successful at the auction.

The auction attracted quite several interested parties. As the bidding got underway, first one potential buyer and then another dropped out. Finally, there was only one other guy and myself still bidding. I felt strongly the bidding was getting at, or very near, the top. It was my turn to answer the bid the other bidder had just made. I was 99 percent sure that if I raised the other fellow's bid, I'd own that equipment. Tony was my only reason for buying this business as I had no time, ability, or interest in running it myself. I turned to Tony before deciding to continue bidding and asked him if he was still with me. He said, "Yes, I am."

I raised the other man's bid and, as I suspected, became the proud owner of a collection of window and door manufacturing equipment. Two weeks later, Tony called and told me he was not going to be joining me in the window and door business!

For a couple of weeks, I didn't do anything about that devastating news. One day, while I was at the warehouse cleaning up and trying to decide what to do next, a twenty-one-year-old man, Tim, came to the warehouse and told me he was aware of my situation and wondered if I'd be willing to hear his reasons for hiring him for the job of managing the business. He told me not to be misled by his age. He had already been in the business for many years and knew it backward and forward. He asked me to give him a chance. He promised that I would never be sorry if I hired him. So, I did.

Under Tim's management, we were making steady progress in all areas. As sales picked up, our business was beginning to grow.

A year or two later, an appeal was circulated within the small business community suggesting that small business owners consider hiring Vietnamese refugees, known as the "Vietnamese boat people," who were seeking asylum in this country. Tim and I discussed it and thought they would appreciate the gesture. We were also aware of their reputation for being hardworking, responsible workers.

With Tim and the Vietnamese, we finally had a team that was an efficient, well-oiled machine. The business became, and remained, profitable for quite some time.

But then, for reasons I couldn't understand, profits started falling off. I talked to Tim about it, and he reassured me that things would turn around. But rather than turn around our lowered profits turned into losses.

One evening, not long afterward, one of our non-Vietnamese employees went down to the plant to pick up some windows for a delivery scheduled for early the next morning. I received a call at home that evening from that employee who told me that he caught Tim and the Vietnamese using our equipment and our materials to make windows that they were selling at night, out the back door!

The cause of my losses was an "inside job." I couldn't believe this about Tim. This was the same young man who had begged me to give him a chance. The one who promised I'd never be sorry I hired him. As for the Vietnamese, they were the needy refugees who we had been asked to help. I was stunned to realize that the ones we had befriended and my most trusted employee were the enemies in the camp!

I've heard it said that locks serve to separate people into three groups. The first group would be those who would never enter, uninvited, any home, locked or not. The second group is made up of those who will try to break-in whether locked or not (if you suspect that someone in your employ is of this ilk, you need to find some reason to get rid of them as quickly as you can). The third group is made up of those who would never try to enter a locked home, but the lure of an unlocked home presents a temptation they often cannot resist. Locks, and other safeguards, are meant for those in that last group; these are the ones who loot the homes of flood, hurricane, or earthquake victims.

Make a decision to place safeguards on your business secrets, checkbooks, bank accounts, material inventories, tools, and assets of the business. No matter how well you think you know your employees, you can *never* be certain about who you can trust. Don't provide a temptation for anyone to take advantage of unprotected assets.

Decide that you will put safeguards on that which you don't want to lose.

BEWARE THE CHARMER

They're so likable! But, almost all con men are charmers.

I encountered a lot of challenges during the development of my real estate project in Mexico. Doing business in another country often subjects you to a different set of rules. It takes time to get acquainted with these rules – both as to what they are and precisely how they work.

In the U.S., land developer faces similar needs; however, there are standard solutions. The installation of infrastructure services (water, electric, telephone, etc.) can be successfully handled by several licensed and bonded contractors who are very competent at what they do. Some of the things that seem rather automatic in the U.S. are not so automatic in Mexico.

We were to learn about this when the day came to begin the installation of our electric system. We began the process by interviewing and getting bids from various electrical contractors.

One day, when Oscar (my right-hand man in Mexico) and I were meeting with our surveyor, Jorge, and our attorney, Max, on another matter, Sr.Arteaga, an acquaintance of both Max and Jorge, joined us for lunch. I felt an immediate affinity for Sr. Arteaga. He was very mannerly and soft-spoken. He was clean and well-dressed, and he had a pleasant, almost disarming smile. I not only felt an instant liking for him but also felt certain that he was a man I could trust.

After attending to the things for which the meeting had been called, the conversation steered toward our need for a competent, trustworthy electrical contractor.

To our surprise, Sr. Arteaga said that he had a very capable man, Juan Carlos, who did that kind of work for him. He said he would be willing to put Juan Carlos on our payroll and allow him to remain with us until our electrical system was completed and correctly installed.

After concluding the discussion about our electric system, Max pulled Sr. Arteaga into the conversation by mentioning that he was a big government contractor who was involved in building roads and other public works projects for the government. This opened the door for me to mention that I had just imported two heavy earth-moving machines into Mexico, a backhoe and an excavator worth approximately $120,000, to sell them to a Mexican contractor.

When Sr. Arteaga heard this, he said he would be interested in buying both of the machines. After some questions, answers, and a brief discussion, he suggested that he would be willing to commit to a payment plan that would provide for the full payout of my asking price for the machines, plus interest, within one year. My only area of concern regarding his offer was the fact that he didn't have any funds currently available for a down payment. But since Sr. Arteaga was just beginning work on a large government road project, he had a pressing need for the two machines. This fortunate timing would enable him to start making money immediately on the two machines and would provide the means to quickly get that money into my hands.

Still wrestling somewhat with the idea of selling such valuable machines with absolutely no security, Jorge and Max each told me that they felt they knew Sr. Ateaga was well enough to assure me that he was good for his word and would honor any agreement he made.

So, I decided to go ahead with the sale. I even managed to get comfortable with it, maybe because Sr. Arteaga was such a charming guy! Although Sr. Arteaga quickly made arrangements to have the machines picked up, many months passed during which only a few payments were made. For *more than a year*, Arteaga had only paid us $40,000. As a result of applying considerable pressure, he arranged to have the backhoe returned to us. After reading the hour-clock in the machine, we determined that the $40,000 he had paid barely covered the number of hours of the machine-time he had used. Upon inspection, we learned that the machine was not in good condition and repairs would be necessary before it could even be operated again. On

On top of all this, I was yet to receive *the first dollar* in payments on the excavator!

After this experience, Oscar made an immediate call to Sr. Arteaga to insist upon the return of the excavator. Many excuses were followed by many phone calls from Oscar. Finally, Oscar began to experience great difficulty in reaching him by phone. Oscar called Max and Jorge to report the disappointing experiences we were having with Sr. Arteaga. Neither of them could believe what was happening. It appeared that they had also fallen victim to his charm. Max then assisted us in taking the bold step of preparing a warrant for Arteaga's arrest!

Upon learning about this, Sr Arteaga quickly called to tell us that he had sold the excavator and had not been paid anything for it. When asked where the machine was, his vague reply was that the "new owner" had taken it somewhere in the Yucatan!

We never saw Arteaga or my machine again. He had successfully stolen an $80,000 machine!

Many of us have fallen victim to charmers. You want to believe their smiling faces and free-flowing compliments. You believe they like you and want to be your friend. But it is important not to allow their mastery of charm cause you to relax your good judgment.

It's best to maintain a healthy sense of skepticism until you can say that you know them well. No matter how impressed with them you may be, or how much you like them, don't allow their charm to cause you to throw caution to the wind in your dealings with them.

Decide to stand the charmer against the same tests of character and reputation as you would with any potential business relationship, and conduct that test as though he was a stranger!

IS HE REALLY YOUR FRIEND?

A true friend is someone who treats you the same when you need something from him as when he needs something from you.

On our first trip to Puerto Vallarta, we were immediately impressed with both the beauty of the place and the incredible weather. My wife had cut out an article from one of her magazines that suggested any journey to Puerto Vallarta should include a breakfast at the Garza Blanca Hotel.

One day, we decided to drive out there for breakfast. It certainly was not a disappointment. We liked it so much that we decided to inquire about a banner on the back wall of the restaurant that advertised villas for sale. Before we headed back to Denver, we had signed a contract for the purchase of one of their villas.

Over the years of our ownership, we got to know some of our neighbors. One, in particular, was a family from Guadalajara who owned the largest soap factory in Mexico as well as a vacation home near our villa. The patriarch of the family was an older gentleman, but one of his sons, Eduardo, was my age. Eduardo and I became friends. We played golf together, we were invited to their house for lunch, and he and his wife even traveled to Colorado for a visit and stayed with us at our home.

Years later, Eduardo called one day saying that he and his family had decided to sell the land between our villa and their vacation home. They had decided to subdivide it into four parcels, one-quarter of an acre each. Because one of those parcels was adjacent to our villa, I agreed to buy it. During the discussion about that purchase, I asked Eduardo if we could gain access to it from his entry road since the only other way was to cut a hole in a beautiful retaining wall that had been constructed by the Garza Blanca Hotel. After cutting through the wall, we'd still have to negotiate a steep bank that was behind the wall. All of this did not even address the issue of getting a permit from the hotel to destroy the wall. That whole ordeal would ruin the appearance of the courtyard on one side and create an unwelcome intrusion into that piece of land for the driveway access. The other point of concern for me was if I were to ever sell that piece separately, I knew the hotel wouldn't provide water for the buyer. So, I asked Eduardo if my purchase of his parcel would include access and the provision of water to that parcel. He said, "My good friend, Gary, this is no problem. I will make sure you have access and water should you ever wish to sell off that piece." Because of our friendship, I felt it would be insulting to request a written guarantee of those items.

Years later, we decided to sell the villa. A prospective buyer came along who, wouldn't you know, wanted to be guaranteed water and satisfactory access to the piece we had purchased from Eduardo. I called Eduardo to alert him to the need for the water and the access he had promised me years earlier.

He said, *"Gary, I'm afraid that I can't do that!"*

Floored, I reminded him of his commitment to me. I told him that his promises were not only pivotal in my agreement to purchase this piece of land from him in the first place, but were also crucial to my being able to sell the parcel to this prospective buyer. He weakly apologized but reaffirmed his unwillingness to provide the things I needed. *Some friend!*

Looking back, I felt that I had treated Eduardo like the friend I thought he was. I had assumed a depth of relationship that obviously wasn't there and in the process, I let my guard down.

A similar story was part of an old Frank Sinatra movie, *A Hole in the Head*. The character who Frank played, Tony Manetta, was the owner of a hotel and was a widower with a twelve-year-old son. Due to his rather free-living lifestyle and irresponsible money management, he was about to lose the hotel to foreclosure. At one point, things became so lean that all the cash Tony had to his name was $200. He desperately needed to raise some money to save his hotel.

Upon hearing that an old college buddy, Jerry Marks, who had become wealthy, was coming to town, Tony got his hopes up for some financial help from his friend. Tony's reunion with his long-lost pal came amidst a great round of backslapping and "old buddy" recollections.

To stay close to Jerry, and hopefully secure some financial assistance, Tony readily agreed to Jerry's suggestion that they go to the horse races together. At the beginning of the first race, Jerry said that he was going to bet several hundred on that race and offered to take Tony's bet to the window for him. To imply that he was financially OK, Tony said, "Sure, count me in." Attempting to impress his friend and keep up with Jerry's wager, Tony picked a horse and bet his last $200 on it. As the race began, Tony swallowed hard realizing that he just bet his last $200 on a horse he'd never heard of before!

As his horse began to fall behind, he panicked. His highly emotional, and excessive rooting for the horse tipped off Jerry. Jerry quickly sized up Tony's situation and brushed him off as a deadbeat bum. Tony's "friend" showed himself for what he was…insincere. Jerry would never have given Tony a dime. The decision to count on this "phony" as a a friend in need led to a sad ending.

But, Tony's friendship was of no greater quality. Tony's only real interest in his visiting friend was in his wallet. In the end, each of these men realized that they didn't have a friend in the other.

How many friends do you think you have?

Many are guilty of using the word "friend" rather loosely. A friendship that is based only on social interactions is yet to face the trials brought about by the introduction of more serious issues. Regrettably, these issues may expose the relationship for what it is… *an acquaintanceship.*

True friendship is based upon a mutual interest in what is best for the other, with personal gain not being sought by either party. Genuine friends will not usually be found in any group of people

for whom relationships are a fourth-level priority – behind money, status, and things. Thus, you are wise to decide not to count on someone as a friend for whom these things are all important.

People who are your friends only because of who you are or what you have are not friends. Hopefully, the friends you pick will also be picking you as their friend using the same criteria.

HE'S YOUR COMPETITOR...DON'T FORGET IT

Competition can do strange things to friendships.

I began playing golf when I was twelve. By age fourteen, I entered my first tournament. At fifteen, I was playing in many tournaments and practiced religiously to improve my game.

Around this time, I met another kid my age, Frank, who was also very enthused about golf. It wasn't long before we were talking on the phone almost every day and sharing stories about golf, our girlfriends, school, our parents, etc. We never ended a conversation without planning our next golf game.

Early on, it became apparent that we competed with each other. Frank thought he was a better golfer than I was, and I thought I was a better golfer than Frank. Because we usually entered the same tournaments, direct comparisons became possible – each wanting to outperform the other. A victory enjoyed by one was always met with congratulations that were little more than a "disguised jealousy" on the part of the other. The only time we genuinely rooted for each other was when we teamed up in a partnership format, called a 4-ball tournament. Even then, whenever one of us was monopolizing the limelight, the one who was looking for his game felt a measure of discomfort.

After college, we went our separate ways, and I do mean separate! I've only talked to Frank *once* in the 40-plus years since, and then only briefly – not what you would call a deep friendship.

True friendship should be characterized by a genuine desire for the other's success or well-being. This becomes extremely difficult if you compete with each other.

All relationships are subject to the possibility of some form of competition between the parties in that relationship. Tragically, competition can destroy a relationship. No matter how close the parties might have been before the appearance of competition between them, its arrival will change everything. The introduction of competition produces envy and jealousy that can become poisons as corrosive to a relationship as battery acid.

The greatest chance for true friendship lies in three situations. The first is to be in partnership with the other person where the success of one benefits the other – like two horses pulling together, as in a marriage.

The second situation is when each person is seeking success in a different arena. While levels of differing achievement might result in some feelings of jealousy on the part of the less successful of the two, the dissimilarity of their circumstances calls for different measuring rods. Hence, direct comparisons become more difficult to assess, and any feelings of inadequacy or superiority are somewhat diluted.

The third situation sees the two friends relating to each other in a mentor/student dynamic. In this case, the mentor shares in the student's rise to success by being partly responsible for that success. The student, of course, feels respect for his mentor as he looks up to him as the maestro. He's dependent upon his mentor for instruction, guidance, and inspiration. However, should the student's abilities, understandings, or accomplishments one day surpass those of his mentor, the future of that relationship will rest upon the attitude of the mentor. If he can genuinely feel as though he too has achieved victory through his student's achievements and restrict his focus to having produced something of excellence, he will have found joy in the fact that his student surpassed him. But if he views his student's ascendency as a threat to his authority and position within the relationship, fallout from the resulting competition will rear its ugly head and the relationship will probably be headed south.

This principle isn't suggesting that true friendships are impossible to find. But it does explain as to why most people have a lot of acquaintances and not nearly so many real friends.

A true friend is an extremely valuable and rare asset – one worth the time, attention, and effort necessary to develop and keep it.

If you desire genuine friends, look in the places where you are likely to find them. That won't usually be from the arena of your competitive encounters or from relationships where envy or jealousy exists.

Look for associations in which each of you can bring benefits to the other. An investment in a mutually beneficial relationship is most likely to bring the love, joy, and camaraderie friendships are supposed to bring. *This can only exist when you and the object of your friendship are not competing with each other.*

Friendships take time to build and develop. If you are willing to give it that time, *make sure the relationships in which you are investing your time and energy have the potential to succeed long-term.*

Any competitors that you've included on your list may prove disappointing.

IDENTIFY THE DOMINATOR

Most people don't change. The outcome of your wishful thinking may be a dismal existence.

Like a scene from the movies, a couple is enjoying a romantic dinner at an expensive restaurant – soft lights and piano music. The restaurant is filled with "beautiful" people.

As the couple in question enjoys a cocktail together, all seems well… until the woman remarks that the man finds offensive. Reacting to the sting, he returns an offensive remark. At this point, the woman insists that her gaffe was unintentional, but she insists that his insult wasn't. As the exchange continues and grows more heated, she finally jumps up, douses him with her martini, and storms out. He's left to mop up, pay the bill, and face the beautiful people as he hurriedly exits.

Unlike her, he was unwilling to make such a scene. If he's ever again up to another challenging evening with her, you can be certain he'll carefully censor any remarks that might cause another tantrum.

When two people have mutually established which of the two is willing to go to the greatest lengths (make the biggest scene or resort to the most extreme actions), that person will "win" all the arguments. They effectively gain control of the other person as a result of their willingness to go to any extent to have their way.

This principle suggests that any person or group of persons can be controlled by that one person among them who's willing to push their point farthest or resort to the most extreme measures to prevail.

The person who cares the least about a relationship can control the outcome of any differences of opinion – and they may do so even if the cost of that control damages, or worse, destroys the relationship.

Power over people, or groups of people, doesn't necessarily require the use of emotional outbursts or threatening tactics. Some people can gain control of people or an organization so subtly that virtually no one is aware of what's taking place. They are opportunists who use sly maneuvering to establish their mastery. Their goal is to gain control over those who are importantly placed – *particularly those in a position to either help them or stand in their way.* They can accomplish this by becoming involved in strategic groups, committees, or boards. They work to arrange positions or assignments that happen to be at critical crossroads in the corporate circuitry. Everything has to go through them for approval. They become formidable foes. Their subtle strategies succeed in making "friends" with all the right people. Eventually, no one dares to buck them.

You need to be aware of any proposed partner or associate's tendency to "bully" people to get their way. It's also wise to try to understand the intentions and anticipate the actions, of that crafty person who manages to control everything. This knowledge should provide a measure of self-protection and give you reasons to reconsider any thought of allying with them. This information will also prove valuable in helping you avoid ever saying or doing something to alienate them or, worse, cause your name to appear on their enemy list!

No matter whether you're dealing with a shrewd manipulator or an explosive, threatening individual, you don't want to be in business with them, or involved in an organization under their control! You will wish you hadn't! They'll thwart anything you do that threatens their position or their ability to wield control over you or your ideas.

This principle should be applied to all relationships, particularly marriage. Someone who's displaying dominating characteristics during courtship won't change after the marriage. To marry someone who needs to control those around them is to live a life under their thumb. If you go ahead and tie the knot, only two choices remain: endure the domination or seek a divorce. Don't expect this leopard to change its spots.

Think about all the life-wrecking marriages and costly divorces that could have been avoided if this principle had been applied to the warning signs that appeared before the marriage ever took place. As the saying goes, love is grand but divorce is one hundred grand.

The application of this principle should help you avoid unhappy relationships, costly split-ups, and martini showers.

Before any important association is formed, carefully note any evidence of the other person's tendency, or need, to dominate.

Before committing to a relationship with a dominating personality, *be certain you can handle it.* **If in your heart you know otherwise, end the relationship! That association is much better left unformed!**

DON'T BURN BRIDGES

A bit of advice you shouldn't ignore!
Many people are guilty of burning a bridge with someone only to greatly regret it later. Sometimes the cause is an emotional outburst where something is said that badly damages, even ruins, the relationship. Some remarks may never be forgiven much less forgotten.

You delude yourself if you think it will be worth it. *It's never worth it* because you never stand to gain anything. The Bible wisely compares the tongue to a spark that's able to set an entire forest on fire.

In the late 1800s, Denver, Colorado was the beneficiary of a flourishing mining industry in the nearby Rocky Mountains. Henry Cordes Brown had come from Ohio to build his luxury hotel, The Brown Palace. The hotel's theme was that of a very upscale, luxury accommodation. It was perfectly suited for those whose success at their mining ventures enabled them to pay the extravagant rates charged by The Brown Palace. The Brown Palace Hotel was qualified to serve, and capable of attracting, the wealthy of that day – as it still does over one hundred years later. Though the guests may have just struck it rich in their mining ventures and might sometimes have been a little rough around the edges, the employees were trained to treat guests with respect and dignity.

An interesting story that has often been repeated down through the years features a rather ordinary-looking man named Charles. He traveled to Denver from one of the mining towns in the mountains, where he owned a hardware store. He decided to stay at The Brown Palace Hotel. After having his bags taken to his room but still in his "mountain clothes," he decided to go to the dining room to enjoy a nice meal.

Once he was seated and given the menu, he waited for the waiter to come to his table. After what seemed like a very long time, his waiter sauntered over to his table. He told the waiter what he wanted for dinner, but the waiter told him that they were out of that. So, Charles reopened the menu and started searching for another selection. The waiter started drumming his fingers in a nervous gesture suggesting that this customer was taking up too much of his time and needed to make up his mind. Despite the pressure from the waiter, Charles remained civil and placed his order. If he thought the waiter was slow in arriving to take his order, the speed of the food's arrival would put that all in perspective.

When the meal finally arrived, Charles saw that his steak was very well-done. Adding to his frustration, the salad had a different dressing on it than what he had ordered. When he informed the waiter of the errors, the waiter muttered to himself, glared at the guest, and gruffly snatched the plates from the table as he walked off in a huff. Charles had not conformed to this waiter's image of a big tipper. Charles finished his dinner and asked for the bill. When the waiter eventually arrived with the bill, Charles informed him that he wasn't going to leave him a tip because of the bad service. He told the waiter that his disturbing attitude put a damper on his enjoyment of the meal. The waiter uttered a few insulting words and stormed off. Though the incident was upsetting to Charles, he kept it to himself and didn't register a complaint with the management.

Years later in 1922, Charles returned to The Brown Palace Hotel. At this point in his life, he had become enormously successful. His investment involvements included banks, meat packing operations, utilities, railroads, ranching, the Ideal Cement Company, and the Great Western Sugar Company. Charles Boettcher was *very* wealthy!

Charles went into the restaurant for a meal and when he spotted his old waiter, he called him over. As the waiter approached, he recognized Charles and braced himself for a few choice words. Well, Charles did have a few very choice words for the waiter and said, "Guess what? *I just bought this hotel…and you're fired!*"

———⸺◦∘◦⧫◦∘◦⸺———

Hold your tongue and refrain from outbursts that are capable of forever altering, even ruining a relationship. You will seldom regret *not* saying something. *Creating enemies never makes sense.*

TRADE VIEWPOINTS

And you thought they couldn't possibly have a viewpoint you'd find worth considering.

When my wife and I traveled to England, we rented a car and had our first experience driving on the left side of the road behind a steering wheel that was on the right side of the car. Adding to that stress, country roads in England are very narrow and twist through the hills with someone always right on your bumper. The freeways, though wider and straighter, encourage bumper-to-bumper traffic moving at speeds of around one hundred miles per hour.

After helplessly watching me barely miss curbs, hedges, and parked cars on her side of the car, my wife finally looked over at me and asked if I had any idea where her side of our car was! Defensively, I reminded her of the extreme skill I had been displaying as I navigated these narrow little roads, all the while dodging the various obstacles along the way. My assurances did nothing to alleviate her anxiety.

I sarcastically suggested we switch places, half expecting her to decline the "opportunity." I was, nevertheless, somewhat relieved when she took the wheel and seemed to relish it! Not long after, however, I became even more uncomfortable than before as I watched her sideswipe two curbs and barely miss a head-on collision.

Until we each had a chance to experience the problems of both the driver and the passenger, we failed to appreciate the challenges and anxieties of the other.

You begin to realize that it is difficult to reach accurate conclusions or make good decisions when your basis for judgment is limited to just your perspective. Decide to take the time and make the effort to put yourself in the other person's shoes.

Your success in virtually any negotiation will be enhanced if you decide to mentally switch places with your opponent and pretend to experience the situation from their perspective. This will also help you appreciate some of their wants and needs – the things that are truly important to them.

It will also provide an insight into their strengths as well as their vulnerabilities and thus help you to develop a strategy for properly responding to them.

The principle of switching seats works equally well when applied to buyer/seller, employer/employee, husband/wife, parent/child, plaintiff/defendant, or virtually any interaction between two people with seemingly opposing interests. Most interactions with people should begin with this simple principle serving as the foundation for building a relationship.

Remember, most people are out to get everything they can for themselves. Decide to take a ride in the passenger seat to get a peak at exactly what it is they want. Then you will begin to understand things from their point of view, even the things beyond just their needs and wants – such things as their hopes and fears

To the extent you can come to some insights as to their position, you may also begin to understand what it might take for them to come to some agreement with you. Additionally, you gain the opportunity, in the privacy of your mind, to ruminate about your ability and willingness to accommodate what you now believe to be their wishes as well as evaluate what might be their counterproposal to your position.

Trade Viewpoints provide an opportunity to understand what is important to the other person by helping you experience the situation through their eyes. You will be assisted in your negotiations when you mentally put yourself in their shoes. This will aid you in perceiving what's important to the other person... *which may not necessarily be what he's telling you is important.*

VII. SUCCESS AND GOAL SEEKING

Being successful is of interest to a great number of people. Yet, its realization eludes most who seek it.

In many ways, success is relative. As an example, a mere millionaire may not feel successful when he compares himself to a billionaire. The first chair violinist in the village orchestra may not feel successful after he hears the master from Carnegie Hall create music from his Stradivarius. On the other hand, the man who is a hero in the eyes of his wife and children is a success no matter the existence of others who have exceeded his "other" accomplishments.

For a breadwinner, the focus is usually on their accomplishments in their job, career, business, or investments. As important to him and his family's survival as these may be, these accomplishments, by themselves, can surprisingly leave some breadwinners with feelings of emptiness. There may come a time, later in life, when they begin to second guess themselves. It's then that they may wish they had invested their time and efforts in other directions, into something that would have given their life deeper meaning.

For a wife or stay-at-home mom, success normally centers on relationships. However, some women choose to enter the business world. Once there, they find themselves in a similar role to that of a male, striving for the same goals common to male breadwinners.

For young people, success is measured in the areas of the school, developing relationships, and extracurricular activities. As they get older, however, their goals change. Their initial goals, having been subject to adolescent interests, may have been poorly defined. One day, these interests and goals will most likely be replaced by new interests and goals that more closely align with their changed circumstances and growing responsibilities. Their former goals may now give rise to some bewilderment.

No matter your station in life, I am defining success as setting goals and meeting them. To avoid the disappointments just mentioned, give the goal-defining process a lot of your attention. Make sure you are devoting your efforts to goals that are worthy of the efforts their realization will require. These should be goals whose cost of accomplishment won't bring later regrets.

The principles presented in this section represent the essentials needed for achieving success – hopefully, your definition of success now agrees with mine.

This section begins with three rather fundamental principles: Make Setting Goals A Habit, To Get There You Must Begin, and Goals You Shouldn't Pursue. They are followed by two important ingredients of the success formula: How Much Pressure Can You Stand? and Is Your Commitment Strong Enough? The latter concept discusses the meaning of commitment and the discipline usually necessary to achieve any notable goal. Together, these should help you better understand yourself and more correctly align your pursuits with the realities of that self-discovery.

The next principle, When In A Battle, Fight to Win! reveals the tenacity that's sometimes necessary to avoid defeat and finally achieve the sought-after prize. It urges your willingness to persevere, fighting for what's important to you. But, be advised, sacrifices may be required. Expand Your Options urges your use of a tool that can lead to a better batting average when it comes to winning battles or overcoming problems.

The next three principles: Focus On Your "A" skills, Passion Separates The Best From The Rest, and Stepping Outside The Box deal with creative approaches to personal development and achievement that have been the reasons behind some remarkable success stories – stories of people who utilized their best skills. You will Pay a Price To Be The Best offers insights regarding the things you should consider about the costs involved in being the ***best.***

MAKE SETTING GOALS A HABIT

How can you hit a target you're not even aiming at?

For years, I had been buying small rental properties. In the process, I had become acquainted with several realtors. One day, a very successful realtor named Mary called me with a proposal. Now, Mary was known for her passion for older buildings, the classic structures that were built in times when handcraftsmanship was still attainable. They were often adorned with handsome woodwork that imparted a richness that their newer counterparts had long since abandoned.

Her proposal involved a twenty-six-unit apartment building that had to be one of the most elegant apartment buildings in the entire historic section of town. Her idea was to turn this Mediterranean-style building into condominiums.

The place had beautiful woodwork, fireplaces in each apartment, a maid's room in some, an extremely attractive built-in buffet cabinet in the dining rooms, and hardwood floors throughout. The rooftop party room had a very classy Mediterranean-style court with a large outdoor deck.

Today, investors and developers would clamor for a building like that. Its potential as a condominium conversion would be obvious to everyone. But as of the year 1974, not one apartment building in the city of Denver had ever been converted into a condominium. If I decided to go along with her proposal, this would be the first. It was a pioneering idea and was referred to as such in the articles written about it in the Denver newspapers.

An old friend, Tom, had watched my success with the smaller apartment buildings and had offered to loan me money on any deal that was too big for me to handle. I was extremely enthused to take on the project. So, I called Tom. With his help, I bought the building and in the process created the most imposing goal of my life.

We hired the most expensive designer in town, Jim, whose list of clients included the wealthy of Denver. We spent a great deal of money putting expensive touches on the building, both inside and out. One apartment was selected as our model which we furnished with antique furniture, oriental rugs, and beautiful artwork.

Jim had great contacts at the Denver newspaper, *The Rocky Mountain News*, and was able to get the head of the home and garden section, Marge, to come and take a look at what we'd done. Fortunately, she became very excited about this novel concept and showered us in the Saturday edition with publicity that we could never have afforded. There was mention of our project on eleven different pages of that edition, one of which was the *front page* of the paper! Because of the unexpected gift of that extensive coverage, I was unprepared for what happened on that Saturday.

Over three hundred people came to see our project and were wandering all over the building. I would be talking with someone in the sales office when three other people would come up and interrupt with questions. Sunday was the same scene only this time I had enlisted help. After two days and over six hundred people, I had *only one signed contract!*

When I arrived at the sales office on Monday, that contract had been slipped under the door with the word "cancel" written across it! What an unpleasant jolt that was. I sat there for a long time wondering what we should do. I realized that we had spent so much money improving the building, that the rents we would be collecting would be insufficient to support the substantially increased investment. It was also clear that we wouldn't be able to resell the building for enough to get our money back. With over six hundred seemingly enthusiastic lookers and no buyers, the prospects for the success of our condominium conversion project were looking grim.

This made it apparent that no investor was going to pay us a premium for its condominium conversion potential since we were already demonstrating the difficulty of getting that done, and to continue with the conversion project would require more money (and more risk) which might turn out to be throwing good money after bad. Needless to say, we were in a tough spot.

About an hour later, Tom called and asked, "Did you sell out?" I sadly related the events of the previous weekend to Tom. There was dead silence at the other end of the line. We both realized that things were going to be tough. He knew that he'd have to invest more money. I had already figured out that I'd have to invest a lot more time.

After hanging up with Tom, I knew the option of returning the building to its former function as an apartment building wasn't one of our choices. I also knew that we couldn't just walk away.

For just a few moments, I indulged myself in a little goal review by imagining the complete sellout of the condominiums. The pleasure of the creation, the satisfaction of doing what no one else had ever done, and the profit potential (more than I had realized on several of my previous projects combined) offered more than sufficient incentive to continue with the project. *This goal review process proved to be an effective antidote for the poison of quitting*!

All that was now needed was a plan to successfully solve the problem of marketing our condominiums. Nothing else had changed; the goal was the same. Nevertheless, continuing with the conversion idea seemed like an enormous challenge, *but not impossible*! just needed to keep my eye on the goal. "We're continuing and going to succeed" was the battle cry.

I immediately put an ad in the classified section of the newspaper. I had a For Sale sign placed in the yard, and I contacted a jazz radio station and placed a series of ads with them. Not long after, I received a call from one of the local TV channels. They were going to air a documentary about the Capital Hill area of Denver. Since my project was in Capital Hill and was such a unique idea, they reasoned that an ad might do wonders for the promotion of my project. They helped create the ad which ran in tandem with their documentary a couple of Sundays later.

As unbelievable as it sounds, after several weeks of all this advertising, I wasn't able to identify so much as *one response* that could be credited to any of those advertising efforts!

So, what now? Was the goal still a viable pursuit? While the only possible answer still had to be *yes,* what *possible* marketing solutions yet remained to get excited about?

Sitting there in my office and feeling so alone, my mind began to wander. I lost myself in the music that was playing on my radio – classical music! Although I usually listened to classical music, I had assumed that my target market would be lovers of jazz music; thus, my ads were on the jazz station. It never dawned on me that buyers of my unique product might prefer classical music.

I immediately made a call to KVOD and asked for Gene Amole, the owner of the classic music station and the very charismatic host of the morning programming.

In addition to placing an ad on Gene's program, I pulled out the list of people who had bothered to sign in on that infamous weekend and decided to conduct a campaign to reignite the interest that had brought them to the building a few weeks prior. As an enticement to encourage their return, I decided to remodel one of the empty apartments to show people what they'd be buying. I had the place painted, the hardwood floors refinished, added new plumbing fixtures, and replaced the countertops in the kitchen.

In a very short while, Gene's ads (which were all cleverly ad-libbed) started attracting between three and four people to the project *each day*! That, coupled with a new reason for former visitors to return, kept that pace of visitors constant. I could begin to imagine people buying. My goal was, once again, starting to feel possible.

Another reason for my growing optimism was that I was starting to attract supporters – people unknown to me when I began. My unwavering determination was convincing some doubting onlookers that I might succeed. That's often how it is with goals. You may start alone, even remain there for a time, but eventually, your persistence will be the magnet that attracts the support and assistance of others.

I also remember receiving valuable insight from a message I had heard at a seminar years ago. One speaker, a direct telephone solicitor named Thom Norman, *demonstrated* a message I'll never forget! That message centered on the value of "statistics" as a tool of prediction and encouragement. "Dial the phone ten times and you will have three prospects" was his message. If that was true, all that remained for me to do was determine how many prospects I needed to make a sale.

I eventually felt comfortable counting on one sale for every ten prospects. Using Thom Norman's formula of three prospects for every ten contacts, meant that thirty visitors would have to walk through the door to make a sale. It was now early October. If the current number of daily visitors continued unchanged, I estimated that I would be sold out in approximately seven months, or by May 15 of the following year. Though I was yet to witness the value of this theory in actual practice, it was still very uplifting to my spirits. This was probably true because I was able to switch my focus from making sales (a task that was proving difficult) to attend the much simpler task of attracting visitors and letting the "statistics" do the selling.

Throughout the experience, my goal continued to burn brightly. It became a reality as *I signed the contract for the sale of the twenty-sixth and final condominium unit seven and a half months later, on May 28!*

Many have achieved impossible dreams, but how'd they do it? First, the realization of their dreams and goals involved their passion/s. Without the inspiration of their passion/s, successfully enduring the inevitable obstacles becomes problematic.

Second, they made sure their passion/s fully embraced their goal, and vice-versa.

Third, it's a goal they are determined to accomplish despite the appearance of obstacles. They never allow these roadblocks to cause them to waver in their pursuit.

Finally, they committed to a tireless quest of establishing a deep understanding of all the subtle nuances and details that might, in some way, contribute to the successful pursuit of their goal.

As these steps fall into place, you'll be pleased to see the progression of your accomplishments that your passion/s wrought in bringing your dreams into reality.

TO GET THERE, YOU MUST BEGIN

Some people (achievers) don't have any problem getting started. Others frequently do. Why?

One of my best friends, Jim, is one of the most unique individuals I've ever known. My first awareness of his uniqueness was the consequence of what began as a rather ordinary dinner out.

Jim had heard good things about a rustic little restaurant, the Northwoods Inn, and one night decided to give it a try. One of its attractions was a complimentary bowl of peanuts at each table. People just threw the shells on the floor which, when walked on and crushed, created a rich roasted nut aroma in the restaurant. The more important attraction, however, was the live music provided by banjo players.

Jim liked the restaurant, and enjoyed the food, but was particularly drawn to the banjo music. So much so that the next day he went out and bought a banjo and began to teach himself to play it. After a few months had passed, Jim had become confident in his newfound skill with his banjo.

He went back to the Northwoods to have dinner – *banjo in hand*. After he'd finished dinner, Jim pushed his chair back, picked up his banjo, and from his table played along with the hired band! If you ask me, that took nerve. Jim knew what he was doing, as the band members quickly invited him to join them on the stage. From that night forward, Jim became part of the band.

Jim was never a procrastinator, and he still isn't! He's a doer. Today, Jim lives in Nashville and is now one of the *top five* banjo players in the country! His "do-it-now" attitude prompted his initial commitment to buy the banjo and his persevering attitude resulted in the rich rewards he enjoys from his music today.

But there's more. Neither Jim's accomplishments nor his "do-it-now" attitude ended with his mastery of the banjo. One summer evening, Jim reunited with a friend who had been away at college for the best part of a year. Jim couldn't believe the transformation he saw in his friend. During his time away at college, his friend had taken up bodybuilding and had built an impressive physique. Jim wasted no time in getting started on his muscle-building program and began to pump the iron. Later, Jim had not only patented a training device but today, at age seventy, he still works out and can boast an eighteen-inch arm!

While Jim's stories speak to an attitude of "do-it-now", many of my personal stories speak to never getting started. This is well illustrated by the difference in my early encounter with bodybuilding as contrasted with Jim's. When I was in my early teens (before I met Jim), I remembered being attracted to those muscle-building ads on the back cover of the comic books I liked to read. As a skinny kid, with flagging self-confidence, I was one of those teenagers targeted by the ad, an ad that promised to ripple biceps and popularity.

Nevertheless, despite the attraction of having big muscles, I failed to follow through. Unlike Jim, *I never responded to any of those magazine ads.* For various reasons, neither do most men ever "get around" to committing to this muscle-building thing….despite a desire to experience the promised results. Procrastination deserves full blame for their continued roles as skinny weaklings.

Another example of Jim's "let's start now" approach to life took place when I was in my late twenties. At the time, I was in the latter days of my career as a stock and bond broker. I remember reading a book on how to invest in income real estate properties. I was so impressed with the author's rock-solid approach that I loaned the book to Jim. Equally impressed with the advice given in the book, Jim immediately went out and bought a little three-unit apartment! Again, Jim took the first step and got started. He acted on the book's recommendations. I didn't. That was something I knew I should have done. I was so envious. Why didn't I "get going" as Jim had done? Fortunately, he soon invited me to join him in a real estate investment partnership, and this time I didn't procrastinate.

A postponement of the decision to begin is to unwittingly shorten the time to enjoy the anticipated benefits! Worse, the decision to postpone is more likely a decision to never begin. Stories of those who never *began* comprise a long list, while the list of those who did is much shorter.

What needs to be remembered is that the amount of "pain" or "cost" necessary to gain the promised benefits is the same irrespective of when you commence. It's amazing how fast six months pass. I have thought about all the times I told myself that I would get involved in "such and such" a program, but didn't. Six months later, I realized had I begun, I would have already been six months into the "program."

It's sad to realize the number of lives that could have been special, but neither they nor anyone else will ever know what could have been because they never decided to start! *The attainment of any goal requires a decision to begin.*

Once you get underway, it becomes more difficult to quit. However, the price of never starting is the loss of the goal itself. If the goal is worthy, it's deserving of your immediate commitment. Once started, you'll find that there's something special about having begun; you may then find it difficult to quit!

GOALS YOU SHOULDN'T PURSUE

It may all seem so innocent when you first begin, but decisions of this kind can mess up your life.

When I was a kid, I lived in a quiet neighborhood where large trees lined the street. We used to play hide-and-seek behind these trees as well as climb them. The squirrels also loved those trees. I always thought they would be a lot of fun to play with. I spent more time chasing them than I would care to admit. One day, I saw a dog catch one. Wow, did he fight with his hands! Those cute little squirrels have very sharp teeth, razor-like claws, and most likely rabies! Moreover, they can move and wiggle with enormous ferocity and at lightning speed. Fortunately, for me, I never caught one. But, I remember pitying the dog that did.

At the time, I never gave a thought to the "what next" question that I would have soon been asking had I caught one. It wouldn't have taken long for me to realize that I had made a huge mistake in ever pursuing a squirrel in the first place.

But, it isn't just squirreled that we should avoid chasing, as the kind of "squirrels" referred to by this principle come in many forms and have many disguises as you'll see in the following story.

My son spent three and a half years in South Africa studying the art of diamond cutting. After he had been there for some time, I flew over to see him. It was a beautiful trip. We toured most of South Africa and saw a few other countries as well. One of our favorite places was Cape Town. It's beautiful. The town sits at the base of Table Mountain which rises some 2000 feet above the city of Cape Town.

One day, my son and I decided to climb Table Mountain. It's a hard climb since the mountain has exposed, natural rock shelves. These two to four feet high shelves formed a crude stair system. The problem was the height of those steps; it was like climbing up onto a table each step of the way. Nevertheless, we were both determined to make it to the top. Along the way, I spotted a tail of "something" sticking out from the crevice in a rock. I walked over to it to pull it out and see what it was. As my son saw what I was about to do, he yelled, "Dad, don't touch it!" I jumped back. Without saying anything more about the incident, we continued our climb.

When we finally reached the top, we came upon an information panel that had pictures of the wildlife one might encounter on Table Mountain. Part way down the list, there was the creature whose tail I was reaching for – a puff adder! We learned that the puff adder is the leading cause of death from snakebites in Africa with 60 percent of all the fatal snakebites coming from these snakes. They can strike from *any* position (even resting) and *in any direction*. They strike with *lightning speed* that must be seen to be believed. A lethal dose of venom is 100 mg. A single bite can inject from 100-350 mg.!

As I so stupidly demonstrated, it isn't just kids who hunt things they shouldn't want to catch. I'd reached for a puff adder which would probably have been a *fatal* mistake. I still have no reasonable explanation as to what possessed me to think of toying with that creature! I was going after something that I would not have wanted to catch!

Kids chase squirrels, fools chase poisonous snakes, while adults chase other things –things that can ruin their lives.

A flirtatious urge with that attractive person at the office can be exciting. Such an indulgence may seem innocent enough since the "what if" question is seldom considered (at least not initially). A decision to continue the quest is often irresistibly tempting, and thus easily made. Such foolish pursuits may begin in the "safe" surroundings of the office, but these "innocent" dalliances lead farther and farther down *a path one shouldn't be traveling* – a path of enormous hurt and probable divorce.

The thrill of gambling with danger can find its outlet in "recreational" experimentation with drugs. Like catching the squirrel, the problem for some (maybe many) becomes the terrifying realization… they are addicted. It rules their life and is ruining them!

The thrill of the chase is all that's needed to lure many people into an adventure. But, *the pursuit of some thrills can lead to huge problems.*

If you ever find yourself contemplating a decision to sample one or more of these kinds of squirrel-chasing activities, take a moment and ask yourself this question: "What if I catch that squirrel - what then?" Remember, bad things can happen to those who pursue things they may not want to catch! Is it worth it?

Your *honest* answer to these questions should make some of your decisions much easier!

HOW MUCH PRESSURE CAN YOU STAND?

Most people are not immune to feeling pressure, and they often, unwittingly, expose themselves to pressures they can't handle.

I'm personally not very comfortable calling attention to myself, particularly not unfavorable attention. That's why I was so embarrassed when I was the one responsible for a large traffic snarl-up…during rush hour!

My wife and I had decided to build a house using reclaimed beams and salvaged cinderblocks. Before we ever began, we realized the need for some way to transport these materials to our house site. We happened upon a large farm dump truck. It was very old and had many mechanical liabilities –there was no way it would ever pass any safety inspection. But, it promised to be of immense help in getting these materials to our house site, and it was cheap. We decided to buy it.

One day when loaded with almost 7,000 pounds of cinderblocks stacked above the wooden side panels, I came to one of the *busiest intersections* in town at rush hour. In racing through a yellow light, I turned the corner a little too sharply and it rained cinderblocks into the intersection. Traffic backed up amidst glares and honking horns. I didn't know what to do. Leaving the scene of the spill seemed like an inviting way out. Just leave the blocks there in the intersection and get out of Dodge.

But I knew that some angry motorist would likely call the police on his cell phone and provide them with my license number. The police were certain to take a dim view of that decision (they might also take a very dim view of the condition of my truck). But if I stayed to clean things up, a policeman might happen by and see the mess I had made and take notice of my transportation. I had visions of a large fine and the impoundment of my vehicle! I jumped out and rushed into the intersection, throwing the fallen blocks back into the truck. I was about halfway through the pile when a police car pulled up right behind me!

To my great surprise, the officer asked, "Do you need any help?" I couldn't believe it! I quickly replied that everything was under control and thanked him for his offer. I reloaded and got the heck out of there. Talk about discomfort! Talk about a lucky break!

Accident scenes present good opportunities to observe people under pressure. I used to believe that anyone caught in a "busy intersection" collision would feel just as uncomfortable as I had felt. However, subsequent exposures to situations that were causing nightmarish traffic jams convinced me of the existence of a wide range of reactions on the part of those involved in such mishaps.

On some occasions, you might expect a fistfight to break out. At other times, I witnessed the victims holding each other and crying. But, I also observed behavior and demeanor on the part of a few of those involved in busy intersection wrecks that displayed a total calm, almost nonchalance. From these observations, I began to realize that there were great dissimilarities between the way people handle pressure and how much of it they can stand.

Exposure to stressful stimulus seems to result in degrees of discomfort that varies from person to person. The widely used term "comfort zone" describes it well. Each person's comfort zone is unique to their emotional fingerprint. It's important to be aware of the defining boundaries of your comfort zone. Once armed with this knowledge, you'll be able to avoid situations that place you at or beyond the limits of your zone. A little story explains how I began to define my comfort zone.

When I was just a kid, I happened across a toy roulette wheel. My friends and I had great fun playing roulette with Monopoly money. Years later, I read an article that outlined a "betting strategy" for roulette wheels. The strategy was quite simple. You picked a so-called even bet (red/black, odd/even, etc.). Then you decided upon a comfortable "betting unit" (my term for the amount of money you would begin wagering). Let's say that the betting unit was ten dollars. The idea was to place your ten dollars in the red. If it came up red, you received your ten dollars back, plus an additional ten dollars. If it came up black, you lost your ten dollars. So, on the next spin of the wheel, you put twenty dollars on red. If it came up red this time, you would get back the twenty dollars you had just bet and receive an additional twenty dollars, thus making up for the lost ten and giving you an overall ten-dollar profit. So, when you won, you are always ahead by the amount of your original bet. However, if it had come up black, you would bet forty dollars on red for the third try, and so on.

Once, when passing through Las Vegas, I was itching to try my surefire theory. Going immediately to the roulette wheel, I confidently pulled out ten dollars and placed it on red. It came up black – I blushed a little. I put twenty dollars on red for the next spin of the wheel, and it came up black again. I felt a little pressure in my chest as I put forty dollars on red for a third time.

As the wheel was spinning, the croupier remarked, "A little martingale?" I didn't know my unique theory had a name. Then he asked, "How *far* are you willing to go?" Somehow, I had never thought about that aspect of this "sure thing." But he had seen this one before, and he didn't seem to be applauding my strategy! That did it! In a flash, I realized that this doubling thing could go through the roof fast. This wasn't a reasoned investment; it was pure gambling. I realized that I had already hit my comfort zone limit for gambling and started to reach for my forty dollars. But, it was too late, the little ball had already settled into a numbered slot – we were now just waiting for the wheel to slow down so we could "read" the result. *Wow, it was red!* I *quickly* picked up the money and left the casino, *never* to place a bet in one again.

I realized my tolerance for losing money gambling was very low. "Investments" in which I have no control over the outcome (I call it gambling) are not for me. However, over the years, I have developed a great deal of confidence in the investment decisions I make because I don't venture forward unless I feel confident about the outcome. Thus, my ability to withstand pressure in the area of my investments is much greater.

Yet, I still have my limits as to the amount of pressure I can withstand. It's hard for me to imagine anyone who doesn't. Accurate knowledge of your limits will allow you to prevent exposure to situations that exceed them. From my own experiences and that which I've witnessed in others, success becomes infinitely more difficult when a person is operating outside their comfort zone. In so doing, they are exposing themselves to pressures that are pushing them beyond their melting point. Under such circumstances, they tend to make one bad decision after another.

Success is threatened when the pressures rise to levels beyond your ability to perform normally. One reason many good ideas fail is the introduction of intolerable pressures.

No matter what pressure levels you anticipate, they'll probably be exceeded. For this reason. many a winning idea has been torpedoed by mounting pressures that have exceeded that person's limits. Thus, know the limits of your comfort zone. Don't risk failure by opting into pressure cooker situations when you already know they will threaten your ability to perform, should they push you beyond your emotional limit.

Know the limits of your comfort zone, and be sure that you don't commit to anything that you *already know* will push you beyond that limit…because…

When stretched too far, things break. However, those same things if stretched in small increments, a little at a time, *can be* stretched well beyond that breaking point. So it is with comfort zones. Work to expand yours.

IS YOUR COMMITMENT STRONG ENOUGH?

The true level of commitment necessary to a successful conclusion is something we often fail to properly calculate or even take into serious consideration. So, what does a proper level of commitment look like?

Some sports require movements that demand 100 percent commitment just to accomplish the maneuver. One that quickly comes to mind is the karate chop. The objective is to break a stack of bricks with your hand. Injury results when the speed of your hand decelerates before reaching the top brick. You won't even succeed in breaking that top brick, let alone the entire stack. To break any bricks, your hand must be accelerating at the point of impact. A decelerating hand speed is caused by fear which speaks to the lack of a 100 percent commitment. Anything short of a total commitment will fail to break the bricks, but will succeed in breaking your hand!

Not all tasks that require 100 percent commitment result in injury when your efforts don't measure up. Moreover, not all tasks even require a 100 percent commitment. But those that do demand that level of total commitment can be separated into two groups:

The first category of things requiring a total commitment applies to all do-or-die challenges – like crossing the ocean in a balloon or rowboat, climbing Mt. Everest, or entering the ring with the World Heavy Weight Champion. Anything short of a 100 percent commitment results in injury or death – failure by definition!

The second category doesn't involve the threat of physical harm. Nevertheless, it requires the same 100 percent resolve that stretches all that you have and all that you are. If there is to be any chance of success in this endeavor, you can't hold anything back.

But what does a 100 percent commitment look like? For starters, it's the willingness to go that extra *ten* miles. It's deciding to continue working when everyone else has gone home. It's working weekends. It's canceling vacations. It's deciding to take extra pains when most would say that's good enough. It may involve putting all your earthly assets on the line. It may demand that you pull out every possible stop, enlisting the help of anyone and everyone you can imagine as being potentially helpful. In short, it involves total commitment and intense focus!

The following inspiring story illustrates the depth of such a commitment.

The time is the very early years of the twentieth century and the setting is a fifty-five-acre piece of ground in British Columbia on Vancouver Island. The couple that owned the land had been attracted to it for its limestone deposits. These deposits enabled them to successfully turn the land into a cement-producing facility. And the cement business was able to provide a very bountiful livelihood for the couple.

When the limestone deposits were finally exhausted, they decided to close down the cement manufacturing operation and ease into a life of relaxation.

The wife, however, felt a sense of guilt about the ugly pit they were leaving behind. They had started with a beautiful piece of land blessed with ideal growing conditions. Plants loved the cool temperatures and abundant moisture which typified the marine climate of the Pacific Northwest.

She began to feel that their wealth had been accumulated at the expense of the beauty of the area. As a consequence, she decided to beautify the old quarry. Her goal immediately took on a grandeur and scope that could only be realized with a 100 percent commitment. What she had in mind was significantly beyond the planting of some trees and bushes. Soon, she began to think of this as an opportunity to create something of extraordinary beauty – maybe even surpassing the exceptional natural beauty that existed before they dug it all up for the limestone.

Having committed to do it "right," she decided not to do any planting until she had properly prepared the bottom of the old limestone quarry for healthy plant life. She went out to all the farms in the area and bought topsoil from them.

This was not to be a simple task. At that time, there were no earth-moving machines to load the dirt, nor dump trucks to haul it. The only means of transporting the topsoil were horse-drawn wooden carts which had to be loaded by hand! The quantity needed was enormous as she planned on filling the entire bottom of the forty-*acre* quarry with topsoil up to a depth of *six* feet! That decision, alone, would deter most people, but once carried out, it provided the very foundation for the dream that would now be very difficult to back away from.

The level of commitment to the beautification of the land was convincingly evidenced by the infusion of quality into everything. This was demonstrated by such things as the annual planting of over one million bedding plants to provide continual flowering from spring through fall. They, and all the other trees and bushes, provide a scene that is now viewed by over a million people every year! (I've personally been there four or five times myself.)

The final result, now widely known as Butchart Gardens, is a world-famous botanical garden. Mrs. Butchart's commitment was total.

There are some undertakings whose success will require your 100 percent commitment. With such endeavors, anything less may result in total failure. This principle isn't about pursuits where an acceptable outcome still results even when your effort falls short. It's addressing issues of success or failure.

In that context, the difference between a successful effort and one that failed can invariably be traced back to a lack of sufficient commitment.

When contemplating any undertaking, you must be careful to accurately assess the type of commitment necessary to ensure success. If the project you're wishing to pursue is of a "do or die" nature, decide before you even begin that you are prepared to make a 100 percent commitment…if not, don't get involved!

WHEN IN A BATTLE, FIGHT TO WIN

Many quit on the eighteenth tee, but I wasn't about to give up.

The construction business, as any contractor can tell you, is an up-and-down business. There are times when you are so busy you can't imagine accommodating another potential client. Then there are times when you find yourself fiercely competing for that rare piece of business.

For some strange reason, the down times are the times when other things also seem to go wrong. Such was the case when a company I owned was awarded a $750,000 contract to do subcontract work for a major hotel chain that was building a new hotel. The contract stipulated payments for the work to be made in three installments of $250,000 each. Naturally, the contract required predetermined levels of completion before any payment would be released. Fortunately, our crews were very competent and we were always on, or ahead of, schedule.

Our request for the first installment was submitted well before its due date. Needless to say, we were disappointed when the payment didn't arrive until thirty days after it was supposed to have been paid. We felt uneasy about the amount of money still wrapped up in those last two installments as well as the increased likelihood of continued tardy payments. This was a poor way to start and gave me a reason to expect the possibility of some unpleasantness before it was all over.

We had completed the work required under the contract before invoicing the hotel for the second installment of $250,000. We called the hotel construction office to alert them of our expectation of prompt payment. Given the difficult times, slow payment caused an additional hardship for us since we had already spent 90 percent of our expected payment of the second installment on our costs for labor, materials, and office overhead.

As I feared, the payment didn't arrive on its due date. We didn't see it for another sixty days! This gave me enormous concerns about the remaining $250,000 and the pressures that seemed sure to come. But, not to finish was to invite a lawsuit that would probably seek damages well beyond the amount of our total contract. Reluctantly, we continued. We finished our part of the contract and submitted our request for the final $250,000 payment – a payment that never came!

We agonizingly realized that the only hope of ever getting paid was to file a lien against the hotel and take the matter to court. A big fight was about to begin!

Our first interview was with a recommended attorney whose fees were said to be very reasonable. Given my feelings on the low probability of ever getting anything, I reasoned that maybe some representation was better than none. But as I was briefing him on the case, I asked him a simple question: What was the order of priority our lien would have versus the other obligations that were recorded against the title, such as IRS liens, deeds of trust, property taxes, and other mechanics liens? He said he'd need to look up the law about that and get back to me. I walked out of his office realizing that regardless of the reasonableness of his fees, he was not the attorney for *this* job. I'd be throwing good money after bad. I also realized that I'd be paying a lot more than a "reasonable" fee to get an attorney of the quality I needed.

In the meantime, the hotel corporation had already shown its hand as to its intentions. They maintained that we had caused delays for all the other subcontractors. In addition, they insisted that our workmanship was shoddy. Their position was that they owed us nothing! It was at this point that I became angry and was prepared to fight them to the end. I decided that I needed to find the best lien law attorney in the city of Denver to pursue our case against this hotel. Fortunately, we found one.

We were invited to a preliminary hearing at the offices of the hotel's defense attorneys. As I arrived at the hearing, I became aware of the large number of other subcontractors that had also filed liens because of similar nonpayment. One by one, they were ushered into the hearing room. Usually, they were told that there were errors in the filing of the lien that nullified their lien rights (wrong property address, incorrect names of the owners of the hotel, incorrect dates, etc.) Any minor error in their lien filing meant that these poor subcontractors walked away empty-handed! Because of our attorney's competence, our lien withstood the scrutiny of the hotel's lawyers. They couldn't find anything wrong with it.

Time passed, and court proceedings continued, but still no decision from the court and no money. Their attorneys kept hammering on their two claims against us: poor workmanship and costly delays.

Finally, before a decision from the court, the attorneys for the hotel scheduled a "settlement hearing." The remaining contractors with lien claims (those whose liens had not been dismissed), as well as myself, came to the meeting expecting to get "beat up."

This turned out to be a particularly tough time for me as my wife was dying of cancer, and my company was dangerously short of cash having funded all the work for the final phase of the hotel project without being paid. For the moment, we were out of that money. Moreover, the prospects of ever getting it were highly questionable. If that wasn't enough, we were now racking up some heavy attorney fees.

As I entered the meeting room, I was greeted by nine lawyers sitting around a very long conference table that had stacks of papers six to ten inches high covering most of the top of the table. I assumed that this was all of the paperwork for each of the cases they were fighting; my papers, no doubt, constituted one or more of those stacks.

The meeting got off to a rather bad start as one of the lawyers stood up and yelled at me. He accused me of being a crook, seeking damages that were in no way warranted. I certainly didn't see it that way. My lawsuit was only for the amount of the unpaid balance of the contract. I wasn't seeking punitive damages. or even any interest. All I wanted was the $250,000 that was due on the last installment. When the offensive attorney finally stopped yelling at me and sat down, the spokesperson for the group of attorneys, a woman, suggested that I accept a settlement of $50,000!

It was at this point that I said the following: "You start this meeting with someone yelling at me and calling me a crook. What you have done by withholding the payment that was due to me has put my company in serious jeopardy. I'm here merely trying to collect for work we've legitimately performed. And…my wife is dying of cancer! I no longer feel that I have a whole lot to lose. It's an understatement to say that I'm not in very good humor right now. Your despicable offer has only worsened it. It wouldn't take anything for me to come in here and *shoot you all in the kneecaps!*"

Without smiling or in any way giving the impression that I was merely joking, I looked at each one of those slimy attorneys. Their eyes were as big as pie plates. They knew I was serious and none of them said a word. After an uncomfortable silence, the spokeswoman invited me into a private conference room for a one-on-one discussion.

She had no sooner shut the door than she offered me $150,000! I then told her that I wasn't there to bargain. We performed the agreed-upon work and are now expected to be paid the agreed-upon price of $250,000. I got up and walked out of the room. *I was not going to give up on this fight.*

The day of the court's decision finally came. The judge awarded us the full value of that final installment, $250,000! The only bad part was that we were not awarded attorney fees – which came to $50,000.

Nevertheless, I was very happy with our attorney and very pleased with the outcome.

Had I stopped fighting early on (as did many of the other poor sub-contractors), I would have ended up with nothing. Capitulating when the attorney yelled at me and accepting their $50,000 offer would have left me with virtually nothing since that was the amount owing to my attorney – a $200,000 difference. To have allowed them to wear me down to the point where I accepted their final offer of the $150,000 I would have still owed the attorney the same $50,000. By continuing to fight, I realized an additional $100,000. The court's ruling convinced me that all those who gave up and walked away, unpaid, could have been rewarded the full balance they were owed had they just continued to fight.

Real examples of determination and vows to never give up can be found in virtually every success story. The road to success is littered with roadblocks and obstacles — obstacles that must be overcome or failure looms.

Colonel Sanders created a chicken recipe that he believed in. He wanted to sell the idea to someone who would run with it and develop it into a national fast-food chain. He approached person after person, *always* getting a "no." It has been reported that he met with rejection over one thousand times before he ever heard a "yes!" Think about the cost Colonel Sanders paid in terms of time and discouragement. But look at the reward his decision to keep fighting brought him.

Tom Monaghan, the owner of a pizza restaurant, paid an even greater price for his eventual success. Because he believed in his idea, he decided (early in the game) that he would never allow the temptation to quit to get the best of him. Many times, setbacks pushed him to the brink of bankruptcy. But, no matter how tough things got, he continued to fight. He wasn't about to give up. Whatever money he made, it always went back into the business. His commitment often resulted in great personal sacrifice as he was often reduced to *living in his car!* Nevertheless, he always chose to keep going and keep fighting. But this decision to continue to fight always meant returning to long days (fifteen to eighteen hours) and long weeks (seven days a week) for years… making pizzas *himself*. To remain faithful to his commitment, these setbacks required the continued renewal of his resolve. His determination and dedication were severely tested as these setbacks plagued him for almost *twenty years*. His eventual reward, however, was the successful pizza franchise now familiar to everyone — *Domino's Pizza* — a reward that made Tom an extremely wealthy man.

If you are taking your first step in pursuit of a worthy goal, remember: the battle has just begun. What may not become apparent to you until later is that few successes ever occur without the need to overcome obstacles — often severe, heart-stopping obstacles. Success is a difficult pursuit, almost always hard-won. The person who stops fighting, and quits, won't find it!

Success will depend upon whether you decide to continue the battle and keep trying even when all your attempts fail…or do you allow those failures to convince you that you should throw in the towel? Success is the result of believing that you will find a path, a solution…somewhere, somehow.

To decide to abandon your efforts while you still have the strength or the will to fight may be to have given up on the eighteenth tee, stopping just short of trying that one last solution that would have unlocked the key to success.

Winston Churchill, the legendary British prime minister during World War II, had the daunting task of trying to keep the morale of his countrymen buoyed. London was being heavily bombed and signs of defeat were appearing everywhere. To boost the people's resolve, Churchill gave his famous *five-word* speech: "Never… Never… Never give up!" That was all he said. But you know the rest. England didn't give up, and with the help of her allies, won the war!

Many seem to think that success is the automatic consequence of merely tossing their hat into the ring. They give little or no thought to the difficulties they are likely to encounter.

At the first sign of trouble, they want to quit. A decision to do so is usually the easiest one to make. As one failure piles on top of another, this pattern of quitting becomes ingrained. Quitting is easy – a lot easier than continuing to fight. At the very core of most success stories is the ability to persevere. And persevering depends upon your willingness to enter the ring and face a fight.

If after the first few setbacks, you find yourself saying, "One more of these and I'm done." – you might as well "be done" right then! That attitude will never see you through the difficulties that you've failed to anticipate and most likely still lie ahead.

Seriously consider this advice before you ever decide to begin. Once you've committed to begin, also make a decision that you will also persevere!

EXPAND YOUR OPTIONS

Some ask "why." You should be asking, "why not?"

When you are trying to solve a problem, it's nice to have a potential solution in mind. Better yet, it's really helpful to have several potential solutions.

Strangely, for some people, having options causes them a sense of discomfort. Maybe the availability of several choices is confusing. They may even serve to further discourage them.

A very close friend of mine was devastated by the risks he foresaw as the result of the outcome of the 2012 presidential election. With no solution in sight to the country's enormous debt, he felt hyperinflation was probably unavoidable. Anticipating the erosion of the purchasing power of his savings, he feared they would no longer be able to support him and his wife.

Frozen in dread, he told me that the mere contemplation of his predicament was injurious to his health and for that reason he was going to assume the role of an ostrich and bury his head in the sand in hopes that the perceived danger would, one day, have passed and things would be alright again. I was saddened by his decision to ignore the existence of other possible options that might be able to solve his problem or at least lessen his risks.

A young acquaintance, Fred, was just getting started on his journey as an adult. Along the way, he would occasionally be faced with the harsh realities of the responsibilities adulthood brings He was enamored with the idea of turning his monthly living quarter's rent expenses into equity-building payments on a home. At about the same time, I encountered a luxury condominium unit in a great inner-city location that was available at an exceptionally discounted price. Fred was all excited and wanted to buy it. The problem was his inability to qualify for the loan based on his limited income-earning experience. I offered to co-sign a loan which enabled Fred to move forward with the purchase.

Sometime later, his hours at the place of his employment were cut back. Soon, his surplus funds were gone and his ability to keep up his payments had evaporated. Despite all this, he was still far from being without other options. He could get another part-time job, or find an alternate source of full-time employment. Maybe he could sell some of his belongings or get a bridge loan to carry him over until other employment prospects surfaced. Surprisingly, Fred chose to fire-sale his home, selling it just for the value of the mortgage against it! He walked away from the equity that he'd already built up, all because he was unwilling to consider any other options.

I like having options. They give me a certain comfort amid problems. The bigger the difficulty, the more time I spend trying to create the longest possible list of potential solutions.

Threatening situations have even prompted me to list options that have only a remote chance of helping me out. As senseless as that might seem, it nevertheless gives me a much-needed measure of hope. If nothing else, it serves to dispel any growing feelings of hopelessness by fortifying a belief that a solution *must* yet exist…somewhere…somehow. Such was the problem when I purchased a 5-unit row house (five houses joined by common walls). It contained commercial space upstairs and offices in the basement. Once I rented the upper area to a restaurant, however, renting the space below became a virtual impossibility. To reach the office's entrance, one had to pass by the restaurant's dumpster (filled with rotten eggs and all manner of other smelly garbage). For many, such a problem would cause them to become despondent and efforts at finding a solution are never undertaken.

Fortunately, I didn't subscribe to that attitude. Instead, I composed a list of practical options that I hoped might provide a solution. I talked to all of my contacts, past tenants, and rental agencies, and placed ads in the newspaper. Unfortunately, none of that was working. I couldn't find a tenant! Having exhausted my list of options, I began to ask myself what other options might I have overlooked. I decided to pursue an option that seemed almost farcical. I opted to take a chance on the following ad: "Nice office but a horrible entry. I included the price and my phone number and placed the ad in the classified section of the newspaper. I got two responses. One of those callers rented the office!

The overwhelming majority of the problems I've ever faced have benefitted from my efforts to find an answer. A list of these potential answers, or options, always brings me back to my belief in the value of options – the mother of all solutions.

Once the list of options has been assembled, three steps yet remain. First, you must *believe* that the answer or answers you seek are contained somewhere within your list of options. Second, the items on the list must be "worked." Each suggested solution must be analyzed and researched to determine its likely value and method or manner of implementation. Third, you may find that your investigations have uncovered some multifaceted options. These fresh revelations may effectively expand your collection of options by leading you in the direction of some truly worthwhile ideas – even an eventual resolution to your troubles.

FOCUS ON YOUR 'A' SKILLS

This is one of the most valuable things you could ever do for yourself.

The author, Sir Arthur Conan Doyle, wrote several successful novels about the criminal investigations of the legendary detective, Sherlock Holmes. Doyle's character development was so brilliant that to some, the person of Sherlock Holmes had almost become real.

Yet, despite the countless number of people who have read the Sherlock Holmes novels, or watched the movie adaptations of Doyle's stories, few are aware of the circumstances surrounding Holmes and Dr. Watson's first meeting and their early days together. This meeting and Watson's later musings about the curious talents and interests of Holmes were described by Doyle in the *Scarlet Letter*, his first book in the series.

It all began when Holmes was engaged in a casual conversation with an acquaintance, Mr. Stamford. Holmes mentioned that he was looking for a place to rent, but had become discouraged by his inability to find a comfortable place at a reasonable price. The only place he deemed suitable would require a roommate for him to afford it.

Later that same day, Dr. Watson ran into someone from his past, the same Mr. Stamford. Watson told Stamford that he was recovering from wounds received in the war and was becoming concerned about his dwindling finances. He realized he needed to change his living arrangements and stated that he wished to find a comfortable place at a reasonable price. Stamford remarked that he was the second person that day who had expressed a similar desire. Stamford quickly arranged a meeting between Holmes and Watson.

When they met, Holmes remarked, "A doctor from Afghanistan, I presume." After exchanging personal information about their less-than-desirable traits (a disclosure of sorts), they agreed to room together.

Early on, Watson realized Holmes was a very unusual man and was quite curious about his mysterious new roommate. Somewhat intimidated by Holmes, Watson's hesitancy to ask him any questions placed him at a loss in figuring out what it was Holmes did for a living. At first, a little conversation took place between them. Watson, being a retired physician, had time on his hands and began to entertain himself with musings about Holmes, such as the remark at the time of their first meeting – the one about Watson being a doctor from Afghanistan – as well as other curious aspects about his interests, activities, and personality.

The more Watson delved into the person of Sherlock Holmes, the more interesting and unusual he found Holmes to be. He observed Holmes's daily activities and made note of his unusual assortment of interests and skills, which contrasted sharply with his unbelievable lack of knowledge about certain other areas.

Here was a man, Watson noted, who had an encyclopedic knowledge of the history of crime, was a master at the art (or science) of deductive reasoning, and had commendable knowledge of chemistry and soils, as well as a respectable skill in the art of self-defense. He had little or no social life, his spare time is largely spent playing the violin. While Watson was intrigued, he was also quite confused by this strange assortment of knowledge, skills, and interests until…he learned that Holmes was a private detective.

As Watson began to piece together this odd blend of attributes, he realized that it all fit. He theorized that Holmes troubled himself only with those things for which he had a natural affinity and were beneficial to his career or were of personal interest and pleased him. For Holmes, as the stories revealed, this focus paid off handsomely as Holmes was the best in his field.

You can apply the same reasoning to your selection of the things to which you should devote your time.

Weed out aspirations that are not worthy of the time and effort they'll demand. Then devote your unrelenting pursuit to those goals you consider worthy of your most enthusiastic commitment.

This would apply to the increasing mastery of an area of knowledge or the development of skills you already have… your "A" skills. Carefully selected, this mastery will further your career, moneymaking efforts, and even your leisurely pursuits.

As you adopt the philosophy of this approach, you will find yourself eliminating many of those things which just waste your time. Like Holmes, you'll profit by channeling your time into exercises that will improve your existing career skills or provide recreational enjoyment.

In a televised interview, Alexander Solzhenitsyn (the famous Russian novelist and historian) was asked, "If he could live his life over, what one thing might he do differently?" His answer (in a Holmes-like manner) was that he would pick a subject, no matter how seemingly insignificant, and become the world's greatest expert on *that* subject.

Achieving this expert status, it has been said, is the result of consistently disciplining yourself to spend one hour a day on your chosen task and remain faithful to it for five years. At the end of that time, it is generally conceded that *you will have achieved expert status.*

When you commit to this exercise, you'll soon notice that spending time improving your skills, or understanding, regarding this subject about which you are already naturally gifted, and passionate, is something you'd probably do without the promise of compensation.

Choose to take a page out of Sherlock Holmes's book and decide to immediately begin working to perfect your "A" skill/s – handsome rewards await that effort. If there's a road to *greatness*, this is it.

For additional encouragement on your journey, identify a role model to emulate. Also, enroll supporters who appreciate what you're attempting. You'll benefit from their encouragement as they hop on your bandwagon.

Forget trying to "bring up" your "B" and "C" skills. When you've fine-tuned you're "A" skills, they'll provide the necessary means to hire professional help in your areas of weakness.

PASSION SEPARATES THE BEST FROM THE REST

Passion is one ingredient common to all maestros.

Since this is the companion principle to the previous concept, Develop Your "A" Skills, it is designed to culminate in the *ultimate development* of your God-given talents. It addresses the rewards of an increased dedication to the development of your special abilities or understandings and seeks to point out the "secrets" of success enjoyed by some of recent history's most astounding people by providing insights into how such people think and what they did to develop their mastery.

People have been forever curious about the secrets behind the extraordinary achievements enjoyed by a few very gifted people. Many would attribute these attainments to diligent study, hard work, persistence, or just plain old luck.

Of course, study, hard work, and persistence matter. However, upon a closer examination of the lives of the super-successful, a different understanding emerges. It appears that the responsible agent behind their extraordinary successes was the passion they felt for that which they hoped to master.

The stories you are about to read are all examples of people who sought the perfection of their passions (typically linked to their "A" skills). Their pursuit typically involves "looking through a microscope" to see the "little things" most people don't see…or somehow overlook.

As you begin to grasp the importance they place on details, you will begin to understand and appreciate the intense interest they invest in the little, seemingly unimportant, things that play an important role in their accomplishments.

This principle means to acquaint you with a process that leads to *pinnacles* of understanding…otherwise known as mastery.

Everyone recognizes the name, Ralph "Polo" Lauren. As a creator of fashion, Lauren may be one of the most successful designers of all time.

As is true of our passions, they are often evident at very early stages of life. Lauren's passion for clothes was evident when he was in the seventh grade. Though he was the best-dressed twelve-year-old in the neighborhood, he didn't start rich.

In 1967, he was hired by Beau Brummell Ties as a designer. His wide, colorful ties were the opposite of the narrow dark neckties common at the time. He was convinced he was right and Beau Brummell went along with this daring change in styles. His ties sold well and started a new trend. Shortly thereafter, Lauren started his own company and launched his now-famous Polo brand, a mixture of English and American styles that projected an image of class. One of the keys to the success he would enjoy was his tireless attention to detail, attention sparked by his passion for excellence in design.

In designing the costumes for the movie, *The Great Gatsby*, he began what was to become a widespread influence of his design statement: "I believe in clothes that last, that are not dated in a season. The people who wear my clothes don't think of them as fashion." His vision was to present a dash of British elegance and the comfort of natural fibers.

Lauren's passion shaped his whole world. Because he lived the image he projected, he was able to step into the role of the master marketer of elegant living. It became a lifestyle marketing philosophy – the old money look. His name became synonymous with status, class, and taste. His line of products portrayed a rugged romance and timeless elegance. They presented the seamless front of a wealthy, adventurous lifestyle. He always stood for providing quality products, creating worlds, and inviting people to take part in the dream. *He was marketing a lifestyle.*

The whole issue of the design was so important to Lauren that he was known to have designed a whole wardrobe of clothes for an upcoming trip to a foreign place. Such was the case for an extended trip he had planned to take to England. His experiences on that trip caused him to make the strange remark that England wasn't English enough – a remark that provides a very revealing insight into his sensitivities.

In an *Architectural Digest* article written about Lauren's beautiful ranch property near Telluride, Colorado, the interviewer wrote of his meeting with Ralph. Possibly expecting to hear deep, hidden secrets of great design from the mouth of this fabulously gifted designer, Lauren rather abstractly started commenting about leather – old leather. He said that there was "something" about it. He added that he looked for the old one and just tried to add a little juice to it. It occurred to me that Lauren had indirectly communicated much more about the basic nature of great design than was apparent to the interviewer. Because the world of fashion design has seen about everything: endless creations of styles, cuts, different kinds of fabric, patterns, colors, and combinations of apparel accessories, it's hard to imagine what one designer might do to stand out above all the others. Lauren did so by venerating and capturing those qualities that had proven staying power: *timeless, traditional, and comfortable* good looks. In this age of imitation, he believed in that which was real – things venerated by a timelessness.

He sought an understanding of what made an article of clothing timeless by starting with what had always worked and sought to add that which made it comfortable. His passion for design led him to discernment and wisdom not available in books. He arrived at his appreciation for the value of things that had that patina of "age." He capitalized on the genuine and just "added a little juice."

Frank Sinatra has been gone for almost fifteen years. But, his music lives on because he is still regarded as one of the greatest vocalists of all time. Some may think he was just a great singer who was just *somehow* "discovered." Instead, if it was something more, what was that "something more" that separated him from almost all of the other singers? You may be surprised by what he added to that which he began with. You will see that it was what he added that was largely responsible for what he became.

Frank was born with charisma. Some people have it and some don't. Frank had it! But that's not where the story ends. It's where it begins.

Frank's decision to become a singer happened after attending a performance by Bing Crosby. Dolly Sinatra, Frank's mother, wasn't in favor of his decision and was shocked to see Crosby's pictures all over Frank's bedroom walls. The inspiration and motivation he sought were obvious. But getting started is not easy. Sinatra worked tirelessly to find singing engagements. He courted radio offices, plugging himself and offering to sing for free. He did the same in his pursuit of nightclub performances – all just so he could gain exposure. He'd also go from music publisher to music publisher seeking free music sheets and orchestrations which eventually led to dates with local bands who lacked this material. He began to gain a reputation for his music library, but not necessarily for his singing. These were lean times for the young Sinatra. Had he been less convinced of his talent, he might have given up hope!

His efforts, however, led to several engagements, with some very tough and hard-to-please audiences. But learning to maintain his composure in front of this kind of gathering resulted in confidence and ease that never let him. It wasn't long before not many audiences could throw him off his stride.

With each opportunity to perform, he sought to improve his techniques. Some weren't just singing, such as his absorption of comedy routines. Tommy Dorsey taught him things like the showmanship, discipline, and endurance. Mechanically, he learned many valuable techniques that would begin to separate him from all other singers – things like breath control. He learned to greatly increase that control by swimming underwater while mouthing the lyrics. He was thus able to hold the flow of a song without the mechanical interruptions of having to take breaths at the wrong times. He also learned about phrasing where certain words are stretched and rephrased – "mine" became two syllables instead of one. He projected the meaning of the mood as well as the meaning of the lyrics. You could tell he believed a kiss was still a kiss and a sigh was still a sigh.

His presentation became enhanced through attention to seemingly minor issues. Like control of the mike. He liked black mikes because they would blend in with his black dinner jacket. This allowed him to move the mike, unnoticed, away from his mouth and disguise his need to take a breath. Also part of his presentation was what one interviewer described as a romanticist, dreamer, and careful dresser. "He loves beautiful words and lives his songs. From them, he learned that emotions can grow from music and lyrics." There was deep emotion in his treatment of a song. While men felt the excitement generated by the beat of his music, women felt he was singing to them…*personally*!

He was very particular as to the band he'd pick to accompany his recordings. When singing with big bands, he learned the tricks of "voice survival" against the big band noise. He also gained knowledge of which phrases and notes to hit hard to draw attention away from the dance floor or the band leader. Early on, Frank was a hard worker. He was not tolerant of the lazy or the mediocre. This was Sinatra's signature style, a style that separated him from almost all other singers. He had a passion that resulted in the mastery of his craft. Close attention was paid to detail upon detail.

Together, it was those details that set him apart.

Ted Williams still holds the record for the highest batting average for a full season in the major leagues, 406! Even though he set that record in 1941, no one has yet to break it. Like all those who accomplish the astounding, the question that begs an answer is how did he do what no one else could do? Was he that gifted? Did he have some special advantage we don't know about? Let's start with the givens: He was a great athlete with unusually keen eyesight. He worked very hard at becoming a great batter by devoting hours and hours to disciplined batting practice. An article in the *National Post* newspaper wrote of Williams, "the 406 season was a result of his tireless dedication to what he labeled the science of hitting – refining that science consumed him. Predictably, his baseball conversations usually didn't include talk about fielding, base running, or bunt strategy. Instead, he would ask strangers to show him their batting swing. Then he would correct their flaws."

But, the thing that separated him from all other batters was his passion to overcome the pitcher's strategy to defeat him at the plate.

Part of Ted's unbelievable skill as a batter was the consequence of his intense interest in the opposing pitchers' techniques, particularly concentrating on their strengths, and weaknesses. He would take notes on what he and his teammates observed when confronting another team's pitcher. When he stood at the plate, he had more than just hope that he would know where the ball would be by the time it reached him. But since Ted didn't face all of the pitchers with any predictability or regularity, he began to pursue a rather ingenious way to fill in the gaps in his knowledge inventory of pitcher information.

It seems that Ted was never the kind to argue with an umpire – even if he thought the call was wrong! For that reason, he had made no enemies among the umpires. He went out of his way to be friendly to them. This led to opportunities for Ted to discuss the various pitchers – most particularly focusing on their strengths, weaknesses, and their particular techniques. Ted began to acquire a virtually encyclopedic knowledge about each pitcher in the major leagues! His batting average would suggest that this little exercise paid off.

Harry Houdini's passion for showmanship first surfaced at age nine when he dreamed of being a trapeze artist. By the time he reached age 17, the pursuit of trapeze artistry was replaced by his decision to become a magician. Like all the other magicians of the day, Houdini attempted to draw audiences by performing card tricks – without much success.

He quickly realized he could not hope to enjoy any exceptional notoriety unless he separated himself from all those card-trick magicians. Since the stage for this kind of magician was already overcrowded, he succumbed to the influence of a business manager named Beck, who encouraged him to concentrate on escape acts.

Houdini began his new career with a trip to England. As a master of self-promotion, he publicly challenged Scotland Yard to try and restrain him with handcuffs. The newspaper eagerly printed his confident challenge to Scotland Yard as he boastfully promised that their shackles would not be able to confine him. Eager to protect their reputation, the police stripped and searched him for any hidden "things" that might come to his aid in escaping. Despite all of that, his escape was not only successful but also led to six months of booked tours throughout

England. Houdini was to become proficient at opening locks, of any kind!

This skill became the foundation for a logical transition to daring escape acts – a different slant on what a magic act ought to look like. These acts not only involved the mystery of "How did he do it?" but also joined that curiosity with the intrigue associated with the risks to his safety. These risks were to become the increasing hallmark of his later career. His career was greatly aided by his "passion" for enlisting the nuances of escape techniques from all manner of restraining devices.

During his career, he would free himself from jails, chains, ropes, handcuffs, straight jackets, water-filled milk cans, nailed packing crates, (often lowered into water), riveted boilers, mailbags, and even the belly of a beached whale. Sometimes an element of extreme drama would accompany an escape routine – such as freeing himself from a straight jacket while suspended from a crane…hanging upside down. He'd alter the act by conducting his performance at the end of a rope dangling over the edge of a tall building (such as the local newspaper building).

Another variation of his escape routines involved extrication from live burials. One incredible incident featured a live burial, without a casket, under six feet of dirt. Just the weight of the ground on top of him almost did him in. One arm finally broke through the surface as Houdini fell unconscious. A variation of this act involved placing Harry in a sealed casket and lowering him into a swimming pool. It was reported that some Egyptian mystique had remained in a similar circumstance for one hour. Houdini didn't emerge for one and a half hours! Houdini's only "trick" in surviving this act was "controlled breathing."

Houdini's passion prompted him to continue to taunt ever-increasing levels of the impossible, even challenging his audiences to come up with new ideas for "inescapable" contraptions. One Englishman spent five years constructing handcuffs and leg irons that he felt were escape-proof. It took Houdini three hours to get out of them! One daring escape was made from a nailed, roped, packing crate (loaded down with 200 pounds of lead) while he was handcuffed and in leg irons and then lowered into the East River. He was out in less than one minute! His most famous act was the one performed inside the water-filled Chinese Water Torture Cell, a glass case into which he was lowered into it upside down while his feet were secured in stocks that were locked to the top of the tank.

Like all magicians, Houdini had his tricks. He gained wiggle room within straight jackets by expanding his arms and chest, enabling him to dislocate his shoulders and thus free himself from a supposedly impregnable restraint. He learned to hold his breath for over three minutes, regurgitate keys, and maintain mind control under threatening conditions (such as a limited supply of air). All of that combined with his mixture of showmanship and stage magic eventually made the name Houdini synonymous with the subject of magic.

Archie Leach, a handsome boy from England, became one of the all-time great matinee idols. With unrelenting effort, Archie pursued the traits of the consummate gentleman – his passion was self-improvement.

This started with the identification of several formidable figures to emulate (persons for whom style was a way of being). Two notables among those he selected were Douglas Fairbanks Jr. and Noel Coward. He learned that clothes are the raw material of self-creation. He had a tremendous passion to achieve sartorial excellence. He began to realize that details make the design. He also became aware that all great artists recognize that even the smallest details are keenly important to the larger creation. They are the larger creation. He was persuaded that to be truly great in the little things is an extremely worthy virtue.

This included certain special looks to offset physical detriments such as a thick neck from all his years as an acrobat. He adopted high collars, scarves, and turtle necks to hide this defect. He even broke with convention by effectively mixing patterns. This attention to his clothes even extended to his choice of underwear and pajamas.

The look he hoped to achieve included great attention to his hair. He changed the part to the right side of his head which changed his facial proportions – something plastic surgery could not have accomplished. His hair always looked neat and in place as a result of his use of brilliantine and other mousses to hold it in place which gave it a black/blue sheen.

His discernment led him to pursue areas beyond that just his clothing. Nobody talked like Archie talked. He did something to his voice – such as the perfection of an accent that was neither British nor English, but a unique blend of the two. It was so appealing that President Kennedy used to call him just to hear him talk.

Noel Coward's relaxed demeanor and natural wit provided the template for Archie to become a master of nonchalance and the projection of confident sophistication. This was something he worked on until it became him. He would also practice, in front of a mirror, the art of nonchalantly putting his hand in his pocket (he "invented" side vents in his suit coat to prevent unsightly wrinkles from forming in the front of his coat when attempting to put his hand in his pocket). Thus, he made this ordinary gesture of putting his hand in his pocket seem extraordinary – as he did when lighting a lady's cigarette. He achieved a casual look in even the most mundane of gestures. His mastery of the art of nonchalance, including the way he "moved," placed him in a class by himself, Only Fred Astaire ever "moved" as well as Archie Leach.

He was eager to improve his style by adding things that would advance him toward the image he had envisioned for himself. Thus, he paid close attention to things like table manners, the art of light conversation, and pleasant after-dinner story-telling. He made certain that he was always well-tanned. It complemented his ever-present smile.

It was his passion that made him what he was, the dashing gentleman. Archie Leach's mastery had successfully separated him from all other actors who might once have been grouped with him as handsome, well-dressed men. He was in a class by himself with his creation of this unique character, a character most of us only know as CARY GRANT. As he once remarked, "Everyone would like to be Cary Grant. I'd like to be Cary Grant!"

Identify your "A" skill and you will have probably also identified your passion. In developing that area about which you are passionate (your "A" skill), you will begin to see that you've always been naturally drawn to several curiosities about that subject. As these curiosities deepen, they will lead you to unique insights and bring you to new ways of thinking about the subtleties involved in the area of your particular passion or skill. Your grasp will soon prove to be well beyond that of all those who lack such an "A" skill and its accompanying passion. It certainly turned five nobodies into somebodies.

Such people understand their field so well that they can zero in on the heart of any problem, know what's needed, and effectively sort through the strengths and weaknesses of all the possible solutions. They sense when they should turn to the right or left. They know where to look to find the answer to the problem, or any need, that's confronting them. They have an almost unerring ability to separate that which has a good chance of working from that which doesn't. Because they are operating out of their area of strength and natural understanding, they have an uncanny feel for the thing.

Mastery is attainable only if you answer to your passion and follow its dictates. In so doing, you become attentive to the countless details that combine to form an incredible understanding of the nuances and complexities of your pursuit. Because of your passion, you become captivated by the subject (whatever it might be) and are insatiably curious about *every* aspect of it…THIS IS WHAT MAKES THE DIFFERENCE!!

STEPPING OUTSIDE THE BOX

Your career does not have to conform to the dictates of societal expectations.

Upon graduating from the University of Houston, I began searching for a career position which began with an interview with J.C.Penny. After discussing my background, I asked the interviewer, if I were to be hired, what my beginning assignment might be. He said I'd initially be placed in men's underwear where I'd remain for roughly two years. I then asked what my next position would be and he told me that I'd then most likely be transferred to women's underwear. I left that little meeting discouraged, even depressed, and severely questioning the value of my degree.

I later realized that what would have been in store for me as an employee of J. C. Penny could best be described as a "trap." Many men make career choices that unwittingly land them in this trap. It goes something like this: they need a paycheck, so they look for a job. The greater their financial need, the lower the bar becomes as to the kind of job they'll consider. Should job offers not to be forthcoming, a sense of desperation is apt to set in. It's at a time like this that they may settle for any job…and any job usually turns out to be a job they don't like.

Unfortunately, they are now caught in the trap! Looking for a new job is made difficult by the demands of their current position. They certainly can't quit their job to free up the time to look for a new job because of their desperate need for a paycheck to feed their family. They are forced to keep their job.

So, what's a man to do? Can this dismal outcome be avoided? A glimpse into the lives and career paths of three men should open your eyes to a new way of thinking.

My friendship with Jed dates back to our teenage days. It was during this time that Jed's father, Bud, decided to open a golf driving range. Though things were going well for Bud, he sensed that he could enhance his profits if he had a golf instructor available to his patrons. To solve the problem he posted a sign offering the services of his 15-year-old son, Jed, as the "resident" pro.

Knowing little or nothing about golf, but being a conscientious person, Jed set about learning the fundamentals of a correct golf swing. Many years later, Jed and his wife moved from Colorado to Tennessee. Needing to identify a source of income, he decided to create a golf video that would provide instruction as per the understanding of the golf swing that he gained at this dad's driving range. He believed that the majority of golf instructors overcomplicated the mechanics of the golf swing and thus, his approach was a very simple one. Because his teaching philosophy was in direct opposition to the complicated swing theories of the establishment golf instructors, he decided to promote himself as the "anti-pro." His promotional approach, his swing theories, and his video… all worked! For years now, his sales have provided him with a *very* good living.

Jed had decided that he would not rely upon a corporate paycheck. Rather, he was aware of the disappointment felt by many beginning golfers about the quality of the expensive golf instruction they'd paid for. He knew that he had been successful in developing the skill of those he had previously instructed. Following the counsel of the famous promotional speaker, Zig Ziglar, he identified a need and filled it.

My son spent over 3 years in Johannesburg, South Africa studying to be a diamond cutter. During his stay there he met a man named Fritz. Fritz, it turns out, was a very enterprising guy who repeatedly proved himself capable of figuring out ways to create money-making ventures… fascinating and exotic ways of making money. The common thread to all of his ventures was anticipating perceived demand or meeting a need. The first example was his decision to gather ironwood stumps and limbs which he stored in his backyard. He then hired African wood carvers from one of the nearby townships to create carvings of African animals and furniture pieces out of his collection of wood. Once he had enough carvings to fill a container, he would ship his overflowing container to Los Angeles. He would then begin fulfilling a series of prearranged appointments, across the U. S. with big-game hunters he had previously met during their safaris in Africa.

One of his creations was a bar (the drinking kind) whose tremendous weight necessitated the reinforcement of the floor upon which it was to sit. Its weight was consistent with its $ 40,000 price tag (and that was just one of the several hundred items in his container). Once he had sold all the carvings and emptied the container, he returned to South Africa, several hundred thousand dollars richer. He immediately started the process of filling another container.

On another occasion, Fritz noticed Americans' interest in Zebra skins. Over some time Fritz gathered roughly 500 skins and shipped them to New York. Then he flew there himself, rented a room, and put an ad in the paper. Not long afterward, he had sold all 500 skins and once again returned home. Fritz recognized a need, or demand, and filled it. He was confident of the skills he brought to the table and aware of those he lacked. He found those who could do what he couldn't and created an enterprise that rewarded himself and his South African wood carvers.

I once attended a real estate seminar where I met a quiet fellow, Richard. After one of the sessions, he invited me to join him for lunch where he began to relate his real estate investment experiences. Though he had very few investible funds, a casual search through the want ads convinced him that he could afford to buy a home if he could just secure a loan from a savings and loan organization. He knew he could make the payments from the rent, with money left over. So, he decided to approach the Savings and Loan. Agreeing to make the loan, the Savings and Loan provided the money necessary to purchase Richard's first building. Soon, he had accumulated enough surplus funds from the rental income for another down payment. Again, the Savings and Loan came thru for the purchase of his second building…and then a third, fourth, fifth, etc. He then reached into his briefcase and proceeded to unroll a three-foot-long scroll of single-spaced addresses of properties he had bought! It didn't happen overnight, but it did happen. Richard acted upon his convictions, and it netted him a multimillion-dollar fortune! He told me that he's committed to putting a wing in the local hospital.

You have just read about three people who approached the challenge of making a living in unconventional ways. Jed had a skill – he just needed to exploit its value. Fritz had an idea – he only had to find those who could do what he couldn't. Richard recognized a path – he only needed to identify a source of the funds necessary to implement it. Let their stories serve to expand your thinking.

Avoid the paycheck trap by deciding to honor your areas of skill or knowledge. Identify a need *you* can fulfill through their use.

YOU WILL PAY A PRICE TO BE THE BEST

A look behind the scenes into the lives of the most successful might reveal things you've never considered.

The sport of golf has enjoyed great champions from each generation since the days of the great depression. Two generations ago, the world of professional golf was dominated by Sam Snead, Byron Nelson, and Ben Hogan. The generation that followed featured Jack Nicklaus, Arnold Palmer, and Gary Player. The current generation boasts of Tiger Woods and Phil Michelson.

However, one golfer from each of these generations has supporters who insist that the great champion from their era was the greatest ever. Currently, that would be Tiger Woods. From the generation before, it would be Jack Nicklaus. In the generation before that, it was Ben Hogan.

But which of these players was truly the greatest? The answer isn't easy to come by since the equipment has changed, the golf courses have been lengthened, and the standards for judgment aren't set in stone. The most accepted standard would be a player's tournament record. But even by that standard, the quality of the competitors, as well as the depth of the field, differs from generation to generation.

Since the identity of the greatest golfer of all time can't be agreed upon, allow me to divert your attention to a golfer that nearly everyone would agree was the greatest striker of a golf ball who ever lived. No one from any era could equal his ball-striking skills. His pursuit of excellence in this area *exceeded* that of any other champion who ever lived. That golfer was Ben Hogan.

Because they starred in different eras, Woods and Hogan never competed against each other. Each perused excellence, but in different ways. While both wanted to be the greatest golfer ever, they approached that goal differently. Woods pursued excellence in the mechanics of his golf swing and a mastery of all departments of the game, including trouble shots. Hogan sought the perfection of his golf swing and excellence in ball striking.

Though a champion of the mid-twentieth century, Hogan's fame and reputation continue, not only in the minds of those who played golf in his day but also in the minds of even today's touring professionals. He still deserves the label as the best striker of a golf ball who ever lived. No other player in the history of the game ever matched the precision of his golf shots – not Bobby Jones, Jack Nicklaus, or Tiger Woods. In his prime, even his competitors would take time out *just to watch him hit practice balls!*

Since this principle is directed at those who deeply desire to excel at something, an examination of Ben Hogan's journey to excellence provides a look into what that involved. It's fair to say that Hogan did things that were uncommon to any other golfer, either before or since. So, if you wish not only to excel but secretly hope to become the very best, you might ask yourself this question: "Am I willing to pay the price?"

The book, *Hogan*, written by Curt Sampson and published in 1996, relates his life story, a captivating account of an extraordinary life. Sampson shares details that often expose the heart-wrenching challenges Hogan faced. It gives the reader a view into his disciplined life of radical devotion to an almost impossible standard. It chronicles the regimens and sacrifices Hogan endured while seeking to become the greatest golfer to have ever played the game.

At age nine, Ben *watched* his father commit suicide! Times were not only lean, but without the primary breadwinner, sheer survival was in question. The entire family had to find employment. Ben got a job caddying at the local golf course.

Being around golf all the time exposed him to the "golf bug," which bit him and never let go. Early on, Ben wanted to play golf – tournament golf, championship golf. Yet, his first performances were anything but those of a champion – failing in one tournament after another, never winning. For a long time, he didn't even place in the money! At one point in time, he and his wife survived by eating oranges they took from the orchards found along the fenced boundaries of the courses he played in southern California.

Unlike his fellow golf pros, many of whom lived lives of playboys, Hogan took the game and his mission seriously. In those days, most professional golfers rarely put much time into their practice sessions which usually served as little more than warm-ups. The tedium of hitting practice balls didn't hold much appeal for most of them.

But while his counterparts were in the bar having a good time, Hogan was out hitting practice balls – something that he felt was critical to the attainment of the excellence he sought. As a testimony to his devotion, it was well-known that he often practiced until his hands bled. It was reported that some of the other professionals saw him hitting golf balls in the rain – even in the dark. Few, if any other golfers then, or since, have devoted as much effort to perfecting their golf swing. Yet, even with that amount of practice, success refused to come Hogan's way. Nevertheless, nothing could deter him.

A typical day would have Hogan hitting hundreds of practice balls before lunch. After lunch, he'd go do it again! I can personally attest to the grueling prospect of hitting hundreds of practice balls in a day. While I was in college, I hit 500 balls a day, every day, for one entire week. It's a lot of work. Your hands hurt, your back hurts, and tedium becomes your biggest enemy. But for Hogan, it was routine.

Eventually, as he continued to persist in the discipline of hitting thousands of practice balls, his efforts began to pay off. Hogan started to win, and win...and win.

Yet, at what seemed like the peak of his game, things went drastically wrong for Ben Hogan.

One foggy night, on a lonely country road, a bus in the oncoming lane pulled out to pass a slow-moving car in its way. Hogan's car and the bus entered opposite ends of a bridge at the same time. The concrete abutment of the bridge left Hogan with no way to get out of the bus's path, nor was there enough time for either of them to stop. The two collided head-on! Hogan's life was saved only because he instinctively stretched across his wife's body to protect her from the impact. The steering column was driven through the back of the driver's seat. A broken collarbone along with tremendous damage to his legs threatened his ability to ever walk, let alone play golf again. Hogan would never again be without pain.

But through the same discipline he displayed in his practice, Hogan relentlessly pushed through the pain. He forced himself to walk, eventually hit a few practice balls, and finally played a round of golf. Eleven months later he would win the U.S. Open for the second time!

His same practice regimen continued to be as religiously observed as before. His ability to hit precision golf shots continued to reach new heights. But the time finally came when the fine-tuning of his mechanical skills had become so acute that he had to look elsewhere for any continued improvement. His focus turned to his equipment.

If you can't even keep the ball in the fairway, it matters little that the balls or clubs might be a bit "off." But Hogan began to realize that his errant golf shots were now more likely to be due to manufacturing flaws in his equipment than the result of any flaws that could be found in his golf swing. Hogan decided to remedy the situation. He would fill a bathtub with water and Epsom salts, take a large number of golf balls, and put a dot on each one. He then placed them in the tub to float. If the same side kept rising to the top, that ball was out-of-round. After removing all the balls that were out of round, he would then take a magnifying glass and look at every dimple on each ball – all 280 of them. He was looking for any sign of excess paint that could cause an off-centeredness that might result in a slight aerodynamic imbalance. To the other pros, who thought little about their clubs and nothing about their balls, *this was unbelievable!*

The extent of their concern was wrapped up in an annual visit to their equipment manufacturer to pick out their new clubs for the year. In roughly one hour, they would walk away with their new set. For Hogan, this exercise took three days. His perfectionism knew no bounds. One club was too upright, another too flat. He wanted others to be more rounded on the tow of the club. Some needed some loft removed; others were too hook-faced, etc. When he finally walked out with his new clubs for the year, he knew he had the "perfect" set of golf clubs. Like the world's greatest violinists who all want to play their music on nothing but a Stradivarius, Hogan's golf equipment was the Stradivarius of golf clubs.

You have just read about the depth of commitment that Hogan felt was necessary to becoming the best. It differs from the commitment necessary to pursue *mere* excellence. Hogan defined that difference when he answered a question posed by that great champion, Gary Player. The player asked Hogan what he'd need to do to become the best. Hogan asked Player if he practiced a lot. The player answered that he did (and he did practice... a great deal). Hogan replied, "Double it!"

To be the *best* at something, you must gain a full understanding of what "best" *really* looks like – in all of its details. Start by carefully examining the stories of those who have exhibited extraordinary mastery at their chosen pursuit and determine what they did that set them apart. Then create a plan that promises to deliver a mastery of those nuances and details.

Once you've developed your plan and have begun your journey in search of excellence, don't ever allow the temptation to avoid the grueling, often monotonous rigors of your program to lure you into taking shortcuts. You're foolish to think that you can somehow avoid the extreme hardships that will be a part of your commitment. Those who aim at being the best have all paid a *big* price for their attainments. Before you begin, assess your willingness to make the necessary sacrifices. If you question that willingness, abort the pursuit.

The realization of excellence is reserved for only those who are willing to make that commitment by extending the necessary effort. To be the best takes nothing less than superhuman discipline, effort, and a matching commitment. Remember: arriving at the top depends upon having *persistently sought the mastery of each of the details that might appear on that enormous list of all the details that might, in any way, define the subject at hand.*

VIII. BUSINESS AND INVESTMENTS

Most people find it easier to accumulate money through success in their business or career than to successfully invest that money in other areas…areas they know less about.

Most people accumulate money as a result of an income that exceeds their expenses. Sometimes it's the result of a good job or the profit realized by their well-run business. A few come upon their nest egg as the beneficiaries of an inheritance. Fewer yet are the recipients of large sums that are the result of some windfall such as an insurance settlement, divorce settlement, a winning lottery ticket, or some other *one-time* event.

Once you retire, you must find something that will replace your former means of support. Many make money in something they know a lot about and lose it in something they know little about.

The principles in this section shed light on what you can reasonably expect from your investments. They will expose unwise investment prospects, and familiarize you with the merits, as well as the hazards, of placing your money in the hands of reckless advisors or questionable monetary vehicles. The following concepts should provide you with some understanding of business strategies and investment principles.

The first five principles, There Ain't No Free Lunch, Getting In Is Often Easy…But, Is It Too Good To Be True?, How Much Do You Deserve To Make?, and Unrealistic Expectations. They expose faulty assumptions, unrealistic expectations, and dangerous schemes.

Understand The Nature Of Opportunities, People Value Things Differently, Partnerships?, Value Your "Trump Cards", and The First

Rule Of Risk Taking will introduce investment strategies and provide instructions on some fundamentals involved in successful investing.

Finally, four valuable business and investment principles are presented in the following concepts. Overlooked Wisdom, Know When To Hang In There, Know When To Retreat, and The End Game Strategy.

THERE AIN'T NO FREE LUNCH

That windfall you've long dreamed about may not be all it's cracked up to be.

Everybody would love to get something for nothing, "a free lunch." Unfortunately, that lunch is never free. Take the cow in the feedlot: even she ought to wonder why she's getting a free lunch. The cost may be delayed or disguised, but there is always a cost. You can count on its existence and the eventual demand for its payment. Nevertheless, huge numbers of people believe otherwise as they place their hopes on some "get rich quick" scheme. Others engage in gambling, which for most people spells "lottery."

The appearance of sudden wealth, which you did not earn, often carries a price tag that far exceeds the riches received. The following accounts (chronicled on the internet) are just a few of the tragic stories of those who have gained the very thing so many seek.

A Texan, Billie Bob Harrell, won $31 million in the lottery. Before his win, he was just a shelf-stocker in a Home Depot store with a wife and three children. Given his meager income, he was deeply concerned about the welfare of his family. He saved a little money out of each paycheck to buy lottery tickets, one of which resulted in his $31,000,000 windfall.

Accompanied by an entourage of family, friends, and attorneys, he accepted his first check. He gave an acceptance speech wherein he said that life had been tough, but he had persevered. He mentioned that everyone kept telling him that things would get better – he just didn't know that they would get this much better.

He bought a ranch, a half-dozen houses for various family members, as well as a new car for each of them. Being a religious man, he also gave generously to the church and was always ready, cash in hand, to help a congregational member in need.

After a while, his life began unraveling. He believed in being generous but the unending number of "people -in-need" finally began to place an unexpected strain on his finances. Family members, friends, fellow worshipers, and even total strangers came to him for money. His out-of-control lending and spending shattered his already strained marriage. Billie Bob confided to a financial advisor, "Winning the lottery is the worst thing that ever happened to me!"

Twenty months after receiving his prize money, Billie Bob went upstairs into a bedroom, placed a shotgun against his chest, and pulled the trigger! Billie Bob was gone, but the children and grandparents continued with their bitter struggles over the money. A family war loomed over the remnants of a fortune that was so depleted that it became questionable if sufficient money remained with which to pay the estate taxes!

William Post won $16.2 million in 1988. He was quoted as saying: "I wish it never happened. It was all a nightmare." His problems started when a former girlfriend sued him for a share of his prize money...and this wasn't his only lawsuit or problem. Hoping to inherit a share of the earnings, his brother was arrested for having hired a hitman to kill him. Two of his children urged William to make investments with them. He invested in a restaurant and a car business in Sarasota, Florida – neither of these investments ever brought any money back to William. Within one year, he was one million dollars in debt! After declaring bankruptcy, William's relationship with his children crumbled. He now lives *quietly* on the $450 he receives each month from his social security!

Evelyn Adams won the New Jersey lottery, not once, but twice for a total take of $5.4 million. Today, the money is all gone and she lives in a trailer! Adams admitted to being a big-time gambler and having lost "a lot of money" on the slots in Atlantic City. She complained that everybody wanted her money – they all had their hands out! "I won the American dream, a dream other lottery winners have called a nightmare." But she lost it all. "It was a hard fall called rock bottom. Winning the lottery isn't always what it's cracked up to be!"

A chance encounter further illustrates this principle. One day, as I was walking down seventeenth Street to return to my office from my lunch break, I ran into an old high school friend, Joe, whom I hadn't seen in years. After our greeting and some brief small talk, he asked if he could accompany me back to my office to discuss a few things with me.

Once we were comfortably settled, he opened up and told me that he was struggling. It seemed that his wife had just inherited a large fortune. He said, "None of my friends can understand the feelings I have about this situation. I'm a school teacher and love what I do. But I don't make much money. Nevertheless, I was quite content and we were living comfortably on my salary. Now, it no longer matters what I do. My abilities will never earn an amount sufficient to compete with what has been 'handed' to my wife. I have become irrelevant!" For Joe, the free lunch carried an enormous price tag – his entire self-worth!

The free lunch for these winners wasn't free after all. It had its price. The knowledge of how to manage wealth is usually the result of your efforts to build that wealth. Those who inherit or win large sums typically can't fathom the money they now have. Unequipped to deal with their new fortune, they think the money will never run out! For this reason, they usually overestimate how much they can buy, underestimate what it will cost to maintain all they've bought, and thus miscalculate how long it will last.

The majority of recipients of large sums rush out and buy all the toys they ever dreamed of having. But the more things they buy, the more their maintenance and overhead rises. They quickly find themselves burdened by the heavy costs of maintaining their purchases.

While charity is a wonderful thing, no one can meet all the needs that come knocking at their door once word of their sudden wealth gets out. Family members, many of whom they barely know, as well as "friends" they haven't heard from in years, all come calling. Add to this the toll taken by bad investments (making and keeping money require skills that go hand-in-hand). Having not "made" the money themselves, they are usually lacking the necessary abilities to keep it! It's amazing how rapidly the money disappears.

Man is meant to be a hunter-gatherer. He wants to feel needed. So he doesn't usually respond well to having everything handed to him.

Stop seeking the free lunch – this means saying "no" to gambling. The odds are overwhelming that you will lose way more than you will ever win. And…once the money's *gone,* you'll be able to think of a thousand things you'd rather have spent it on.

Decide to be content with what you can earn with your talents and effort. The fruits of your labor will always taste better than that free lunch which seldom brings happiness,

Be forewarned: once in possession of a big windfall, *you can never return to your former life.* In that life, you felt respected because whatever money you had, you had earned it. That respect (at least your self-respect) could easily drift away …because the money now in your possession is money you didn't earn! Books have been written, and counseling services are available, to help recipients of sudden wealth cope with it!

GETTING IN IS OFTEN EASY...BUT

The ease of getting involved versus the difficulties of getting uninvolved can be quite pronounced.

This principle speaks directly to a certain real estate investment I was very intent on making.

A real estate agent friend of mine, who had been the source of several profitable ventures in the past, called me with what looked like another such venture. The project was a four-building, 28-unit, apartment complex that my friend strongly felt should become a condominium conversion project. It had already been legally separated into 28 separate titles which eliminated the need for me to spend the time and legal fees to get that done. The apartment building was located in a Colorado mountain town that was right in the heart of many fabulous ski areas. In fact, within one hour's drive, you could be at any one of eight ski resorts. Several 14,000-foot peaks were in the town's backyard – a big lure for hikers. Rafting and fly fishing were also popular summertime activities. The town itself had some colorful historic aspects to it as it figured largely in this country's 19th-century mining activities. Similar to many Old West towns, it could boast of famous legends who helped create the mystique of the place. The old-timers insist that Doc Holiday once shot a man outside one of the saloons

As far as the business aspects of the proposition were concerned, it was very promising. A very large mine was an important source of jobs in the area. When I first visited the property it was almost fully occupied and generated a very impressive cash flow. The manager was also a valuable asset as she was one of the locals who knew everybody and didn't have much trouble filling a vacancy. Additionally, the condition of the apartments was a big plus. A great deal of renovation had already taken place, which left little need for expensive outlays to bring the units up to a saleable condition. The final plus was a very pleasant young woman who had extensive experience in the sale of condominium conversion units having sold several thousand in her career. She was willing to decorate one of the apartments as a model and move in for an on-site commitment to market the project. She and I were both convinced that sales of the condominiums would be easy since, remarkably, we could sell the units for a lower mortgage payment than the rents they were now paying. Additionally, the owner was even willing to carry back these mortgages as full credit against our note to him that represented the balance of our purchase price. That owner was a wealthy older gentleman who was primarily interested in shedding the responsibilities of management, preferring to reduce his involvement to getting checks in the mail. This was great. We wouldn't have to conduct the tedious and uncertain task of finding mortgage sources for our buyers.

Quite naturally, the existing tenants figured important in our marketing strategy. I was secretly hoping that we might be able to sell a large percentage of the apartments back to our tenants. Everything was coming together nicely.

You are probably wondering what could be wrong with this deal. Embarrassingly, it was the size of the down payment. I didn't have it. *No matter how hard I tried*, I couldn't seem to raise the money. I offered the owner a trade for some of my other properties. I went to various lenders, but due to the underlying economic circumstances at that time, I was unable to find anyone willing to help.

Several months passed and I called my realtor friend to see if the apartment building was still on the market. He said he'd call the owner and get an update. His call back revealed that things hadn't changed, the building was still available….but other things had.

The manager's husband had died and she had moved out! No one was now managing the project! To make matters worse, the miners that figured so importantly in the occupancy statistics, were of two types: permanent employees who worked in the mine and contract engineers who were short-term employees hired to design labor-saving mechanical systems to help reduce the dependence upon full-time mining employees.

The latter group had finished their work and had all moved out! The building was now suffering a 50% vacancy rate – resulting in the loss of thousands of dollars every month! The town's other apartment owners were now desperately hanging on to their tenants.

To have undertaken this project would now have meant making the mortgage payments to the former owner with dollars from sources *other* than the apartment building's revenues – revenues that might not even be sufficient to cover the building's operational expenses.

And the talented young woman had, in the meantime, take a job away from the real estate business – no longer available to assist me with the marketing of the project.

The final nail in the coffin was the fact that most of the sales would probably be made in the summer months. At the beginning of the summer, news reports carried the story of a large sinkhole that had occurred on the only road into the little town from the north, the primary source of visitors. Several weeks later, other reports estimated the repair time to be at least a month!

Had I possessed the money for the down payment, getting in would have been a lead-pipe cinch! The owner had already approved a preliminary purchase contract that we had submitted to him.

But once involved and knowing what I now know, imagine the problems in trying to get out of that mess! All solutions to the problem of getting out of it promised to lead to enormous losses! It would have been so easy to get in but almost impossible to get out (whole).

As you can now appreciate, getting out of a losing situation can be extremely challenging. You've bought a business that's now losing money. You'll soon discover that buyers for your business will indeed be tough to find. Maybe you own a backyard full of ostriches. All the hype that convinced you to become involved has proven strangely incapable of attracting other ostrich buyers. Such situations represent daunting challenges to "getting out" as these "sure-fire" investments now stick to you like a tar baby.

Anyone who handles another's money is capable of misappropriating some of it for their use. The money you just "temporarily borrowed" from your boss's bank account has a way of never being repaid. Taking the money was so easy and seemingly so innocent. Things will not end well when you can't replace them and are then discovered in your embezzlement. Most excuses won't save your job and may not avert a little stretch in prison as criminal charges are likely to be filed against you. Getting out of this nightmare may prove to be one of your life's greatest challenges!

This is also true of the married man's casual affair that results in a *very* unwanted pregnancy. This may have been a situation where those involved just viewed it as brief, no harm done, dalliance. But getting free of this fishhook is more than just a flesh ripper; it can be a life wrecker!

These situations all have a similar theme: the signing of the contract, the signing of the check, or an ill-considered decision can all be deceptively appealing. But reversing the situation can often be very costly and painful. Unwittingly, you may have become involved in something you should have *never* touched!

Acknowledge the possibility that your "deal" could go bad, and decide upon an exit strategy before making any serious commitment. If you don't have one, suspend your plans until you do. It's better to miss a good deal than to ever take on a bad one!

Since you may be blindsided by numerous difficulties you failed to anticipate, it's critically important that you not make the mistake of dismissing the ones you did anticipate. They alone could cause your undoing.

However, these precautions will be of no help to you if you've incorrectly concluded that a need to "get out" will never occur.

When applying this principle to investments, remember that as you are trying to "get out" of your bad deal, the number of sellers looking for money greatly exceeds the number of buyers looking for deals.

IS IT TOO GOOD TO BE TRUE?

Wow! Was this ever a slick idea? Or was it?

Moneymaking schemes come and go. I've always considered myself too "smart" to ever fall victim to one of them. Yet, when I heard about this business of raising chinchillas, it somehow seemed different. I was told that they are clean, inexpensive to raise, can be kept in small cages, and reproduce like rabbits. Moreover, most furriers would acknowledge, that chinchilla furs are expensive and highly desired luxury furs.

The more I thought about it, the more excited I became, and the more my current way of earning a living seemed both tedious and unexciting. Looking back on it, I was gullible – like all the others who were lured in.

To my credit, however, the more I thought about it, the more it seemed too good to be true. Still, despite that glimmer of caution, I couldn't spot the fly in the ointment. My discomfort finally led me to seek expert advice. I decided that I would call the New York fur market and expose my plan to them. If the experts there could find no fault with the idea and better yet, if they were in any way encouraging, I was ready to start ranching.

When I telephoned the New York fur market, I found myself talking to a very knowledgeable man who was nice enough to listen to my plan and answer my questions. What he told me stopped me cold in my tracks! He explained, in great detail, that the fly in the ointment that I hadn't been able to identify was the exacting standards the New York fur market placed on the quality of chinchilla pelts they would accept. They were only interested in buying the best. If you sent them pelts that were anything less, they would reject them.

Now, I must admit that I didn't immediately grasp the significance of this emphasis on the quality of the fur pelts. The fur market employee then explained that unacceptable characteristics will inbreed. This adversely affects the quality of the fur, making it unsalable. If the chinchilla rancher isn't extremely careful, it isn't long before his entire "herd" has become contaminated. Once this begins to happen, the rancher finds that his only "marketable" animals are his best ones. So, to keep his operation going he pelts (kills) those marketable ones and sells their pelts (the best of his herd) so he can continue to feed the ones he'll never be able to sell.

In no time, all that will be left are the chinchillas that can't be sold. Furthermore, these chinchillas are only capable of producing offspring that can't be sold either.

Chinchilla ranching, ostrich farming, and other ideas like this might properly be labeled, "investment scams." These and other more sophisticated "schemes" are often responsible for *life-altering* losses for the uninformed investors who invested their money in them. Among these people are those who finally accumulated enough money to think they needed to invest it someplace. As novices in the area of investments, they are totally at the mercy of the *competency and honesty* of those they're trusting with their money. Unfortunately, most novice investors are unable to render a reasoned judgment about either of these qualities.

One woman's attitude about her experiences in dealing with a swindler highlights the problem. Though she was the victim of a scam, she never contacted a law enforcement office to report her horrible experience. After the scam had come to light publicly, investigators interviewed some of its victims. When an investigator called upon her, he asked her why she had never made any investigative inquiries about either the promoter or the investment he was promoting. She told him that she was afraid someone would burst her bubble and tell her it was a bad deal!

Scam artists cleverly choose just such people as targets for their schemes. They know that some people greatly need to believe the stories of the sudden riches that are being promised. When the deception is discovered, they are often too ashamed to report the problem, not wanting to call attention to their stupidity. Those who refuse to verify the information they are being fed – information that lures them to invest – are sitting ducks just asking for trouble and loss.

Even successful people who are financially responsible get suckered into misguided or fraudulent investment schemes. These are people who made their money in one area but entrust it to someone else to invest it in another area about which they are not familiar. Surprisingly, they often fail to embark upon even the most rudimentary of investigations. They are no better off than novice investors. Both are at the mercy of the person who now has their money! Starting over may be in their future!

"Starting over" doesn't have to happen to you. The lesson to remember from this is that when something seems too good to be true, it usually is. Many don't want to investigate their "good idea" too thoroughly as someone might try and talk them out of it. So, they forge ahead only to watch their investment turn sour and brace themselves for devastating losses and huge regrets.

When something seems too good to be true, *decide that you will search out experts in the field and subject your investment idea to their critical eye. If your idea can't convince them, don't touch it!*

When you are being urged to place your money with someone who is going to invest that money in something about which you have little knowledge, say NO! Stick with the things *you know* a lot about.

HOW MUCH DO YOU DESERVE TO MAKE?

This principal won't tell you what you want to hear. But, don't ignore it!

Making money by selling your time is called a job. Making money through the use of your money is an investment. It might come as a surprise to many to realize that a great number of "investments" also require some of one's time – time for which no direct payment may be received.

Pure investments, those that require none of your time, are fewer in number than those that require some of your time. For all those that do require some of your time, two principles shouldn't be ignored. These two principles, taken from elementary physics, comprise the very foundation of what's required to reap financial rewards from your investments.

Inertia and friction both speak to the need for a force, or energy, to move an object at rest. Inertia says that an object at rest tends to remain at rest unless acted upon by some force or energy. Friction causes objects in contact with each other to resist being moved - unless acted upon by some force or energy. These two principles explain why the perpetual motion machine has never been invented. To keep something constantly in motion requires an unrelenting application of energy to overcome the forces of inertia and friction.

The train, and all the cars it's pulling, won't move down the tracks without fuel (energy). In like manner, energy is required in every manufacturing process, whether it's building a house, manufacturing a car, or the growth of crops. We are all required to exert energy to sustain ourselves. To expect otherwise is to ignore those two laws of physics.

Surprisingly, these principles also happen to apply to the creation of wealth. To put money in the stock market, or any other investment, and then expect that money to just grow without the input of *some exertion*, is to deceive yourself. And what's true of the stock market is also true of any other business investment. They all require an input of a great deal of knowledge to realize any measure of success. That accumulation of knowledge takes schooling which takes time and energy.

This begs the question: If someone isn't willing to invest any time or effort into their investment results, what kind of results can they expect? What do they deserve to make? My answer: *"nothing!"*

One friend complained that he had lost money in the stock market. Our conversation revealed his serious lack of knowledge about the workings of the stock market. Since he knew very little about it, he innocently assumed that the mere act of putting his money in the market was all that was required to realize profits. My answer, which may have offended him, was, "How much do you think you deserve to make?" As you might guess, he didn't answer my question.

In the early days of my career as a young businessman, I was employed as a stockbroker. I spent the last four and a half years of that career with Lehman Brothers. At that time they were the scions of wealth and financial power. Collectively, the Lehman partners had corporate board directorships on 250 of the largest corporations in America (maybe the world). As one of the leading investment bankers in the world, they had their "ear to the ground" in terms of what was going on in the world of high finance. There was an unmistakable aura of wealth and intrigue about the firm as well as about the famous members of the higher echelons of the Lehman partnership.

For me, a nobody stockbroker, the reputation of the firm I worked for was all the credentials I needed to gain access to some very high places. Wealthy people everywhere had respect and desire to rub shoulders with the Lehman mystique.

I remember one day getting a notice from the New York office that each of the brokers in the Denver office had been invited to a luncheon at the Brown Palace Club – Denver's most exclusive private luncheon club. The purpose was to hear a presentation by one of Lehman's brightest gurus on the stock market, investments, money, and money management strategy. The Lehman management suggested that we include our best client or clients in that invitation.

My client and I were both extremely excited to hear what this man had to say. I brought a notepad to take notes on his thoughts and predictions. Both my client and I fully appreciated the opportunity..

I kept those notes regarding the predictions and recommendations made that day by the brilliant guru. Sometime later, I decided to review my notes to see how well his suggestions had performed. I was astounded to discover that his predictions and recommendations had turned out to be *86 percent wrong!*

At that point, I decided to educate myself. Aiming at a master's degree in finance, I enrolled in graduate school. I signed up for two very extensive courses in technical analysis (the prediction of future stock price movements by observing and analyzing past movements). Over the next year or two, I also read fifty books on the stock market and twenty-five more on investments in real estate. One of the books was an old, out-of-print book, which claimed that for every one hundred people who are involved in the market, one person makes a lot of money, two make a little, and two break even. *The other 95 percent lose varying amounts*! I didn't want to believe what I had just read!

Over the next two years, I carefully analyzed my clients' investment results. What I observed was a very disturbing confirmation of that book's statistics regarding the relative success of those who invest money in the stock market. I finally arrived at the point where total verification of the book's statistics only lacked my meeting that one person in a hundred who was making a lot of money. I never met him! But, by that time, I had already become convinced of the book's assertions about the other 99 percent. I left the stock and bond business. From that day to this, I have never bought, nor sold, another share of stock!

Many investors have the mistaken impression that all they need to do is put their money "to work," as if that mere act of putting some money in the market is deserving of a profit. What investors fail to realize is that the market isn't some giant charity that provides profits to all participants.

Remember, you are competing against some of the most brilliant financial minds in the world. Moreover, you will never have access to the quantity and quality of information that's available to them. What you are buying, someone else is selling. What you are selling, someone else is buying. What do they know that you don't? Gains that may take months or years to accumulate can be lost in days, even hours; to me, that's very troubling.

If you insist on putting money in the stock market, hire a conservative money manager. Otherwise, decide that you will limit the scope of your investments to just a few areas. The first would include investments in any area about which you can claim expert status. The second is to become a money lender who deals in well-secured loans to people with good reputations. The third is residential rental properties (not warehouses, office buildings, or commercial properties). Fourth, raw land (beware: it typically provides no income but does require the payment of property taxes, every year!)

Avoid aggressive money managers who promise enticingly generous returns – this is the ploy of all Ponzi schemes. Instead, limit your choice of money managers to those who are *genuinely* conservative.

Successful money management takes the same degree of effort and knowledge as does the attainment of success in any other field. *Don't expect profits without one, or both of those ingredients.*

Assure yourself of success by seeking to personally gain *expert status* in matters of money management. This means taking responsibility for your investments by being personally involved and knowledgeable about what is being done with your money! By paying the price of educating yourself in this area, you will then have earned the right to expect a profitable outcome.

UNREALISTIC EXPECTATIONS

Many dreams big. Few see those dreams come true.

Dreaming: It's something we all do – an enjoyable escape that allows you to lose yourself in a fantasy. Where would the world be without the dreams of some of the great inventors, statesmen, explorers, artists, developers, etc.? These visionaries were the responsible agents for the untold advances that have become the way of life that we now enjoy.

Today, people of relatively modest means can explore the world. At one time, such exploration required a budget available only to royalty. Communications that once took weeks to accomplish (Pony Express, etc.) can now occur in seconds from just about anywhere in the world. These and countless other advances are the legacies of the dreamers. These are the people who have stepped into the world of the unknown, thumbing their noses at the hazards

For visionaries like this, their dreams often translate into wonderful realities that benefit the life and health of individuals as well as society as a whole. Unfortunately, many people cannot distinguish between realizable and unrealizable dreams. For them, dreaming can become a substitute for doing. Unrealizable dreams are a waste of time and should be recognized for the flights of fancy that they are. But even those that are realizable must be weighed against the cost in time and money that will be necessary for their accomplishment. But how does one differentiate between the achievable as opposed to the castle in the air that has little or no chance of becoming a reality? A longtime friend's pursuit of his grand imagination provides insight into the heart of this question.

After returning from his wife's thirtieth high school reunion, my friend, William, began to think about the successful career and tangible rewards of one of her classmates he had met at the reunion. The man had a nice home, a new car, a pleasure boat, and a beautiful fifth wheel (all debt free). All this, plus an adequate pension, and no worries! Who would believe that this was the story of a retired postal worker?

William felt envious. He had long dreamed of making it big in the business of real estate investments. He had made liberal use of bank borrowings which had enabled him to acquire several investment properties. Because he was highly leveraged, his equity didn't amount to much – certainly, nothing compared to that of the little postal worker. Yet, he had no desire to change places with that postal worker or settle for his accomplishments.

Nevertheless, the postal worker and his achievements were to become the motivation for my friend's goal…to show the world that he had made it "really big" – never again needing to take a backseat to someone like his wife's former classmate.

As the picture began to take shape in his mind, he sought to acquire some visible evidence that would elevate his stature to that of a man of wealth and accomplishment. After a visit to his friendly bank, William was able to "shoehorn" himself into one of the most expensive building sites near the most exclusive country club in the Denver area.

One of William's sage friends, who was aware of William's finances, feared that William was heading in a dangerous direction and proceeded to caution him about the implications and further obligations that would become an expensive part of his purchase. He reminded William that with the purchase of the lot, he had only barely begun. In a sense, he had merely succeeded in "nailing down" a very small piece of his dream. For starters, he'd need to build a house that "fit." After all, this was the ultimate upscale neighborhood. (It's worth noting that it's no fun to live in a place where all your neighbors can outspend you. It has been my experience that I'm most comfortable living in a neighborhood where I'm convinced that I'm *five percent wealthier* than my neighbors, not rich enough to feel smug or arrogant, but comparatively a *little* wealthier – just enough not to worry about keeping up with my neighboring Joneses.)

If you're fortunate enough to build a "fitting" house for this classy enclave, you'll need furnishings to match. He'd also feel pressure to drive the "right" cars, send his children to the "right" schools, fill his and his wife's closets with expensive clothes (as well as adorn her with some stunning jewelry), dine at the best restaurants, and vacation at the posh resorts. He would eventually discover that because of their great wealth, his neighbors all had financial advisors, personal trainers, and charity foundations. In addition, most of them had serious art collections. After all this, he would need to round out his luxury portfolio with a second home in some ski area and maybe a third in the desert, otherwise, he'd never break into their inner circle and connect with his new neighbors. And where would all the money necessary to do those things come from? Most of his neighbors didn't need to borrow money to buy their lot. Nor did they borrow the money they gave to charity or paid their trainer.

He impatiently rushed things...the result being the death of his dream.

He never got that far. Within a year, his other highly leveraged business ventures had failed which made it impossible for him to make his lot purchase payments to the bank. They foreclosed on his country club lot.

The total of his achievements was financial havoc and an unhappy marriage that ended in divorce. His concluding thoughts about his sad state of affairs were summed up in his telling statement: "I guess I'll never have the Lear jet and the billions."

In pursuing the most (and skipping all the intermediate steps) he ended up with the least. Had his dream been a vision of a staircase of intermediate goals and accomplishments, the steps from one level to the next would have represented a series of realizable dreams – each successively within reach. His approach, however, was to vault from the first floor to the top floor in one step! Now, he's starting over – a sad example of an unrealizable dream.

This concept isn't meant to discourage your dreams. But it does seek to alert you to the folly of risking what you've already achieved in an unwise attempt to bypass intermediate steps on your way to the grand finale. Without the benefit of intermediate successes, reaching the pinnacle will prove to be infinitely more difficult than you might imagine.

Decide to focus your efforts on realizing success with the first minor step – that success will provide the impetus to pursue the next step. The lessons learned, as well as the wisdom gained from these struggles, will play an invaluable role in helping you keep what you've already earned!

View the journey forward as a staircase of the economic pursuits of life: security, comfort, leisure, and luxury – all successive steps on the way to the realization of your dreams.

Decide that you will continue to entertain dreams, dreams that will spur you on and inspire you to succeed. But, decide that you will not allow your eagerness to cause you to attempt to vault to the conclusion of that dream without having laid the proper foundation for its realization and sustainability.

UNDERSTAND THE NATURE OF OPPORTUNITIES

Many wouldn't recognize an opportunity if they tripped over it. Even when they do, they often fail to act quickly enough.

This concept deals, in part, with opportunities that often escape people's attention. These are the ones whose attractions are either derided or hidden from the view of the opportunity seeker because of the way he commonly looks at such things.

This principle deals with two different kinds of opportunities and the basic approaches to successfully dealing with them. The first is the opportunity that exists despite a majority opinion that no opportunities exist.

The second type of fortuity might be generally conceded to be an opportunity in the making, but the time to properly check it out isn't available. Most people pass on situations like that.

The "no opportunities exist" mindset describes the situation my wife, Ellen, and I faced on a last-minute vacation to Hawaii.

My wife had just endured a grueling regimen of chemotherapy in her fight against lymphoma. I felt a little time away would be therapy in and of itself. After waiting a few days for her to regain some strength we headed to California. When we arrived, however, it was raining and the forecast was for it to continue for the entire duration of our planned getaway. I made a quick visit to a nearby travel agency and booked us on a flight to Kauai. For whatever reason, I didn't make a room reservation. This oversight, however, didn't cause me a moment's concern since there are lots of hotels on that island. Immediately upon our arrival, I went to the electronic board that had direct dial lines to all the major hotels. To my astonishment, every one of them was full and none had any suggestions as to where we could find a room. Each told me that a large convention had convened there and the entire island was sold out.

I began to have visions of my wife and me sleeping in the rental car. In her condition that seemed like the cruelest irony of all. I stood there stunned, not wanting to tell her the dismal news. Frantically, I racked my brain for some possible solution to the problem. Suddenly, it occurred to me that I knew someone who was involved with the Princeville development project. After spending some time with long-distance information, I was able to get the number for his office. He was out but his secretary took an immediate interest in my problem and gave me the number of a woman who managed a condominium project's rental program there in Princeville.

I held my breath as I rang her rental-office number. When she answered, all my problems melted away. It seems that she had been away for two weeks. As a consequence, all 32 units within her project were available. And what units! They were beautiful two-bedroom apartments perched on a cliff just above the crashing waves below.

Never forget, the minute you begin to entertain the belief that there are no opportunities, you will logically suspend all your efforts to find one – which also increases the likelihood that you'll fail to recognize it even if one does appear!

But, *there are always opportunities!* However, you must remember that the type of opportunity that's hidden from common view will remain hidden unless you begin to view things uncommonly. Such a way would be to adopt the mindset of a *contrarian*. By realigning your thinking in this fashion, you will face little competition, and no lack of viable opportunities Such opportunities are readily recognizable by anyone who separates his thinking from that of the crowd.

So, when the headlines in the newspaper shout "No End in Sight to Prosperity" it's time for you to start selling! Both ends of the cycle, though opposite in nature, offer a great opportunity. Those who have amassed great fortunes have often been those who have exploited such opportunities as these by moving in the opposite direction from that of the popular sentiment. *Your first venture in this direction will take nerve.* But after a few successes, you will find yourself able to "smell" these opportunities. In time, you will find yourself becoming increasingly comfortable committing to them – even when popular opinion says you're nuts!

THE KEY: *You must think like a contrarian. When the news is terrible, the prospects for improvement are nowhere in sight, and conditions seem to worsen each day – to the extent you are aware of facts that stand in contradiction to this mass pessimism – the time to buy is nigh. The actual investment vehicle you choose (whether it is a stock, a piece of real estate, or some other worthy expression of value) should also reflect the public's disinterest in it by an abnormally low price in comparison to your estimate of its intrinsic worth. When prices are skyrocketing, the reverse strategy applies.*

As mentioned previously, there is a second type of opportunity that merits your attention. While this potential opportunity might be generally recognized as such, the problem here is that time doesn't exist to thoroughly check it out. It is, so to speak, a window of opportunity that may close at any time. Such was the case with a property that was presented to me for a very last-minute consideration.

During the time I owned apartment buildings, I established relationships with several realtors who understood exactly what would interest me as a potential investment. I usually acted quickly and always made sure that I paid them what I owed them for their services. Thus, when properties they thought would suit my requirements became available, I would get a call from them.

It was probably for these reasons that I got a call at five o'clock one afternoon from one of those realtors. A very special building had quietly come on the market. There were, however, two problems: The owner of the building wouldn't be available until nine o'clock the next morning, and no one else had the keys. There was no way to get to see it before the next day. The second problem was that this realtor knew that a *full-price offer* had already been delivered to the owner. That offer was sitting on his desk just awaiting his signature of acceptance the following morning.

The most I could do was go by the property and, since it was empty, look in the windows. I would not be able to get inside before the owner would have already accepted the offer sitting on his desk. I would also not be able to assess my abilities to get financing for the potential purchase, as all the lenders I dealt with had already gone home for the day. The prospects for turning this opportunity into reality were very poor.

The realtor recognized all of these problems but urged me not to ignore the opportunity. She begged me to go to the trouble of driving to the property and seeing for myself that this whole exercise was more than worthwhile!

Because of my respect for this realtor, I knew that a door of opportunity had opened, albeit just a crack. I also realized that this door was only going to remain open for sixteen hours – most of them in the dead of night!

I rushed over to the property to get whatever feel of the place I could just by walking around the building before darkness. Even in the fading light, I could see enough to know that the realtor had been right about the building's value and prospects.

I quickly went to a phone to call the realtor. She informed me of the asking price which in my mind was a steal. Having completed several condominium conversions, I knew this was a perfect candidate. It was a stately mansion in the heart of the city. I told her to submit an offer that was five percent above the asking price. In those days, nobody ever did that. Fortunately, the strategy worked, and I became the owner of that beautiful place.

But the story doesn't end there. I hired my good friend, Errol, who had always assisted me with renovation plans, and he began to work on plans for turning the building into a four-unit condominium. Several months passed during which time I began assessing my costs, as well as the anticipated sales price for each of the units. By the time the plans had been completed, I was confident of the profit I would realize from the renovation and eventual sale of the four units.

One day, one of the most aggressive realtors in a town called me and asked if I would consider selling this building. I told her that I had already prepared plans for converting it. But she wasn't to be easily discouraged. So, I asked her what price she had in mind. She told me the price and said she and her partner could close quickly with an all-cash deal!

I couldn't believe it. The price she offered would guarantee me more than the profit I had calculated making by converting the building into condominiums! Moreover, I wouldn't have any of the risks of cost overruns, glitches in the market, or any other unforeseen mishap. The best part was that I had yet to drive the first nail!

Needless to say, I was astounded. For a moment, I wondered what she knew that I didn't. If I accepted their offer, I'd probably never find that out. But if I refused their offer, I would be left to perform all that work, take all the risks, and make less than what was now, as a result of their offer, already on the table. I decided to let them take the risks and accepted their offer!

Many months later, I happened to run into that buyer. When I asked her about the building they had bought from me, she informed me that they had encountered deep troubles. They were faced with serious cost overruns, and the prices they had anticipated getting for their units were nowhere in sight!

The key to having taken advantage of the opportunity to buy the building in the first place rested in taking *immediate* action. Situations like this call for a *pre-decision* to act or not act based upon a cursory examination of hurriedly gathered facts. This pre-decision must focus on the few, important things that can be learned in the limited time available. You must get comfortable with the idea that whatever facts can be gathered, they *must* suffice.

I'm referring to opportunities that are suddenly open to you, the doors to which may have been previously closed for a long period …and the time to act is extremely limited as other people will also be exposed to this fresh opportunity.

In addition to the foregone, this principle seeks to prime you to be on the alert for a sudden change in some situation, a change that opens up an opportunity that had not existed previously. Maybe there's a property you've always admired that's just become available because of the death of the owner, a divorce, or some other situation-altering occurrence. Such opportunities are not necessarily hidden but there's often little time to "think about it." This was the reason I missed a great opportunity to buy a beautiful piece of acreage located on the banks of the Arkansas River (with generous river frontage), lots of trees, a neat old Victorian house, and an *unbelievably* low price! The problem: the next-door neighbor knew what was going on *one day before* I did. He beat me to it!

There are times when the popular lament is that no opportunities exist. This principle argues otherwise and insists that opportunities always exist. Your diligence in continuing to be on the alert for them will pay off.

The "public" usually (rigidly) adheres to the belief that investments currently enjoying new highs have a long way (upward) yet to go. Similarly, they believe that the investment that's making new lows will continue to drop in value. Decide that you will take the opposite tack...sell when the public sentiment favors higher prices...buy when the general public expects prices to trend still lower. *This defines your golden opportunity!*

Finally, some opportunities appear rather suddenly, and just as suddenly they may be gone. But when something changes and a door has opened that brings that opportunity into play, you must act without hesitation as that door of opportunity may only remain open for a very short time.

To properly deal with these short-lived opportunities, a "pre-decision" needs to be reached. In an atmosphere of calm, you have time to ponder your ability to handle an unknown opportunity and establish limits to a commitment should a fleeting chance at a good deal arise. In making your decision in this atmosphere of calm, the time to ponder the various pros and cons is comfortably available… also available is the time necessary to arrange a line of credit at the bank!

PEOPLE VALUE THINGS DIFFERENTLY

You will have a hard time believing this *true* story.

In an old, out-of-print book entitled, *Extraordinary Popular Delusions and the Madness of Crowds* which was written by Charles Mackay in 1841, unbelievable tales of the temporary insanity of crowds were chronicled with sometimes humorous, but always true reports of what were often tragic events. In those dusty pages, historical facts reveal the truth about some very bizarre events and strange (even extreme) beliefs. One outlandish story contains a valuable lesson that deserves to be retold.

The story began in the early 1600s when a man named Conrad Gesner first brought tulips, imported from Constantinople, into Western Europe. In just a dozen years, tulips were much sought after by the wealthy, especially in Germany and Holland. Rich people in Amsterdam began to order their bulbs directly from Constantinople, paying exorbitant prices for them. The tulip continued to increase in popularity as more and more people began to notice the beauty of the flower and wanted them in their gardens. As this emphasis on owning tulips continued to grow, the possession of tulips became a status symbol. By 1634, it was considered bad taste for any man of wealth to be without a collection of them in his garden.

This passion for tulips eventually caught on with the middle class. These working-class people were even pitted in competition with each other in their attempts to obtain these treasured bulbs. As the craving for tulips continued, the price of tulip bulbs started on an upward path – and people's focus began to shift from flowers to profits.

This all-consuming desire among the Dutch to own tulips became so great that the country's ordinary course of business started to suffer from neglect. The majority of the citizenry switched their focus and energy to involvement in the tulip trade. The price of tulip bulbs skyrocketed. That price was now on such a steeply inclined path that it would outstrip even the most optimistic predictions that had been made about their potential value.

To put what became that "potential value" in perspective, one thousand pounds of cheese could be bought for 120 florins. It would cost 2,500 florins, enough to buy twenty thousand pounds of cheese, to purchase just one tulip bulb! At its zenith, the price of tulips finally became so inflated that one merchant paid half of his entire fortune for a single bulb! His goal, he said, was not to speculate in the buying and selling of tulips so much as to simply own one for his friends to see.

When the delivery boy arrived with his tulip bulb (singular), he excused himself, leaving the delivery boy at the front door as he disappeared into the house. He quickly unwrapped his "investment" and, in keeping with his stated purpose of tulip ownership, placed his prize on the windowsill for everyone to admire. He was so pleased with his purchase that he enthusiastically returned to the front door to invite the young delivery boy in for lunch. The merchant decided to treat the boy to a fine breakfast of red herring. In the merchant's brief absence from the room, the delivery boy spotted the tulip bulb on the windowsill. Thinking it was an onion, he ate it!

The owner of the bulb had seen it as something of such great value as to make it worth an investment of half of his entire estate. The delivery boy saw it as nothing more than a casual snack!

Two people can look at the same item and reach opposite conclusions. Something that holds great attraction and value for one person can be viewed with total indifference by another. This is the reason why knowledgeable art dealers have been able to purchase valuable paintings from people's attics for just a small fraction of their worth. It also provides windfalls for savvy jewelers who occasionally buy valuable rubies, emeralds, or sapphires from unwitting heirs of inherited jewelry that they thought was of little value.

Unfortunately, this is the way things sometimes go, as one man's trash is another man's treasure. This happens to be the theme of "The Garage Sale Millionaire" written by Aaron LaPedis.

If you are ever in a position that's even remotely like that of the owner of the tulip bulb, decide that you will ask yourself if you have been assigning a value to an "item" that you could successfully defend to a harsh critic.

Decide that you will *always* avoid investing in exotic promises of quick, sizeable profits, even if everyone is jumping on the idea.

Today, a simple tulip bulb has very little value. Yet, the "right" baseball card, or old comic book, can command an astounding price. Both of these items seem to be strange vehicles to consider as sensible investments; so, how does a person discern the difference? Because it's hard to imagine why anyone would risk meaningful money believing they are being prudent when they "invest" in such things, I am not sure you can always know. What I am sure of, however, is that today's baseball card could become tomorrow's tulip bulb.

Several credible investments (water rights, precious metals, stamps, coins, art, antiques, etc.) are narrowly understood and for this reason, don't command the popularity stocks, bonds, and real estate enjoy. Thus, investments in these areas are best left to the experts who have made them their lifelong study.

The conclusion of this principle would suggest that you are best advised to confine your investments to areas, or subjects, about which you can claim expert status. What could be more worthy of your investment confidence than investing in an area or subject about which *you* know *a lot*? Short of this, real estate (land or buildings) has enjoyed a long reputation for having enriched those who've entrusted these vehicles with their investment funds.

PARTNERSHIPS?

A partnership may not bring an end to your problems. It may be the beginning of them!

People with an idea or those seeking to leave their job and go into business for themselves, often seek the *comfort* of a partner. The risk, the unknowns, and the question: "Can I (all by myself) make this work?" makes the idea of involving a partner seem like a good one.

Now, this principle isn't denying the existence of healthy partnerships. But it does suggest that the odds are *against the likelihood* of a long-term success story.

When listing the various contributions that a given partner might bring to the partnership, the most common would be money, effort, knowledge (special skills), and specialties (contacts, the patent, the big client, the product, needed tools or assets, etc.).

Seldom do the partners have similar financial capabilities. Thus, a partnership might recognize this inequality by assigning the bulk of the workload to the partner who doesn't have the money. If his efforts fail to produce profits, the money-man will likely look for ways (a different partner?) to salvage his investment. On the other hand, if the business is making a lot of money, the man doing all the work will realize that he now doesn't need his partner's money and will quickly resent the time he spends making things hum along while his partner is basking in the terms of their agreement, terms which require little, if any, work from him.

A friend of mine made a down payment on a piece of ground. When the time came to make his first note payment, he didn't have the money so he agreed to a partnership with a wealthy man who agreed to put in an amount of money equal to my friend's initial investment in return for a 50% ownership in the land (and they would then share an equal responsibility for the note payments as they become due). When the time came for a second note payment, my friend's circumstances had not improved. So, his new partner said he would pay all the money that was due (including the portion owed by my friend), but the ownership of the land would now be 75/25. With one more stub of his toe, my friend will have lost his down payment as well as his ownership of the land. This isn't to imply that my friend's partner did anything wrong, but he did disproportionately increase the percentage of ownership with each cash infusion he had to make. The same narrative could just as easily be used to describe a similar outcome wherein one of the partners has special knowledge and the other is either the money man or works alongside but in a lesser capacity. The partner with the knowledge will be the one most likely to be the first to become disenchanted with the arrangement.

Sometimes, it isn't so much a matter of who's contributing what, as it is a matter of who's making the decisions. God designed marriages for the husband to be the head of the wife – like a king and queen. Partnerships aren't necessarily designed this way. Therein lies a problem. The following interaction between two partners should make the point.

A decision about a problem needs to be made, and partner Al quickly suggests a solution. But the second partner, Bob, can see a lot of reasons why his partner's idea is flawed. Diplomatically, he tells Al of his better idea. Reluctantly, Bob defers to Al. Then, along comes the need to make another decision in answer to another difficulty. Al immediately jumps in with an answer hoping to prevail in the little tug-of-war he perceives as beginning to form. However, Bob is once again convinced his partner's idea is not the one to be implemented. He patiently explains his reasons for rejecting the solution Al had suggested. This time, Al is less agreeable, but finally gives in. Now, a third problem and another decision come along. Determined to redeem his somewhat bruised ego, Al now takes a strong stand in favor of a decision he's hurriedly concocted. The second partner, Bob, now understands that his partner, Al, is somewhat grasping at straws to regain a sense of importance in the partnership. This is particularly evidenced by the quality of his partner's latest answer to the problem currently at hand. It's, by far, the worst of his three solutions. Bob realizes he must be very careful in stating his objections to his partner's suggestion, but cannot stand by and allow this solution to be acted upon. Bob may win this battle, but it's a sure thing that he won't win the fourth one, which might be Al's idea to paint their office building *pink*!

Even when each partner assumes a different role, and each competently carries out his responsibilities, it's surprisingly easy for one partner to feel like he's carrying the bulk of the load. Moreover, he may even think that his function is vital to the success of the business.

Family members often form partnerships. I know of two brothers, Sam and Fred, who became partners in a contracting business. Upon his retirement, their dad gave them his business. Sam, the older brother, was a very responsible man who had a sterling reputation for honesty and quality workmanship. Fred was a fun-loving guy who was liked by everybody. Their parents, knowing Fred wasn't much of a businessman, were anxious to know that Fred would be taken care of. So, they maneuvered things so that he could be under his brother's wing. They knew this would be important to Fred's financial survival since Fred, among other things, had the habit of writing bad checks. He was not a crook; rather, a very poor record keeper. Fred's problem escalated to the point that he knew he had to do something about it. He cleverly decided to protect himself from these embarrassing shortfalls in his bank account. He instituted a practice of entering a larger amount in his check register than the actual amount of the check. So, if he wrote a check for $15.00, he would record that check in his register as $20. If the check was for $80, he'd enter $100. He smugly believed that he was building a nice cushion in his checkbook that was certain to protect him from overdrafts. One day in need of some cash, Fred "estimated" the amount of his cash buildup, and wrote a check against that amount – it bounced!

Given that history, Sam was understandably reluctant to allow Fred to assume any responsibility for the money end of things. But as you might guess, Fred felt very left out. He kept pleading for some role in the important areas of the business, like bidding plans. Sam finally gave in and agreed to let Fred figure out a set of plans. To Sam's surprise *and concern*, they got the job. Fred's bid was low – very low! Sam reviewed the plans and to his horror discovered that Fred's bid only included one floor. The problem was…there were two floors!

Resist the urge to take on a partner if your main reason for doing so is to bolster your fortitude. When that is the primary reason for entering the partnership, not much time will pass before you realize you didn't need this boost…or the partner.

Partnerships that work are most likely to have certain things in common: an equal cash investment in the partnership, similar salary needs, separate responsibilities but equal competency in their area of responsibility, and an agreed-upon plan regarding how decisions would be made and by whom. This would work best if one of the partners was an agreed-upon "leader" and the other was more of an advisor with limited veto power.

One attorney I met said that when he prepared partnership documents, he insisted upon also preparing the dissolution papers. He said that it would save everybody time and money later!

VALUE YOUR "TRUMP CARDS"

You probably never realized your assets was this extensive.

The card game of bridge has captivated bridge-playing enthusiasts for over a century. The game is complex enough that some people devote their lives to becoming a "master" bridge player. It is, of course, this complexity that gives the bridge its appeal.

A fundamental aspect of the bridge is the inherent value of the cards and how that value can be selectively enhanced. This maneuvering for enhanced card value, as well as how the player who gains it exploits that advantage, can add great intrigue and challenge to the game.

The game of bridge provides the foundational concepts that are the very backbone of this decision-making principle.

Though greatly oversimplified, the essence of the game of bridge is as follows: A full deck of cards is dealt out to four players. Those players assess the cards in their hand as to the presence of aces and face cards, but more particularly they are interested in the presence of any suit that's in abundance over the other three suits. The game begins with bidding as each participant expresses, by way of his bid, how strong he thinks his hand is. This strength closely correlates to the number of tricks he thinks he can take (a trick being four cards which are the result of the play of one card by each of the players into the center of the table). A trick is "taken" by the player whose card, out of the four, has the greatest face value. The value of that trick is determined by the total sum of the face value of each of the cards. The winner of the bid gets to name the trump suit —a suit that will now have greater "power" than any card of another suit. For example, if hearts are named as the trump suit, a two of hearts will be deemed stronger than an ace of any other suit. Thus any trump card in one's hand is of great value since it automatically exceeds the value and power of all cards, except other cards of that trump suit. The person, or partnership, with the greatest total points, as determined by adding together the value of each of the tricks they've taken, wins the game.

The challenge of winning bridge lies in intelligently using your trump cards to take valuable tricks. Every possible attempt must be made not to waste a trump card by using it to take a relatively valueless trick. That strategy speaks to the very heart of this principle.

In the game of life, we each have talents and possessions that become our "trump cards." They should not be regarded casually. The wisdom obtained from this principle lies in recognizing our trump cards, which can be found in the four categories that spawn them, and properly exploiting their value.

Besides money, which some of us have and some don't, there are four categories of items that each person can claim some ownership. These include **things, acquaintances, knowledge**, and **time**. They each have value, though they are not all necessarily of equal value. And depending on the circumstances, those values can be subject to change.

Some people's things are just unwelcome consumers of space. A good friend of mine answered an ad for the sale of an old jukebox. The seller wanted one hundred dollars for it. My friend loved old jukeboxes and knew a lot about them. He paid the one hundred dollars and hauled it off. Once he had cleaned it up and replaced a few worn-out parts, a total cost of about $1500, he was able to immediately resell that same jukebox for $40,000! The former owner didn't recognize the value of what he had.

Another item on the list you should always value is the worth of your acquaintances. Who you know might have greater value than you could ever imagine. My daughter was often called upon to drive her daughter (my granddaughter) to this friend's house or go there to pick her up. Over time, she became friendly with the parents of her daughter's friend. One day, a conversation with the daughter's parents came up about a development project in Mexico that's owned by my Mexican corporation. Eventually, they purchased a lot from the corporation for which my daughter was paid a $10,000 finder's fee.

The third thing of value you are now being urged not to ignore is the value of *what* you know. I heard of a story that has been told about a mechanical problem that occurred on one of Henry Ford's assembly lines in his auto manufacturing plant. None of his engineers could solve the problem. Try as they might, their efforts didn't produce a solution.

There was one man, however, who claimed to know the solution and was called in after Ford's engineers finally said "uncle." As I remember the story, this man solved Ford's problem in just a few hours; nevertheless, he sent Ford a bill for $10,000 – a lot of money in those days!

Thrilled though he was about the repair, Ford called the man and questioned the size of the bill concerning the time spent repairing. He commented that, after all, it obviously must have been a very simple repair. The man answered Ford by saying that it wasn't the time spent that Ford was paying for – he was billing Ford for his knowledge of *what to do* and *how to do it*. This directly relates to placing value on what you know, since what you know has cost you an investment of your time to acquire that special knowledge.

The last thing on the list is the value of your time. You must never forget that your time has value. Decide that you will always place a value on your time. When you don't, no one else will either. Another friend of mine was a high-powered tax consultant. I had not only skied with him but on countless occasions, my wife and I had dined with him and his wife. One day, I needed some tax advice. I approached my friend who told me he charged for his advice. Surprised, I nevertheless agreed to meet with him. One hour later, I had the advice I needed as well as a bill for three hundred dollars. I later realized that because his advice had come at a high price, I paid a great deal more attention to it than I ever would have if the discussion had occurred around the dinner table.

These are the kinds of things that constitute your "trump cards." If you treat them as if they have value, others will do the same. Two men carried this concept even further. In not only acknowledging the value of one's assets, Ted Turner's father additionally advised him to *always* work at improving what he had (his assets). Clifford Roberts, Bobby Jones Wall Street partner in the founding of the Master's Golf Club addressed the club's board of directors during the dismal time of the 1930s depression with a history-making suggestion. While acknowledging the difficult financial times, he nevertheless urged the board to make some costly improvements with wise words of encouragement that things never stayed the same – they either got better or worse. He feared that their decision to do nothing would turn out to be the beginning of things getting worse at the Masters. The board voted for the improvements. Decades later, the brilliance of his insights is evident. The beauty and uniqueness of the Master's Golf Club are all the testimony needed.

Although life isn't all business, everyone is confronted with the challenge of earning a living. What you have or don't have depends upon your moneymaking abilities and efforts. The success of those efforts depends a lot on how well you handle or manage, your trump cards. These are your wealth-building assets.

It's one thing to give of your time to help a friend with some project or to decide that you will make a charitable gift of money, an asset, or your professional advice to some deserving cause or person who has a need but is unable to repay your kindness.

It is another thing to undervalue your arsenal of "trump cards" by allowing those who would exploit your generosity to take advantage of you. It can become quite easy to go through life never realizing the potential of what you are and what you have because you have failed to properly value what you are and what you have.

Decide that you will value what you have, what you know, who you know, and your time. **These are your "trump cards." They can be your ticket to a richer life.**

Don't listen to those *(including yourself)* **who attempt to undervalue the worth of your "trump cards" and don't allow anyone to persuade you to part with them too cheaply. To do so is to negate their value and dismiss their potential for improving your life.**

Their worth will never be more than the price you put on them!

THE FIRST RULE OF RISK-TAKING

The lure of the thrill of the thing explains a lot.

It's hard to understand why some people feel obligated by an opportunity to take small advantages over the "system." As a kid, my friends would climb over the fence at the ballpark to avoid paying the admission fee. One night, I decided to join them. As I was climbing over the chain-link fence, the pant leg of my nice dress slacks caught on the fence and ripped them. The value of the slacks was three times the cost of the admission.

As an adult, I was no longer tempted to climb fences. Instead, I adopted an attitude of shameless irreverence for the City of Denver's fund-raising efforts through their use of parking meters. I recall driving up in front of a drugstore for a quick purchase. I barely gave any thought to the parking meter because I knew that my whole shopping episode would only take three to five minutes. To my surprise, however, I emerged from the drugstore to be greeted by a ten-dollar parking meter ticket stuck to my windshield! Some quick arithmetic verified that my strategy to save a measly nickel by "beating the system" would have to be successfully repeated two hundred times to recover the money I now owed on the ticket!

As I reviewed my decision and resulting actions, I saw that I had stupidly risked the loss of far more than what I would have gained had I won. Today, as a hopefully wiser adult, I'm pleased to report that I've amended my response to any temptation to take irresponsible risks.

In my defense, what tempted me has also tempted others. The cause seems to be rooted in that rather reprehensible desire to gain something without having to pay for it. While my loss was insignificant, losses don't remain insignificant when the quantity of unknowns expands, the money at risk increases, or the penalties for losing become more severe.

The truths of this principle don't just apply to financial risks. Think for a moment about the deceptive self-talk of someone experimenting with drugs for the first time. While attending a party, they are offered a beautiful experience. Their curiosity aroused, they tell themselves surely no harm can result from just this *"one-time"* experiment. They assure themselves that they are certainly not interested in any long-term use. They're also confident that they're strong enough to avoid ever becoming hooked. Given those initial convictions, it's surprising to learn that for a lot of people, it wasn't just *"one-time."* In fact, over time, the beginning thrills diminish and increasing dosages become necessary – addiction follows. But none of this would have happened if the initial sampling had been refused. The drug user is taking a huge risk for a very short-lived pleasure.

Other risks that participants call fun, like bungee jumping, rock climbing (without ropes), skydiving, etc., represent small gains (again, just a momentary thrill) at the risk of one's life – the ultimate high risk!

Ideally, you should be aiming to *risk small amounts in expectation of large gains!* Some might dismiss this principle, feeling that it states the obvious. Yet, these are the very people that frequently ignore its advice.

The true problem, as it relates to the subject of risk, is that most people ignore the existence of risk, or its threat because they underestimate its size. Once you realize that what you are contemplating does involve risk, decide, in advance of taking any action that you won't risk a large amount for a small gain.

***Despite certain appearances to the contrary, the greater the unknowns and uncertainties, the greater the risk.* Therefore, place all the unknowns and areas of uncertainty in the risk column. Resolve that you won't commit until you've fully understood just how threatening they might be to your success.**

OVERLOOKED WISDOM

The true expert may not be anyone you'd notice.

The movie channels are still featuring reruns of a classic old movie that won two Oscars and three Golden Globe awards, *The Flight of the Phoenix*. Frank Towns (played by Jimmy Stewart) was the pilot of a plane that had to crash-land in the Sahara Desert. Although neither Towns nor any of his wartime crew was injured in the landing, they were still facing death. Their radio didn't work, the plane had been badly damaged in the crash, and they did not have enough water to hike out of the desert. For days, they attempted to make any possible search party aware of their location by burning things that would send smoke into the air for anyone who was flying nearby to see – to no avail.

A murderous group of wandering Arab nomads killed two of the crew who had innocently approached their caravan in hope of finding help in escaping their desert prison, or at least the provision of some water.

It seemed all hope for survival was lost as each plan for rescue or escape was dashed. Finally, one of the passengers, a German crewman, Heinrich Dorfmann, approached Towns with his plan to repair the plane and fly out! As the pilot of the plane, Towns' first reaction was one of anger as he saw no way the wreckage could ever be made to fly again.

During the time Towns and the rest of the crew had been exploring all their options for escape, Dorfmann had been working on drawings to modify the plane to overcome the irreparable, damaged portions. With his drawings finally complete, Dorfmann was convinced the modifications he had designed would work. So, he approached Towns, the pilot, with his ideas.

Towns immediately challenged his credentials. How could he make any guarantee that the modifications to the plane would really work? Dorfmann informed Towns that he was an aircraft designer by profession. Still not convinced, Towns shouted at Dorfmann saying they'd all die. Dorfmann answered Towns's insults by pointing out that their death was already a certainty. They had nothing to lose by trying his idea.

Dorfmann's plan was finally given the green light. As work began to reconfigure the damaged plane, the men's spirits picked up. They had a goal and also now a ray of hope. Dorfmann proved to be a tough taskmaster, but as a result of the discipline he instilled, the plane was finished on schedule; a schedule that was largely dictated by their dwindling water supply.

When the day finally arrived for their long-awaited flight back to civilization, Towns offhandedly asked Dorfmann about his aircraft design background. Specifically, what kind of aircraft had he had a hand in designing? Dorfmann's answer was like opening a trapdoor under the feet of Towns and the crew. He said that the largest plane he had personally designed had a three-foot wingspan! Towns took a hard look at Dorfmann and in a tone that hardly masked his shock and anger said that he thought that Dorfmann had worked on the "big stuff." Dorfmann said, "Oh, no, the 'big stuff' is all powered aircraft. I just design model airplanes!" At that, it was all Towns could do to contain himself from tearing into Dorfmann.

Instead, Towns accused him of deceiving them, giving them false hope, and wasting their time and effort on a crazy idea that had no way of working.

Dorfmann's answer speaks to the very heart of this principle. He told them that what they failed to understand was that model airplane lacked the advantages enjoyed by powered aircraft. The excellence of their design was crucial to their flight performance. The powerless model airplane had to be aerodynamically perfect. A powered aircraft, on the other hand, was able to overcome slight design flaws. Dorfmann was telling them that he may well have been the very best man for the moment. Nevertheless, Towns' reaction to Dorfmann's credentials was probably typical of how most people would have reacted.

There exists a brand of an advisor who, though not in the limelight with the other gold-plated advisors, may have far more valuable advice than the blue-chip advisors who charge an arm and a leg for their counsel. However, this brand of advisor might be a person in dirty overhauls who needs a shave and drives around in an old car. For many, he's an advisor who's easy to ignore. But consider: who would best know exactly how to *install* a new roof – the owner of the roofing company or the $10 per hour workman who's on the roof every day installing new roofs?

Who would command your greatest attention regarding statements about the mechanical reliability of a certain make of car – the fashionably dressed owner of the car agency or the man with grease under his fingernails who repairs them? From whom should you seek counsel regarding real estate investments…the Harvard-trained Ph.D. who has spent his entire life in the classroom or the "little" guy who may only have a high school diploma, but owns a sizeable portfolio of rental properties that he manages himself?

Decide that you will not be too quick to shell out the big bucks for advice from the "pros" that may not be worth what it's costing you.

Instead, decide that you will give more than polite consideration to listening to the advisor who, though lacking the luster of some of his glittering competitors, may be better positioned to advise you than their higher-paid counterparts. Such an advisor is the one who's down in the trenches. He's a hands-on guy who doesn't just know what he's doing, he senses what the problem is and knows where to look for the answer. When necessary, he knows how to improvise. When you want to find out how the "thing" works, you don't ask the guy in the coat and tie who occupies the big corner office; instead, find a way to get next to the guy responsible for actually making things work. Don't dismiss such a person's wisdom

and possible value to you just because he makes look a little scruffy. You would be well-advised to search this kind out!

The man who has successfully *done it* may be worth ten ivory tower professors who've spent their lifetimes theorizing in the classroom.

KNOW WHEN TO HANG IN THERE

While many of our prized dreams seem to be within reach, somehow they remain just beyond our grasp.

The rules of wise investing would suggest that you capitalize on your good investments (ideas) while not letting your bad investments (ideas) wipe out the gains you've realized from your successes. Even more important is making sure that the losses resulting from your bad investments are never allowed to run unchecked. Such a mistake has wiped out the fortunes of many hapless investors as they continue to ride with an investment that is relentlessly losing value. Unable to stomach the thought of a loss their common sense turns to a fantasy of false hope.

Obviously, without some success, any losses will put you in the red. And while it's extremely important to know when to call it quits (which is the subject of the next principle), you must develop the ability to recognize worthwhile ideas and projects

I started playing golf at the age of twelve, and over the next twenty-some years, I would devote a lot of time to the study of the golf swing.

I had always admired my dad's swing which everyone thought was great. I also studied the golf swings of some of the best golf professionals of the day. In particular, Sam Snead had a swing that was as smooth as any you'd ever see. I had pictures of his swing in photo-sequence from a book of instruction written by Snead. I would spend hours trying to emulate the positions as shown in the photographs. My dad and I even rigged up a driving range in our garage by hanging a tarp from the exposed ceiling rafters and hitting golf balls off a wooden platform with a rubber mat on top. I remember using those rafters to concoct a type of noose that was to fit loosely around my neck. If my head dropped, the noose would pull tightly on my neck! The idea was to encourage me to keep my head steady throughout my swing – it worked!

Years later, after countless hours spent studying and analyzing the golf swing, an idea struck me as a surefire way to cure a slice, the weekend golfer's biggest lament. My idea involved a simple device that would provide an image of the correct club head path through the golf ball. The device seemed to pose the threat of being in the way of the descending club head should its path be anything but correct, which strongly encouraged the golfer to do it right.

When I tried out my idea on a few of my fellow members at the club where I played golf, it worked! They didn't slice the ball anymore. I was so excited that I decided to make a prototype of my training device. I also created a slick little brochure that fully explained the theory behind it. The prototype guy was so clever at making my training device model function properly that we even discovered another use for it – the improvement of one's putting. It may even have been more valuable in this role than it was in the role for which I originally intended. As a bonus, the device looked cool!

A good friend of mine had become a very well-respected and successful patent attorney. I had him get a patent on my training device. With the patent under my belt, a box full of brochures, and the prototype of my training device under my arm all polished and perfected, I headed for the PGA show in Florida.

Once there, my first assignment was to get the endorsement of the teaching pros who were in attendance. I went straight to the practice tee with my device. I'd walk up to a pro, most of whom were club pros and very involved in golf instruction, and invite him to hit a few balls using my device. Before the day was out I had convinced thirty pros to give my device a try. Of these, one guy didn't like it, another didn't understand it, but twenty-eight thought it was great and agreed it would accomplish what I claimed. That was over 90 percent! One man was extra enthusiastic. His name was Bob Toski, the most famous golf instructor of the time – the swing mechanic (teacher) of the pros. In fact, he even asked if I'd send him one of my devices so that he could use it in his golf school.

I eagerly packed up everything and headed for the tents where all the big manufacturers had set up shop. I remember thinking, *I've got the better mouse trap – everyone is going to beat a path to my door!*

I walked into the Wilson Brothers' tent full of confidence and asked to talk to the head guy. Whether or not he was the head guy, he quickly informed me that they weren't interested. Not to be discouraged, I moved on to Spaulding, the same answer. MacGregor represented the last of the big tents. That visit was equally brief. Taking a deep breath, I approached the lesser manufacturers of golf equipment. After another series of "not interested" responses, I found myself in front of my last possibility, a manufacturer of golf tees and divot fixers. Walking rather slowly, I realized all of my earlier enthusiasm was gone. And why not? What an insult to think that this great idea, which worked, was being so rudely dismissed.

Surprisingly, these people seemed interested. But it was still a big letdown to think that the only manufacturer who could see the merits of my idea was a manufacturer of divot fixers! They asked if they might take my prototype back to their head offices and further examine the idea. I told them that I'd be pleased if they would. Weeks passed but finally, I received a box that contained my prototype and a "Dear John" letter of rejection. It was a bit of irony to realize that the low esteem I held for the product (divot fixers) being manufactured by this company of my last resort held my golf training aid in even less esteem.

I put the prototype in the garage where eventually it became the victim of tires, tools, and whatever else was being thrown on top of it. When I finally threw it away, it was already well beyond any chance of repair. But why think about repair? Why spend more money on a losing proposition?

I decided I had had enough!

Twenty-some years later, my wife and I were having dinner on the patio at the golf club. Who should walk by but my patent attorney and his wife? We invited them to join us for dinner. After the usual conversational subjects, he turned to me and asked, "Have you seen the TV ads for your golf training device?"

"No, I haven't," I answered.

He went on to say that he was sorry about what was now happening with my golf training device. He went on to explain that after seventeen years my patent had expired and all the protection from copycats, who might steal my idea, had also expired. As a result, someone else recognized its merit and decided to resurrect my idea. As I was processing all that he had just told me, he compounded that discouraging news with another question, "Guess who's endorsing it?" When I responded that I had no idea, he said, "Jack Nicklaus!"

I already knew that it wasn't enough to just have the better mouse trap, I also needed to be able to market it. But nothing has happened, either then or since, that has ever led me to believe that the idea itself wasn't as good as I had originally believed. I had just quit one step too soon! What excuse for my failure can I offer? I had virtually made *no* real efforts to market it other than that one day at the PGA show. I took the rejections I experienced there as the death knell for my idea. It was as though those rejections were saying that the idea was not good. Yet, I knew that it was good! If as much effort had been put into the marketing end as had been put into the development of the concept, someone would have surfaced who could have made a success of the idea. I just hadn't been sufficiently determined to tough it out and hang in there! You must fight this urge to give up on your winning idea as long as *any* hope remains. If every time there's a hint of trouble and you quit or sell out, you'll never know success from any project you undertake.

But I'm not alone. When things get *tough*, quitting looks very attractive to many weary strugglers. Some years ago I met a man who owned a real estate development project in Mexico. His instinctive reaction to seemingly unsolvable problems was always to say, *"There must be a way."* One such occasion left him with only *one* way, that even he could see, to solve his problem. He had to get an audience with *the President of Mexico!* Convinced this was his only answer, he went about securing that appointment. Sometime later, I learned that he had met with the Mexican President! As a result, his problem met with a solution. He never allowed *any problem* to deter his belief that "There must be a way." Before you quit, let that be your first response.

If you have invested in a project, property, or service that you thoroughly believe in, but things aren't going as planned, do you continue fighting or fold up? Maybe, the following thoughts will help.

Re-examine your project and expose it to experts. If both you and they are unable to find any flaws in it, take that as a sufficient endorsement of your idea. You *now know* your idea is good. You and they believe in it. *Keep that thought in the forefront of your mind!*

But despite this endorsement, you find yourself facing obstacles, some of which seem insurmountable. When this happens (which is almost guaranteed), you must remind yourself that no matter how good your idea is, you will run into roadblocks to your success! No great idea has ever been problem-free. Thus, when problems arise, be determined not to allow them to discourage you – *keep focused on the fact that you do have an idea worth fighting for!* Most important of all is your determination to turn your "project" into a success. Without a belief in your project and the determination to stick it out, success is highly unlikely.

So, when troubles come, look for your answers in one of two areas: experts and supportive friends and acquaintances.

Seek the help of someone knowledgeable and experienced in dealing with the very things you're struggling with. Keep knocking on doors until you find someone, or a group, who can help you accomplish what you've been unable to do. However, your circle of supporters won't necessarily come from the ranks of the "experts."

Often, the most valuable support comes from those who are just as enthusiastic about your idea as you are. Look to them to help you expand your circle of supporters – they can supply that necessary enthusiasm to help you mount the charge each day. Even if you have to give up a part of the "deal" to someone who can supply the missing component of the puzzle, a piece of the pie is better than a wholly-owned prototype sitting in your garage under a load of junk!

KNOW WHEN TO RETREAT

Professional poker players understand this concept.

After graduating from the University of Houston, I returned home to Colorado to start looking for a job. I recall sharing my ambitions with a friend, Jim, with whom I had played a lot of golf. He was a stockbroker with a small over-the-counter (OTC) firm. He frequently told me how much commission income he was making and how much he loved the securities business.

He urged me to consider applying for a job with the brokerage firm he worked for. Thanks to a good word from Jim, I got the job. To say that I didn't know anything about the stock market was a huge understatement. Despite being unqualified, I was given a desk, phone, phonebook, and a list of their recommendations (but no customers). The good news was that I immediately inherited one client, my dad. Jim had been my dad's stockbroker and had made him a lot of money.

My dad had invested in the firm's recommendations, most particularly in a company called Clute which was the manufacturer of grain cleaners and other farm machinery. Jim's firm, Lowell, Murphy & Co. had underwritten Clute, so one would be correct to conclude that it was the Lowell, Murphy favorite. My dad owned a lot of Clute, most of which he had purchased at prices well below the market value at the time which was around ten dollars per share. Management held frequent sales meetings to discuss the investment merits of the firm's recommendations. Clute usually received the bulk of the attention.

During the months that followed, Lowell, and Murphy continued to make strong pitches for Clute. According to them, big things were happening at the Clute Company. Convinced, I bought some Clute for myself and also urged my dad and my growing client list to take advantage of this opportunity. My dad told me that he had previously invested all the cash he had. To buy more now, he would have to approach the bank for a loan. The bank informed him that by pledging the stock he already owned, plus the stock he intended to buy, they would be willing to finance the purchase of a lot more Clute. So, he pledged his stock and purchased the additional block of Clute which the bank was willing to finance. The stock was purchased at prices from ten to twelve dollars per share. It quickly ran up to seventeen dollars! Within the next few weeks, it settled back to fourteen and a half to fifteen dollars per share. For months and months, it didn't move. *Every day* it hovered between fourteen and fourteen and a half.

At about that time, my dad and I both qualified for the U.S. Amateur golf tournament which was to be held at Pebble Beach in California. Because of the stagnant performance of Clute, I began to fear for my dad. His huge bank loan was making me uncomfortable. So before leaving for California, I decided to get my dad out of debt.

I told Mr. Lowell what I intended to do and he cautioned me to feed it in gradually so as not to upset the market with such a large block of stock. I complied with his request and managed to liquidate enough of my dad's stock to completely pay off his debt at the bank. In the process, my dad even realized a small profit. So, all was well. My mother and dad, as well as my wife and I, boarded a plane bound for Monterey, California. Once there, I found that we were somewhat isolated from the financial markets. There wasn't a brokerage firm in the Pebble Beach/Carmel area that had any pink sheets (a service that provides daily quotes on over-the-counter stocks). I was forced to forget business and enjoy one of the great weeks of my life.

Upon my return to the office, the first thing I did was to look up the value of all the stocks I was involved with, especially Clute. To say that my first day back at the office was a real shock was a gross understatement! The quote for Clute stood out like flashing, neon lights.–It had dropped to *ten dollars* per share. I had to remind myself that just one week ago it had been fourteen and a half dollars per share! This represented a 30% drop in one week! Without saying a word to anyone, I got up from my desk and went outside. For one whole hour, all I did was walk up and down Seventeenth Street trying to figure out what I should do.

When I came back to the office, I called my dad and told him we were selling everything. He was stunned and for a moment didn't say anything. Then, he said, "You are making a huge mistake!" I told him that I was getting everyone else out, myself included. I knew he was mad, but he didn't tell me not to sell. I hung up, filled out sell orders, and made calls to other clients.

About half an hour into my selling frenzy, John Lowell's secretary came over to my desk. She told me that Mr. Lowell (one of the partners of the firm) wanted to see me in his office. When I entered his office, I could see by the look on his face that he was not happy. He asked me if I knew what I was doing. He told me that I was harming the firm. He also informed me that I was doing my dad and the rest of my clients a huge disservice. He pointed out that all of the men in the office were advising their clients to buy, not sell! He emphasized that I was the only one going against conventional wisdom and that everyone was eagerly taking advantage of an opportunity that hadn't been seen in months. Lowell asked how I'd feel if he were to call my dad to tell him what a mistake I was making with his investments. I answered, "Don't do that. I'll take care of it." I excused myself and walked back to my desk.

I took care of it alright. I immediately picked up the phone and called a competing, over-the-counter brokerage firm. I sold everything through them that hadn't been sold before I met with Mr. Lowell! By the end of the day, all my clients, as well as my dad and I, were sold out of all our Clute, as well as the other stocks the firm had been recommending. The lowest price anyone received for their Clute stock was eight dollars and eighty-seven cents per share. Meanwhile, the other brokers in the office were still frantically calling all their clients, begging them to buy Clute. None of them knew what I had done. But, I made an irreversible decision and retreated from my investments, associates, and job. *I felt alone!*

My dad was angry with me. I knew Mr. Lowell was going to blow up when all that stock I had sold through the other brokerage the company finally came back to Lowell, Murphy and they realized where the stock had come from! But that discovery was never made.

Two weeks later, *Clute was at zero!* There was no market for Clute… anywhere! Lowell, Murphy & Co soon declared bankruptcy and closed its doors shortly thereafter! I had been vindicated!

The takeaway from this whole debacle is that the lonely feeling I had because of the stand I was taking is almost always true of those who are *correct* about a *change* in trends. There is a saying in Wall Street, "The crowd is right about the trends, but wrong at both ends." Aligning yourself with the crowd is temporarily comforting because you have the reassurance of so much company. But in the end, it is almost a certainty that you'll end up with losses.

You might ask, "Why was I the only one who sold out?" Unlike the other brokers in the office who had watched the price of Clute decline over seven to ten days, I had been confronted with the shock of the large drop in price all at once. In addition, I was experiencing a feeling (maybe a deep concern) that had been building up for a previous couple of months that a giant tire pump had been plugged into the Clute balloon.

Despite everyone's frantic pumping, it still failed to rise. Moreover, the fundamentals of the business didn't seem to justify a rising stock price. The more I thought about it, the more I began to feel foolish for not having questioned the prospects of a company whose primary claim to fame was a machine that cleaned grain. The minute those manning the pumps stopped pumping, the balloon began to deflate. The confirmation of those feelings came from the pressure Mr. Lowell put on me not to sell any more Clute stock. I felt that something wasn't right. Little did I know just how much!

Kenny Rogers's famous country western ballad, "The Gambler," recounts advice given by an old gambler in the often-quoted lines: "You've got to know when to hold 'em, know when to fold 'em. Know when to walk away and know when to run."

Knowing when to retreat is key to avoiding crippling losses. The problem is that once you've taken your loss, you've eliminated all chances of ever participating in any recovery that might take place later. Some ideas, investments, or plans get off to a poor start, but later get their second wind and end up working out well. Herein lies the source of resistance we all have to take a loss.

Rather than retreating every time a situation turns slightly against you, address the questions listed below. They will prove to be an aid in discerning the difference between a losing deal and one that still holds promise – one that may need a little more time, a little more money, or someone's assistance.

Thus, when you find yourself looking at *a potentially losing situation*, ask yourself these questions:

Is the reason for your initial decision still intact? If it isn't, get out!

Are the fundamentals still sound? If they aren't, get out!

Has anything changed? Are the changes negative? If yes, get out! Have your estimations of the money or the time needed to be changed?

If beyond your capacities, get out!

Have you become aware of risks heretofore unseen? If yes, get out! Has someone or something introduced a new unknown or negative slant on things? If yes, get out!

Have you become aware that you are dealing with someone you can't trust? If yes, don't walk away – run!

THE "END GAME" STRATEGY

Some situations would seem to suggest a strategy similar to the fine-tuned plans employed in the invasion of Normandy.

The pressure increases exponentially when your circumstances deteriorate into a do-or-die situation. When things get to that point, you are faced with a problem that you'll probably get but one chance to solve.

This principle, "The End Game Strategy," was inspired by an intriguing problem-solving concept found in the game of chess. One chess magazine featured "End Game Strategies" in a section called "Chess Puzzles." When a player uncovers the solution to the chess puzzle, it always results in an uncontestable victory for the party that unlocks the puzzle. The opposing player is powerless to avert defeat. Far from easy, these puzzles can be surprisingly tricky. But *it is the strategy common to all these chess puzzles that are the basis for this decision-making principle*, "The End Game Strategy."

The "end game," as the name implies, occurs at the end of the game when both players' arsenals have been reduced to just a few pieces (chessmen). One of these is always the king since under the rules of chess, the king cannot be captured. Any situation that arises where a player cannot move his attacked king to safety from that attack, ends the game in checkmate – victory going to the attacking player.

But until that event occurs, the two players continue their battle, although with differing goals. The player with the stronger or greater number of pieces seeks outright victory. The weaker player can usually only hope to escape with a draw, and clever play on his part might earn him that draw. This outcome will become the focus of his strategies as all his efforts will now be directed at robbing his opponent of an outright victory. The attraction of this end-game strategy to the stronger player is that if he discovers the correct moves, the weaker player will have *no chance* of avoiding checkmate!

From time to time, everyone faces a situation that desperately needs a successful outcome – *a guarantee of victory*. If such an outcome is truly possible, the powerful similarity between the "End Game Strategy" found in the game of chess and the "End Game Strategy" embodied in this decision-making principle sets forth how guaranteed outcomes *might* be realized.

Years ago, I purchased a hotel and restaurant in a thriving area of western Colorado. It was an exciting project for several reasons. First, the owner was willing to take a trade for his down payment. Second, the restaurant was probably the most popular place in town. My mortgage payments were rather hefty, but the tenant who had leased the restaurant building and the motel was paying monthly lease payments exactly equal to the amount of the note payments. All I had to do was hang on for five years and the restaurant and the motel would be mine, free and clear of any debt.

Things went well for about a year, until one day when the lessee operator, Ken, called to tell me that he couldn't pay the rent. I was now faced with having to meet my obligations under the note I signed with the former owner, without the benefit of Ken's offsetting rent payments.

I couldn't believe that he could be in such a jam. Every time I visited the restaurant, it was necessary to put my name on a waiting list and wait for a table. Moreover, revenues from the motel were almost free money since the income from the restaurant covered the expenses for both the restaurant and the motel (including the mortgage payment). The motel's direct overhead was minimal and there were always guests. A mere 30-40 percent occupancy level would come close to making the rent payment for both the motel and the restaurant.

I couldn't possibly imagine what the problem was, but I certainly intended to sit down with Ken and find out. A meeting was scheduled and I made the trip across the state to get to the bottom of the problem.

It didn't take long. Once we had cleared the air, Ken said that he was facing problems with the law for dealing drugs out the backdoor of the restaurant! In addition, he was in trouble with the IRS for nonpayment of taxes.

In my mind the solution was simple: Ken had to go! I didn't need the problems that were sure to accompany his drug business, and I didn't need a tenant who couldn't pay rent.

The only problem with that solution was that Ken didn't want to go. In his mind, the only way to extricate himself from all his problems was to hang on to the restaurant and dig his way out of the hole with the profits he knew he could generate by continuing to operate the restaurant and motel. I informed him that without rent payments I couldn't, and wouldn't, allow him to stay. I told him of my obligations to the former owner which involved hefty note payments every month. But, that was certainly of no concern to Ken. His focus was 110 percent on his problems. I informed him that if he wouldn't hand over the keys voluntarily, I would have no choice but to institute eviction proceedings.

He quietly informed me about a small detail that had slipped by the former owner…and me. The lease for the piece of land across the street, which had become the restaurant's parking lot, was in Ken's name! He made it clear that he was willing to use the leverage of that lease to whatever extent necessary to ensure a solution to his problems. It was clear that he had me over a barrel. The city wouldn't allow parking on the street and there didn't seem to be any other nearby off-street parking available. Without the benefit of "Ken's" parking lot, there was no parking for the restaurant.

For the moment, I was facing two ugly choices: I could evict Ken and have no parking (and no one to run the restaurant), or I could let him stay and keep the parking lot but lose the rent until he solved his problem (if he ever could…or would). I knew that if I acted upon either of the two choices that were currently available to me, I'd lose my whole restaurant/ motel investment. The task before me wasn't just finding the right solution, but finding it fast! And not just any solution, but *a winning solution*. Now's the time to introduce the "End Game Strategy." After some intense brain-storming sessions, a workable strategy began to take shape in my mind. Critical to the success of this idea was that each step of my strategy had to go exactly as planned. I wouldn't have an opportunity to go back and adjust for mistakes in my plan or its execution. I needed to make sure that each segment of the plan was properly choreographed to ensure a certain victory.

My first move was to contact a friend, Tom, who was a big success in the restaurant business. Upon hearing of my problems, he sympathized with me and suggested a solution for at least part of my difficulties. Should I decide to go ahead with Ken's eviction, he knew a fellow named Buck, whom he would highly recommend as someone to take over the management of the restaurant. I immediately made arrangements to meet with Buck and had a very good feeling about him. Buck, like Ken, was very self-assured. In the case of Buck that was a plus – not so with Ken. In addition to all my other problems, Ken's huge ego was quickly becoming another addition to my list of problems. The restaurant's enormous popularity with the young crowd was an ego booster for Ken that he didn't want to lose. To bring Buck into the picture, with an ego of his own, was to light the fuse of a very large stick of dynamite.

The first step of my plan required Ken to sell his lease on the parking lot for the amount of his indebtedness to the IRS. The second part of the plan was for Buck to buy the business for the value of Ken's parking lot lease and be the operator of the restaurant and the motel. I would retain ownership of the restaurant, motel, and parking lost lease. I would receive rent from Buck for the use of those facilities, just as it had been with Ken.

There were problems with my idea. First, getting Buck to pay anything for the right to run the restaurant. I realized he thought he would merely be making lease payments to me. I had to convince him that he was acquiring a business – one of considerable value.

My next problem was to get Ken to release his hold on the business and accept a payment equal to his IRS indebtedness as full payment for his restaurant business. This would be a very tough sell since the entire payment would quickly disappear into the hands of the IRS, leaving Ken with nothing for what had been a very profitable business. What would his decision be when he finally realized that he was walking away from his ego booster, empty-handed? All the success he had built into that restaurant operation was going to slip from his grasp. These were two very difficult assignments. They were made even more difficult by the dislike the two men felt for each other. Ken certainly wouldn't want to think Buck would reap all the benefits of his hard work in building the restaurant's image and success.

I would never accomplish any of this at some joint meeting among the three of us. I was sure that even if they were put in separate rooms, I dared not leave any of the negotiations for that meeting. I began to think of a way to soften Ken to the reality that he didn't have the option to continue operating the restaurant and that the parting price to step aside would be limited to the amount of his indebtedness to the IRS. Ken's position would be critically weakened if he knew that I didn't need his parking lot. It occurred to me that I merely needed an alternative solution for the parking – or at least one Ken would view as potentially viable. At this point, nothing would prevent me from going forward with the eviction and putting Buck in charge. Combing the area, fortunately, revealed a suitable (albeit not ideal) alternate parking location. I quickly met with Ken and confronted him with that alternative plan and convinced him that I was prepared to go forward without "his" parking lot. If that happened, his parking lot would be worthless to him. He would walk away with nothing! He agreed to sell the parking lot for the amount of his indebtedness and signed an agreement to that effect!

I then called Tom and asked if he might know an alternate manager who might be willing to buy the restaurant business and become the owner of the restaurant and motel operation in the event Buck didn't want to buy the business. He said he did have another person in mind and gave me his name. I now felt I had all I needed to approach Buck with the proposal that he *buys* the business. I would be able to tell Buck that Ken was willing to sell the business and inform him of the price.

Armed with that agreement, I met with Buck and told him that there would be a price for the business he was about to take over. I told him that there would be no deal if he was unwilling to assume that responsibility. But I reminded him that this had been a booming business even with the motel facility having been largely ignored. I told him that I would understand if he felt unwilling to payoff Ken's IRS problem, which would constitute his purchase price for the business. However, he needed to know that I had the name of someone else who might step up to buy the business should he decline the opportunity. It was immediate, "I'll pay for it." He agreed to pay the amount necessary to give Ken a clean bill of health. Buck and I then signed an agreement for him to buy the business, including the price he would pay for its purchase.

I decided to take no chances of some emotional blowup derailing the final closing and arranged for Buck and Ken to be confined to separate rooms until the closing was complete. Since I had not allowed them to ever have contact with one another, I became the courier who carried the documents back and forth between the two rooms.

My strategy worked. Buck bought into a great business opportunity, Ken was free of his IRS problems, and I saved my investment.

The key to the successful implementation of this principle is to identify *the correct path* to the problem's solution. It's not just any path, *it has to be the right one!* Similar to the "End Game Strategy" in the game of chess, there are countless possible paths you might take in your effort to find a solution to a big problem or important challenge you face. What you're looking for is that one particular sequence of decisions and maneuvers that can lead to a *certain* victory.

This strategy for victory starts with a detailed outline of the problem as well as all the salient facts, personalities, and peculiarities of the situation. This outline is then broken down into ideas regarding trial solutions for each of the separate hurdles to be overcome. It's a who, what, when, where, and how analysis of every permutation and combination of potential answers you can imagine.

These potential answers must then be ranked in order of their likelihood of success along with thoughts about sources of "outside" aides (references, letters, articles, testimonials, etc.) that might effectively bolster the value of one or more of these potential answers.

Once that path has been identified, the successive steps along the way must be carefully planned to make sure they are executed flawlessly and placed in their logical order. For instance, if you call the wrong person first, you will almost assuredly have to call them back later. Don't anticipate the same level of success with the second call that was obtained with the first. Any unnecessary repeat conversation opens the door for renegotiation of what was previously decided or agreed upon. It's often difficult to sell the same thing twice. Reasons that were convincing the first time, may lack the same punch a second time. You also face the risk that the other party will have had a change of heart during the interim. So, be fully prepared by having the answer to every question you can imagine them asking. When you lack one or more of those answers, you'll end up having to say, "I'll get back to you with an answer." This creates a need to call them back which provides them with an opportunity to change their mind.

Another important aspect of proper sequencing lies in 'nailing down" solutions to certain subordinate challenges. To obtain the other party's agreement, use whatever legitimate levers are available to you. If deemed at all helpful, arrange for backup documentation or expert testimonies to strengthen your case. Once this subordinate problem has been resolved you can take that issue off your list of concerns. This fortifies your bargaining position regarding the situations for which solutions are still pending.

Your mini goal is to get each person to pre-agree with what you need from them. Confine that agreement to the actual role they play. There are many reasons why someone might view their role as different than the bigger picture. Thus, they may alter their conclusions about their part based on their distaste for some aspect of the whole picture. Thus, narrow your conversation and arguments to the necessary. The greater the number of steps successfully in the "bag," the more it provides substantial assistance in nailing down those steps that yet remain to be put to bed.

This process is both complex and tedious. Bolster your resolve to stay the course by *reviewing* the consequences of failing.

IX. ATTITUDES AND HABITS

The principles in this section are attempting to call special attention to the proper ways of looking at life. Attitudes and Habits aim to improve the general quality of your life as well as the amount of enjoyment you'll experience from all your adventures when good attitudes become second nature to you.

Because you can't choose or control many of the circumstances that confront you, unexpected events can result in a wide range of reactions on your part depending on how you choose to view them. Life isn't so much about what happens to you as it is a matter of how you respond to those events.

For this reason, it seems fitting to begin with the philosophy How Do You Know It's Bad? This principle offers a way of dealing with unexpected news, annoying interruptions, or unanticipated problems – both good and bad. If you choose to adopt its philosophies, you will certainly separate yourself from the way most people handle unexpected news. Going one step further, Surprises In The Ashes suggests that you look expectantly for good to rise out of disaster.

The message contained in The Threat Of The Crowd will provide the necessary reasoning to allow you to comfortably sever yourself from the crowd. It urges you to appreciate and properly value your uniqueness and to tenaciously cling to your individuality which sometimes means that you always Take A Stand For The Truth. This principle provides insights into the eventual consequences of allowing the expedient to shape misguided tolerances for untruths just to gain popularity or get what you want. Feeling Sorry For Yourself? is a valuable principle that warns of an attitude that is never rewarded.

On a lighter note, you must retain the ability to let down your guard and allow others to witness your humanity. "Don't Take Yourself Too Seriously" suggests that someone willing to step down from their pedestal and laugh at themselves will win the respect and admiration of others.

Are You Spread Too Thin? will provide you with the needed encouragement to help you embrace an attitude of reverence for living a life of quality – such a life does not shortchange relationships for "duty."

Two principles delve into a couple of very special areas of life: Value Special Moments advises you to take the time to savor those special, irreplaceable occasions. Surround Yourself With Beauty urges you to take notice of the beautiful things that surround you and when possible, incorporate them into your life.

As you near the end of your life, the way others have known you will become your legacy. Unfortunately, many do not begin to think about such things until it's too late. You can't begin your creation of a *worthy* legacy too soon. These concerns are addressed in the final principle, What Kind Of Legacy Will You Leave?

HOW DO YOU KNOW IT'S BAD?

A profoundly insightful story leads to a philosophy worth adopting.

There was a Chinese farmer who lived in an agricultural era long the past. It was a time when a person's entire life came from the soil. Farm machinery was nonexistent. Next to a family member, the horse was the single most important possession the farmer had. The horse was not only instrumental in all crop-planting and harvesting tasks, but it was also the primary means of transportation. Life was extremely difficult, if not impossible, without a horse.

One day this farmer's horse got loose and ran away! Realizing the tremendous impact of this tragic event, the farmer's neighbors all came to the farmer's house to offer assistance in finding the horse, as well as to communicate their sincere condolences regarding this incalculable loss. To their surprise, the farmer's response to their visit and condolences was surprising, "How do you know it's bad?" At best, they thought he was a little flip. Quite possibly, the gravity of the situation had caused a temporary emotional overload. Discouraged in their efforts and not knowing what else to offer, they all went home.

A few days later, the farmer's horse returned – following it was a whole herd of wild horses. Astounded at the farmer's good fortune, his neighbors ran over to congratulate him. Not only had he recovered his horse but, he had now acquired an entire stable of new horses. They were all jubilant, almost envious. That was until the farmer shocked them by asking, "How do you know it's good?" Perplexed, they again all went home in disbelief.

The next day, the farmer's son decided to break one of the wild horses for use around the farm. The particular animal he chose was highly spirited and threw the boy off, breaking his leg. This was a true calamity his neighbors were quick to acknowledge. They again gathered to console the farmer and his son. They all knew the dangers of improper healing or infection. But once again, the wise old farmer answered, "How do you know it's bad?" Not particularly quick at picking up on the farmer's philosophy, the neighbors once again went home, this time a little disgusted. They could not understand how the farmer could display such a philosophical insensitivity, such a lack of sympathy, for his son's misfortune.

A few weeks later, officials from the emperor's court visited all the farms in the area. The emperor was involved in a war and every able-bodied young man was conscripted to serve in the army. Because of his broken leg, the farmer's son was not required to go into battle. Within weeks, every one of the neighboring boys had been killed!

At a minimum, such a philosophy helps us temper otherwise wide emotional swings and greatly reduce our anxieties. To our surprise, as it was to the farmer's neighbors, it might also lead us to valid understandings and proper decisions about the true portent of extraordinary situations and the most effective way of dealing with them.

These same ironies observable in the "How Do You Know It's Bad" principle are a fact of life today. Sports figures, actors, musicians, etc., find fame and fortune. Yet, immorality, drug and/or alcohol abuse, and broken lives often accompany that sudden fame and fortune. Some people win the lottery or inherit fortunes – not always with a happy ending. Studies made of the lives of lottery winners have revealed the almost unbelievable, nearly universal, wreckage of their lives caused by their windfall. Even Christmas day is often the scene of children in grumpy moods, fighting among their brothers and sisters. The letdown after the windfall of all the gifts is the culprit that's usually behind this seemingly irrational behavior. Thus, the wisdom of "How Do You Know It's Bad?"

On the other hand, countless victims of bankruptcy have been forced to discover new careers. These have often turned out to be more satisfying and more rewarding than their previous vocation. Victims of health problems have witnessed profound changes in their priorities – for the better. They have often become, as a consequence of their testimony, of great value and inspiration to others. Calamitous events in some people's lives have forced an entire change in attitude and lifestyle – many times for the better. Keep in mind, things are seldom as good as they first seem or as bad and threatening as you first thought.

In tempering your excitement upon the occasion of a windfall, emotional letdowns can be avoided, or at least lessened. Your ability to relish the good that has come your way can then be savored and enjoyed over a much longer period. By tempering your reaction to a calamity, you will find yourself able to address the repairs and cleanup of that tragedy. That cleanup/repair effort best answers the need, unlike any other response, to return your life to a sense of normalcy. It satisfies that overwhelming urge to "get things back" (or as close as possible) to where they were.

These suggested reactions to the "excesses" of life speak to decisions that can significantly improve the quality of your life since windfalls and calamities occur in almost everyone's lifetime. Incorrectly dealing with these aberrant occasions, you will have successfully addressed that all-important issue…your emotional balance.

Upon receipt of the news of a calamity or windfall, rest in the fact that things seldom turn out to be as extreme as first reported.

Decide that you will temper your immediate reaction and maintain your emotional balance to reports of a windfall or calamity. Wait for the dust to settle so that you can accurately assess the impact of what has resulted from the initial storm of emotional excess or factual exaggeration.

By not allowing an initial report to upset your equilibrium or cause an ill-considered reaction, your subsequent dealings with the situation will be greatly benefited.

SURPRISES IN THE ASHES

You know what's said about the best-laid plans…"things" happen. Look for the silver lining and expect a miracle.

Life can sometimes deliver some nasty blows. Almost everyone experiences them. Even for those who consider themselves to be good decision-makers, "things" happen.

While this entire book speaks to the elimination or reduction of problems through good decision-making, this principle isn't about eliminating unwanted events. Rather, it seeks to encourage two things: First, a mental preparedness to properly deal with the unexpected bad event that will sometimes descend upon you. Second, it hopes to positively influence your thinking such that you begin to treat seeming disasters as moments or events of potential opportunity – like searching through the wreckage for something that wasn't damaged. Even better, the changes brought about by the calamity can be examined for the fresh opportunities they present…opportunities that, heretofore, didn't exist.

Such was the situation when my wife and I decided to go forward with our plans to build our mountain "dream" home. We had put off the project several times. Each time, concerns about the true costs of building and our inability to meet any unexpected costs or expenses, caused us to hesitate. Years went by; we continued to punt.

When we finally decided to begin, we decided to act as our contractor and save the cost of his services. As a result, the responsibility for preparing a detailed list of all the anticipated expenses fell on our shoulders. The bank that was making the construction loan provided a very comprehensive list of all manner of possible expenses one might expect to encounter in the process of building a home. It was a great help as it became the instrument that created "the budget" we relied upon.

The only problem with this whole process is that the bank expects this document to have meaning. When an expense exceeds the amount listed on your budget statement, the bank is very niggardly about advancing funds from another expense category to make up for a shortfall. At the very least, your beginning operations must go as expected.

Our first move was to lay out the house's perimeter lines on the ground and hire a backhoe operator to carve out the area for our foundation. He began with the driveway which traced an uphill path into the lot that would end at the garage. He was only halfway up the hill to the garage area when he hit solid rock. He said, "I'm afraid I can't go any further. You're going to have to blast." As you might guess, that wasn't on our budget. But I consoled myself with visions from a T.V. show of large buildings that had been demolished with correctly placed dynamite charges. It all seemed so simple. A big puff of smoke and a huge cloud of dust eventually congealed into what seemed to be a relatively small pile as the dust began to settle, a pile that was much smaller than I might have imagined. Pieces of heavy equipment came along, "swept" up the rubble, and that was the end of it.

So, we hired a blasting expert. After weeks of delay awaiting the many repairs to their constantly malfunctioning rock drill, the big day came when they set off the dynamite. Expecting similar results to the demolished buildings I'd seen on TV, I was very unpleasantly surprised to watch our huge cloud of dust and smoke become an equally huge pile of enormous boulders.

A nature trail that was used by the owners of the neighboring homes meandered by the site of this disaster. What happened next became the final confirmation of the immensity of all the problems we now faced. As I was sitting on a boulder, somewhat out of the view of someone on the trail, a neighboring couple came walking by and came upon the huge pile of boulders, broken trees, and debris. The man looked at his wife and remarked, "They sure wrecked this site." This presented a whole list of costs we had not expected. I sat there feeling like crying. Later that same day, I even called a man who had previously expressed an interest in buying our lot. Somehow, his price had drastically dropped. A few days later, I realized that I needed to address the problem and began calling around for people who had those huge side-dump trucks. I stumbled upon an interesting man named Colt Simon who owned such a truck and knew four others who also had such equipment. After looking at the huge pile, he told me that it would take his team of five trucks, three days to haul off the boulders. Wow! In addition to the costs of all this equipment, there were dump fees to be paid in order to get rid of all this material. I began to think, "What an ominous beginning to our supposed dream!"

Pure coincidence found my wife sitting in the hair salon wherein she mentioned our predicament to the hairdresser. In a rather excited tone, the hairdresser exclaimed that one of her relatives had been looking for material to fill a large ravine on his mountain property. My wife got the guys number and I called him. We made a deal that resulted in his paying for the material. What he paid us completely covered all the expenses of the blasting and removal of the debris! Getting rid of our entire mess at no cost to us was not all the benefit we realized from this seeming disaster. What had been hidden beneath all the boulders was a generous supply of useable rocks (of the correct sizes) for all the rock work we would later be doing as part of the construction of the house and the creation of the various stone walls around the property! Out of the ashes of the disaster came a miraculous set of answers!

When a true disaster strikes, many find the mere contemplation of where they find themselves to be more than they can stomach. Positive thoughts are totally missing. While this concept can't guarantee positive results from the adoption of the attitudes it suggests in your times of trouble, dismissing its merits leaves you with little hope of an answer.

Sifting through the ashes in search of some kind of answer does have some therapeutic benefits. First, you're forced to come to grips with the problems you now face – and usually, the sooner, the

better. Second, it's surprisingly common for the seeming immensity of the problem to shrink under an assessment of what's happened. Third, and more important, is the distinct possibility that you will actually discover a benefit to be realized from the disaster that's just occurred. Part of this principle's value is this message: you have nothing to lose by adopting its suggested attitudes and giving them a chance to prove their worth.

THE THREAT OF THE CROWD

Adhering to this principle requires self confidence, and sometimes even sheer nerve!

A few years ago, my wife and I went on a journey to the Holy Land. In addition to some side excursions into the countryside, we spent time in and around Jerusalem. The city is divided into four quadrants, one of which is the Arab sector. Wandering from store to store within that Arab sector, we happened on a little shop that sold all of those exotic "trinkets" that would remind you of scenes from Ali Baba. Some of these exotic things included daggers – the ones with the sharp, curved blades. Noticing our interest in them, the shopkeeper began to describe the way they were used. He explained that a person would carry the dagger in his hand, with that hand and arm tucked inside his cloak, hidden from view. He would walk alongside his intended victim and place his other arm around the victim's shoulder – as he did with me in a mock demonstration. A friendly conversation would ensue until the anticipated moment arrived. In a flash, everything changed; out came the dagger which was quickly jammed into the victim's back! The dagger was hastily returned to its hiding place inside the assailant's cloak, allowing him to quietly slip away unnoticed. Shocked, but intrigued, we bought the dagger.

Just as we exited the shop, the eerie "siren" from the minaret (a tall, narrow steeple or tower) sounded the call to prayer for Muslim worshippers. Thousands of Muslims immediately flooded the narrow cobblestone street. Because of the stone buildings on either side, these dark passageways felt threatening, even when deserted. But now, we found ourselves hopelessly confined in a stampede! To make matters worse, they were going in the opposite direction to the one that would lead us out of there. While the people weren't running, they weren't walking either. We were aware that we were in a very foreign place, and we didn't get the feeling that these people liked us. Our eyes focused on those with long robes as we struggled to move "upstream" to get out of that Arab sector. The twenty minutes that we were trapped in the middle of this threatening crowd, seemed like an eternity. Thankfully, we made our way safely out of that situation.

Though most crowds would not seem to present such an ominous threat as the one we perceived, crowds do pose a threat to you. The threat they pose, however, is one you may have never thought about. A bumper sticker I saw recently explained the point perfectly: "You Laugh At Me Because I'm Different; I Laugh At You Because You Are All The Same."

The threat of the crowd isn't usually that of physical harm. But, as the bumper sticker suggests, the threat is being absorbed into their thought patterns and sameness…ultimately mimicking the mediocrity of its members. This principle should serve to alert you to the brainwashing influence the crowd exerts on its members.

Scientific advancements inform us that we've been uniquely branded by our fingerprint, eye print, voice analysis, etc. With the discovery of DNA, the true uniqueness of each person on earth has been proven. No two people in existence are duplicates of one another – this is even true of identical twins. This uniqueness is evident in seemingly insignificant things such as our handwriting, the way we walk, and even our golf swing.

Many people, however, do not view their particular uniqueness as a positive thing. Either they are not willing to accept themselves as they were created, or they don't like what they've become. Their assessment of their personal qualities brings them little comfort as they surrender to the siren call of the "crowd" not willing to stand out as being "different." Their desperate need to "fit in" and be liked is achieved by blending in with the crowd. To assume the crowd's identity is to reject and hopefully bury the image they have of themselves. They begin to dress like the crowd, talk like the crowd, use the same buzzwords – even the same tonal inflections in their speech. They have bought into the crowd's values. They eagerly adopt these attitudes and mannerisms to make sure they have all the identifying marks of the crowd and *don't stand out!*

They eventually melt into the crowd's persona and identify with the crowd's values, often forsaking their values and individuality in the process. Because their reference point is always the crowd, their decisions are all screened through the crowd. Gone is the desire, even the courage, to make a choice that in any way bucks the crowd or speaks to what they are – a regrettable conclusion for those who had something going for them. By "fitting in," people are often denying the very qualities that are their greatest personal assets – assets that make them worth knowing. Rather than denying them, recognizing and using these assets will expose them to their greatest chance of realizing the promise of success and living a meaningful life. Why try to be like everyone else when you are inherently different?

The truth is that the majority of people who have accomplished *anything worthy of note* are those who are not afraid to appear, and be, different! Focus on your unique qualities. A path will begin to open up before you. Your special qualities will become the underpinning of your most promising pursuits.

To be a member of the crowd requires that you blend in and disregard all that separates you from it. It can result in the abdication of personal responsibility for making decisions by allowing the "crowd" to make them for you

Stop trying to blend in. Accept yourself as you were created and treasure what you are by taking advantage of all that makes you special. Only then can you begin to develop the potential that lies within you.

The life of the person who consistently decides to honor his uniqueness looks nothing like the life of the person who enlists in the crowd and in that process rejects his uniqueness.

Since no one else is like you, nor can they do what you can do, decide to honor your uniqueness. If you do, life will be so much richer and more rewarding.

TAKE A STAND FOR THE TRUTH

Reality…efforts to deny it are baffling!

In 1837, Hans Christian Andersen wrote a short story about an emperor who had lived and ruled many years ago. This monarch didn't have much interest in most royal diversions. But he loved new clothes because he always wanted to appear well-dressed. He spent enormous amounts buying clothes so that he could travel around and show them off.

Sensing an opportunity, two swindlers came to the city pretending to be weavers and claimed they could manufacture the finest cloth imaginable, the colors and patterns of which were exceptionally beautiful. The material also possessed the wonderful quality of being invisible to any man who was unfit for his office or unpardonably stupid.

The emperor thought these must be wonderful cloth. He thought that if he had a suit made of this cloth, he would be able to find out which of those in his palace staff were unfit for their positions or would be able to distinguish the intelligent from the stupid. He immediately issued orders to have a suit made for himself and gave a large sum of money to the swindlers who pretended to be hard at work while creating nothing on the looms on which they continued to "work" until late into the night.

Curious as to the status of the weavers' project, the emperor sent his top minister to investigate. The emperor was sure that his minister was both intelligent and eminently qualified for the position he held within the empire and would be the best to investigate their progress. When the minister entered the workroom where the weavers were sitting at the empty loom, there wasn't any cloth to be seen, but he was afraid to confront them with his disbelief for fear of being thought unfit for his position. When the weavers asked him what he thought about the new cloth, the minister said the cloth was exceedingly beautiful. He praised the colors and the patterns and promised them he'd tell the emperor that he liked the cloth. A few days later, the emperor sent another of his trusted ministers to once again check up on the weavers. This minister saw what the first minister had seen (or hadn't seen) and came to the same conclusions as the first minister. But, he too fell victim to fears of being labeled unfit for his position within the royal cabinet. The scam was working beautifully as he also praised the weavers for their beautiful cloth and complimented them on their fine workmanship.

Finally, the emperor himself wanted to be shown the cloth. The two ministers who had previously "seen" the cloth and had reported its beauty to him were there continuing to praise the marvels of the cloth. Now, it was the emperor's turn to be forced to question his intelligence or his qualifications to be the supreme monarch of the kingdom, as he admitted (to himself) that he could not see any cloth.

And so the deception continued, as everyone ignored what each of them had just seen (actually not seen). They advised their ruler to wear his new clothes for the great procession that was soon to take place. They all praised the beautiful cloth and its weavers. Incredibly, the emperor appointed the two swindlers as "Imperial Court Weavers."

As the swindlers put the new clothes on him, they warned him that because the clothes were so light, he would feel as if he had nothing on them. After the weavers had put each article of clothing on the emperor, he looked in the mirror and joyfully praised his new clothes.

The emperor marched in the procession and all who saw him were unanimously admiring of his new suit. No one wanted to let others know that they couldn't see his clothes as that would render them either stupid or unfit for the positions they held within the empire.

As the procession moved through the streets, among the onlookers was a little child who was standing with his parents along the route of the procession. As the emperor passed by, the child remarked, "The emperor doesn't have anything on!"

Finally, someone had called it like it was. But, where was everyone else? Why were the people unwilling to stand up and be counted? It took a child to state the obvious. This was something that had been evident to everyone, even the emperor! But none of them had the nerve to volunteer their true observations!

Taking a stand can be risky; nevertheless, it's best to be recognized as a person who doesn't always have their finger on the wind. Instead, separate yourself from those who are willing to support lies so that never become required of you.

While we all know what happens to whistle-blowers who expose fraud or misconduct in the upper ranks of a corporation, you don't have to do what they're doing or lie for them. When that becomes a part of your job description, it's time to look for another job. A tough call? Yes, but there are many honestly run businesses who would be happy to have in their employ a truthful person…because they know that individual can be trusted.

DON'T TAKE YOURSELF TOO SERIOUSLY

The most comedic genius couldn't have improved on this scene.
My family and I took a much-anticipated trip down the Natchez Trace, a journey that began in Nashville, Tennessee, and finally took us to Natchez, Mississippi, where we stayed for a few days. We planned to tour the old plantations, take in the historic pageant play, and just get a taste of the Deep South. The trip took us along a beautiful drive down a winding, country-type road that journeyed through the lush countryside of the rural South. Arriving in Natchez was like traveling back in time.

The southern culture there was certainly alive and well.

The beginning of our excursion involved interesting tours of the famed plantations of the South's early days. Each of the plantations we toured had "greeters" sitting at umbrella-shaded tables. The women were adorned with historic antebellum hoopskirts. Pots of flowers were generously sprinkled around the entry to each plantation. I remember one plantation in particular because I made the mistake of cutting across the lawn to get to the check-in table. The woman at the table, in an overly polite but stern manner, pointed out my error of insensitively failing to stay on the prescribed path. I later learned that she was the chairwoman of the pageant play. That all made sense as her stern and "proper" demeanor fit the part you might expect of one who would be in charge of an event that had a much deeper significance than a casual Yankee visitor might quickly grasp.

One afternoon, we had lunch at one of the plantations. The dining room was this airy pavilion-like room that was elegantly adorned with white tablecloths, crystal glassware, and silver utensils. Flowers and beautiful indoor plants adorned the scene. The scenery through the large glass windows to the gardens outside framed views of the live oak trees with Spanish moss hanging romantically from the branches. An impeccably dressed black waiter (in a tuxedo-like uniform) came to our table to welcome us and take our order. He enthusiastically gave us a brief history of the place and the continuing role his family had played in the functioning of the plantation. He passionately described three generations of involvement (the waiters, his father, and his grandfather) in the life and care of the plantation. You began to understand the pride and sense of inseparable inclusion he felt regarding the significance of this plantation's place in history, as well as his family's relationship with its owners. That and many other equally special experiences led up to the culminating evening – the pageant play. Even before we arrived at the auditorium where the play was to be performed, we had the feeling that this presentation was *a really big deal*. It marked events and sentiments that were of the deepest significance to these people.

The evening of the play finally arrived and the patrons were very graciously led to their seats to await the beginning of the performance. While preparations for the play were taking place behind the closed curtains, other preliminary events of great pomp and elegance had been planned to help round out the audience's experience of the evening. The formal, almost royal, entrance, introduction, and seating of the officials of the pageant, as well as glamorous flag processions, all took place as part of the opening ceremonies. Special music was provided for a fitting background. As these officials were being paraded in, I recognized the lady that had spoken "special words" to me about walking across her lawn – the chairwoman. All the other ladies wore full hoop skirts, bonnets, and carried bouquets, and were seated around Madam Chairwoman's elevated seating platform. After they were all finally seated, the actors' final preparations took place behind the curtain. By now, I'm sure you get the picture. This was, indeed, a very elaborate deal, even animals had roles in the play.

As the audience waited in hushed silence for the opening curtain to be pulled back, one of those animals (a little dog) crawled out from under the curtain and momentarily stood motionless on the stage. Seemingly oblivious to the large audience, the dog stood there for a few moments looking around. Not finding a handy tree or fireplug, he took a few steps and proceeded, in full view of the audience, to hike his leg and take a leak on the curtain!

The audience (they all saw it) let out a collective gasp. They didn't know how to respond – to laugh or remain silent. They waited in stunned silence for the august members of the pageant board to signal a response. The scene represented the ultimate contrast between the sophistication, formality, and ostentation of the pageant (with all its officialdom) versus the dog's barnyard response to his instincts – instincts that were in total contradiction to the setting within which he chose to "perform." The officials of the pageant all took their cue from the prissy chairwoman who sat there in death-like stiffness and exquisite discomfort. The audience reacted similarly – except for a few uncouth people, like myself, who couldn't control their response to this most hilarious juxtaposition of extremes ever to come together in such a quick snapshot. For me, it was classic humor!

Because the officials didn't see it that way, there was a sense of embarrassment for them and the pageant itself. The audience also felt that embarrassed. However, had the officials of the pageant (particularly Madam Chairwoman) chosen to acknowledge that extraordinary moment of unforgettable humor and responded with a collective roar, that night's play might have gone down in history as one of the most enjoyable, if not most memorable, programs in the history of the pageant.

Embarrassing moments present a rare opportunity. **It's almost guaranteed that you will be better thought of if you allow everyone to have some fun at your expense.**

Decide to laugh at yourself. **Others will relax in your presence, knowing you are approachable and possess a good sense of humor.**

While this requires an act of great humility, it will not go unnoticed by others – the consequence will be the growth of their respect for you.

FEELING SORRY FOR YOURSELF?

This is one ugly emotion!

I began playing competitive golf in my early to mid-teens. At that age, many young players don't concern themselves with guarding their emotional displays – something that hopefully comes with a little maturity. The elation over winning isn't hidden, nor is there any attempt to disguise the upset connected with losing.

During those days when I played a lot of competitive golf, I met some very interesting people. One older kid, Marvin, stands out in my memory. While he was a good player, his golf course conduct could only be categorized as tempestuous. Bad shots would result in burying his club head in the ground in a hatchet-like fashion. A series of bad shots would set one of his offending clubs sailing through the air. A bad round would usually result in some broken equipment!

Marvin never had any money. Neither did he have a decent car – among its defects was a faulty starter motor. Because of this problem, Marvin always parked his car in the golf course parking lot against an old tree trunk so he could exploit the small slope created by the root system of the old tree. When he was ready to leave, he would turn on the key, release the brake, push in the clutch, and allow the car to roll down the little hill away from the tree. He would pop the clutch, wait for the reassuring sound of the motor, and drive off.

Marvin always played with the same group, and they always had money riding on the outcome. One day after a particularly bad round and heavy losses of money he couldn't afford to lose, Marvin was in no mood to stick around. Heading straight for the parking lot, all he wanted to do was get out of there. He quickly turned on the key, pushed in the clutch, and released the brake. The car rolled backward, he popped the clutch, and the engine coughed...*but didn't start!*

In a rage, Marvin got out of his car, went around to the rear of the car, and opened the trunk. He grabbed the tire iron and proceeded to demolish his car! When he was finished, it was doubtful that any of its parts had escaped his tirade. It wasn't even worthy material for a junkyard. Besides being short the cost of a new starter motor, Marvin was now out the cost of another car. Marvin felt ***very sorry*** for himself!

But Marvin isn't alone. We are all occasionally guilty of feeling sorry for ourselves. When feeling down and full of self-pity, an angry artist has been known to slash his masterpiece. Others, in the destructive grip of self-pity, have made the horrible mistake of saying something extremely hateful to the one they love the most, the very one whose love they need the most. The error of these ways, though usually acknowledged later, is often difficult to control because *there's a certain sick, albeit momentary, satisfaction gained in venting one's rage in an ugly display of self-pity.* Beware of its insidious grip!

This is an extremely difficult behavior to remedy because it is always accompanied by extreme emotional upset and behavioral instability. All reason has been lost. Raw emotion has taken its place and rules the moment. The only possible way to deal with this problem is to make a covenant with yourself.

First, promise yourself that the minute you feel this terrible cloud enveloping you...*you will walk away!*

Second, if you find yourself wavering in your willingness to walk away, promise yourself you will take just a second to reflect upon the damage you are about to inflict. Ask yourself these questions: "How am I going to feel about the destruction I'm about to cause...*after* I've regained my self-control?" and "What will others think of me?" If the answer to those questions doesn't prevent another outburst... know this: the image of your rage will *never* leave their minds.

ARE YOU SPREAD TOO THIN?

Life in the "fast lane" can be thrilling...but, it's not free of train wrecks.

That old song, "Slow down, you move too fast" speaks to the way a lot of people live their lives. Taking time to smell the roses is increasingly a lost concept. Evidence of a growing impatience that permeates the life of many is all around us. Presentations, ads, websites, etc., are all designed in recognition of almost universal, ever-diminishing, attention spans – a consequence of moving through life too fast.

A study was conducted by some truck driving schools that measured the amount of shrinkage of one's field of vision as the speed of travel increased. The results have been used and published in the instruction booklets found in places like drivers' licensing bureaus.

This study concluded that the width of the observer's field of vision was the greatest when they were standing still. At twenty miles per hour, their field of vision was cut by one-third. At forty miles per hour, it was further reduced by 60 percent of the range measured when standing still. At a speed of sixty miles per hour, the driver's field of vision has been narrowed to no more than the width of the beam of the headlights – basically about the width of the lane, one's traveling in. Today, most people are "going like sixty." It's no wonder they don't stop to smell the roses; they are moving too fast to even see them.

The real issue here isn't the focus on the vistas along the side of the road that are lost to motorized travel. What should be of concern are the things that have been sacrificed in the process – things like relationships, personal development, and enjoyable diversions. For those who are moving too fast, the "gold-plated" rationalization is that they'll spend "quality time" with their family. What isn't acknowledged is that this concept has become a substitute for "quantity time." We'd rather wait until we can get tickets to the World Series then go out in the yard and play catch with our boys.

As I reflected on my situation, I realized I was moving too fast, spread too thin, and greatly off balance! I began to understand that going through life at the speed of light can also bear other consequences – consequences beyond lost opportunities with family and leisure activities. Moving too fast threatens your way of life with the devastating losses that often accompany the manic attempt to get ever bigger, wealthier, and constantly stimulated in the process.

In the late 70s and early 80s, I felt that I had finally hit my stride. I owned two companies and a nice home in an upscale mountain community. I was able to indulge my wife with expensive clothes and jewelry. We had a valuable art collection and a nice assortment of antique furniture pieces. In addition, we each drove a Mercedes.

I knew I was really on the fast track when I purchased a one-hundred-acre piece of ground that straddled an important interchange on a major freeway. I remember thinking that I was really onto something big.

As I contemplated what I'd do with that piece of ground, I began to imagine my corporate headquarters proudly sitting within *my new one-hundred-acre office park*. I could just picture "Wright World Headquarters" chiseled into the stone entrance to the building. But that fantasy was fortuitously interrupted by a phone call from a man who wanted to buy that one hundred acre and pay me a *hefty* profit. He gave me an acceptable deposit, and we signed an agreement that called for a closing one year from the date of the contract, a date which coincided with the due date on the loan that my seller had carried back for me. The one-year delay also qualified the sale for a capital gains tax treatment.

At about this time, my wife and I became enamored with the idea of owning a second home in Mexico. We decided to buy a villa in a very nice development on the south edge of town in Puerto Vallarta.

Sometime later, I joined a second country club and bought three lots on the golf course. I started designing a spec home that we would build and sell. At about the same time, I also began designing a plan for our own house that was to be built on the best of the three lots.

I had developed a very good reputation with one of Denver's largest banks. It was as though they rolled out the red carpet for me as I was invited to their executive dining room on several occasions. Quite naturally, I approached the bank about a construction loan for the two houses. It couldn't have been easier. They asked how much I needed and I told them $1,150,000 for both houses. The loan was approved and we broke ground on the spec house.

It's a little difficult to recall what started to turn sour first. Sky-high interest rates, however, proved to be the financial death knell for a lot of people – I began to fear that I would be one of them.

Both of the companies I owned were tied to the construction industry. With the advent of high-interest rates (17 percent prime rate), home construction slowed to a crawl. We weren't able to cut our overhead fast enough to escape sizeable losses.

Just three weeks before the closing of the sale of that one-hundred-acre parcel, the buyer informed me that he wouldn't be able to pay me!

Our spec house ran into enormous cost overruns. I was forced to confront the bank with my need for another $250,000 *just to finish the first house!* (*No work* had started on the second house) It was amazing to observe the speed with which that red carpet rolled up. The banker, in a most unfriendly tone, told me that the bank had no interest in loaning me another penny. Moreover, he strongly suggested that I start cutting a few corners if I were to have any chance of pulling this disaster out of the fire!

The final blow was the effect all this had on my wife's health. I had noticed that stress always resulted in some form of physical manifestation such as headaches, upset stomach, and even hives. But this situation was much more than just a little stress. We were threatened with losing everything. Six months into this pressure cooker, my wife experienced some strange symptoms that were later diagnosed as lymphoma.

After a terrible two-year struggle, she was gone,...along with both businesses, the second country club membership, the one hundred acres, the golf course lot we intended for our residence, as well as our mountain residence, and one of the cars – all of it, gone!

I was spread too thin!

Making money is not all there is. Never allow the cruel demands that typically accompany pursuits of success to rob you of things that you cannot buy with your "success" dollars. Slow down!

The gift of life, in all its richness, is a priceless treasure to be enjoyed – not rushed through in a state of frenzy to make more money, gather more things, or accumulate more experiences!

Remember, some people are very important to you, others are worth knowing, and special occasions shouldn't be missed. There's a lot to see along the side of the road.

Make a decision to slow down and take in the view. Decide that you will not tolerate any imbalance that threatens to compromise the very things that make your life worth living!

VALUE SPECIAL MOMENTS

Some things have a value that can't be purchased.
No two sunsets are ever alike – it's a new show every night. While it may not be apparent, each moment within the unfolding of any one sunset is unlike any other. Like the subtle movements of the hour hand on a clock or the aging of our bodies, the process happens at a pace too slow for the human eye to detect. Nevertheless, the hour hand of the clock is continually moving, our bodies are relentlessly aging, and the colors of the sunset are in a constant state of change.

Though the differences between most moments are hardly noticeable, other moments are strikingly contrasting. Such would be the moments just before an accident, or the receipt of some bad news, as compared with the moments immediately following the accident, the bad news, etc.

The important point here is that just as each moment possesses a uniqueness of its own, each day and every occasion also presents its specialness. Don't overlook the importance of these times or the priceless events that sometimes occur within them.

Such was my realization one summer night in Bryce Canyon National Park, Utah. It had its beginning just as our family vacation was coming to an end. Because we didn't arrive at our motel until well after dark, everyone was tired and by eleven o'clock, they had all gone to bed, except me. Just as I was about to turn in, I happened to notice a magnificent full moon that gave the canyon, with its hauntingly beautiful spires, a most incredible look. I rushed around waking everyone up with the suggestion that we all take a walk on the trail that led down into the canyon. My idea met with a mixed response – some saying they could see it in the morning. In the end, I convinced them all. That midnight walk was the one event during that vacation that is universally remembered by everyone. Luckily, we took advantage of that moment.

None of us have ever experienced a moment like it again!

Many special times can slip by, unnoticed, when you deceive yourself into believing there will be other moments, other days, or other occasions like the one you just missed – another chance to do it right the next time. Unfortunately, this belief causes inertia to rule and allows you to again miss another special, *never-to-occur-again,* opportunity. It is, however, within your power to not let this happen.

So, when there's a day on your calendar that's marked for someone's special occasion (a birthday, wedding, graduation, or anniversary) remember, **it is that day that's special to that person**, not the day before and certainly not the day after. Decide now to make a habit of getting it right by making such occasions special.

Just as unique moments can be very precious, there are circumstances in which time itself becomes very valuable. When my wife, Ellen, was diagnosed with lymphoma, life for both of us changed… immediately! Frequent visits to the hospital became her life. On the occasion of one of her overnight stays, I came to visit. As I came to the waiting room of the oncology center, I noticed a rack on the wall that was stocked with brochures containing information about the various cancers under the care of that ward. Tenuously, I pulled out the one that dealt with Lymphoma, her disease. I was devastated to learn that her odds of survival were only ten percent! It quickly dawned on me that *time* had suddenly taken on a very unique importance…for both of us.

Her chemotherapy treatments were very debilitating and required several days just to recover to the point where she could get around comfortably. I decided that I would do all I could to create something for her to look forward to after each chemo session. This usually involved a few day's getaways to some vacation spot. In between, I did my best to adjust my business responsibilities to allow maximum time to be spent with her. My acute awareness of the preciousness of her last days led to me to commit to this plan of action. Though she regrettably ended in the ninety percent statistic, *I never had any regrets* about how I treated her, how I handled her situation, or how I conducted my other responsibilities.

I made sure that time with her would occupy my top priority, and placed all other responsibilities in second place.

This principle speaks to the uniqueness of every segment of time and strongly advises your sensitivity to that fact to exploit those wonderful, serendipitous moments when they present themselves – because a day gone by is a day that will never again return.

Thus, make sure that you enter special occasions on your calendar well in advance of their arrival. Use this lead time to plan and prepare for that event in a manner that won't soon be forgotten.

Decide now that you will value the uniqueness of every special day, each memorable occasion, and those romantic, red-letter moments that occasionally cross your path. Don't allow these special occasions to slip by uncelebrated.

SURROUND YOURSELF WITH BEAUTY

This principle could enrich your life well beyond your expectations.
The world always seems to be changing. Some changes are desirable, while others appear to be moving us backward. Elegant, historic structures have been torn down only to make way for nondescript replacements. In recent years, many lovely buildings suffered the indignity of disfiguring graffiti. Everyone who appreciates beauty finds these things baffling.

Communist party rulers in Russia and Eastern Europe created a blight with the ugly concrete apartment boxes that were built under their direction. No attempt was made to make them attractive, let alone beautiful. What a strange juxtaposition – grey, austere, shapeless masses standing in bold contrast to the elegant architecture of old churches and public buildings that can still be found in those areas. Even today, many visitors to this scene remark about how depressing it is to see this starkness and lack of beauty; they describe it as being cold, even eerie.

A lot of people are unaware of how important their comfort and sense of well-being are to them. Yet, those are two of the reasons why the repugnant landscapes of countries under communist rule impose such a disquieting aspect to life. It is also an explanation for why that quiet table in the corner of the restaurant, removed from the traffic routes to the kitchen and restrooms, is the one most people want.

Some people are also unaware of just how important beauty is to them. But that quality of attractiveness is the reason that one hotel can charge significantly more than another for rooms that are about the same size, roughly the same floor plan, and with the same basic amenities; the only difference rests in the quality of the décor, the beauty of the landscape, or the elegance of the lobby.

Way beyond the attractiveness of any man-made beauty is the artistry God created – it surpasses all else. Millions upon millions of annual visitors to the national forests and parks attest to the importance of the loveliness to be found in nature. A hike into the wilderness reveals peaceful meadows, dense forests, wildflowers, unbelievable vistas, and chiseled rock faces. Sometimes we are lucky enough to round a bend and stand in awe of a magnificent waterfall. Often there are occasions to enjoy a mesmerizing blue sky offset by majestic cumulus clouds. The utter tranquility of gentle falling snow on a forest path presents a quiet allure. Sunsets and the aurora borealis represent some of the most extraordinary light shows on earth. Even the dappled shade of sunlight filtering through a tree onto the wall of a building or the floor of a shaded terrace can be surprisingly captivating. God's creativity is unsurpassed, and it endures.

But you might wonder, "Is beauty just in the eye of the beholder, or is it quantifiable?" One very interesting website, "God, The Creator Of Beauty," suggests that man's appreciation of pulchritude is universal because God created beauty and all the elements that contribute to it – *including* man's ability to appreciate the beauty in what He created. We all have an inherent ability to see loveliness, recognize it, and, ultimately appreciate it.

This website goes on to say that the creation of beauty is a matter of adhering to the basic rules of design which involve the incorporation of one or more of its seven governing principles. These seven principles are scale, proportion, symmetry, balance, rhythm, emphasis, variety, and unity.

These principles are abundantly present in nature. One of them deals with the ratios of ideal proportion, the golden mean. It is a rule of proportion found in the design of plants, animals, and even the human body. Being the proportion that is most pleasing to the human eye, it is not surprising that the human face is constructed from this principle. The more closely facial features conform to the golden mean, the more beautiful the face. This applies to all races and genders.

This concept of ideal proportion is responsible, the world over, for the beautiful being accepted as beautiful.

Because God has provided the template for beauty, you can be sure that when you incorporate these principles you will have succeeded in creating a universally acknowledged loveliness within your environment.

Decide that you will put forth the necessary effort and cost to beautify any area where you spend a lot of time. Don't allow any impulse to the contrary to squelch your intentions in this regard. Surrounding yourself with comeliness will reap great dividends. You will find that the beauty of your special place(s) will provide a haven of safety and escape. You will never tire of the feelings of serenity and the sheer enjoyment your well-planned world of elegance will bring. There is something both soothing and refreshing about the impact things of beauty can bring to your life.

One very famous artist was keenly aware of this truth and carried its application to the extreme. In the 1890s, Claude Monet purchased a piece of ground as the beginning step in a quest to create a garden just so he could paint it! He achieved his dream and the result was his now world-famous garden, known as Monet's Garden. Located in Giverny, France, it's the most visited garden of its size in the Western world. This mere five-acre garden attracts nearly a half million admirers a year!

He pronounced himself good for only two things in life – painting, and gardening. In a letter to the government office in charge of permits for such things as the garden and the pond within it that he wanted to create, Monet stated his purpose for the garden as being the creation of pleasure for the eyes. As one of the most admired artists ever, Claude Monet was eminently qualified to speak about loveliness as it was obviously all important to him.

Judged by his glorious paintings, popular gardens, and the almost unanimous affirmation of the quality of his creations, we have a most convincing testimony to his understanding of beauty as well as to the immense joy he received from it. It worked for Monet, and it will work for you.

The infusion of beauty in your life is much more important than you might think. God felt it was important enough to have gone to tremendous lengths to bless you with the magnificence that's to be found in so much of His creation.

Responsible for all that you find lovely are the principles of design, as found in nature. Observance of this principle will encourage you to create your beauty, a beauty that will enrich your life and calm your soul.

Decide that you will surround yourself with beauty by committing to the cost and effort it might take. You will enjoy your retreat into a world of serenity and allure every day. Rest assured, it will be worth whatever it costs.

WHAT KIND OF LEGACY WILL YOU LEAVE?

You'd better hope that by the time you think about it, it's not too late.

Most of us could name a few people who are nearing the end of their life and have done it right. Their reputations are the result of not only what they did, but also how they did it.

A brief look into the lives of those with enviable legacies would reveal a road map, of sorts, as to how to go about establishing your legacy. You might begin to notice that their legacy-building qualities could be generally grouped into three primary categories: their accomplishments, their character attributes, and the quality of their interactions with people.

In the area of physical accomplishments, sports figures can often attain idol or cult-like status. Despite their "on-the-field" accomplishments, some are rather undeserving of such accolades because of their behavior and unsavory extracurricular activities. To name just a few, such was the fate of Jim Thorpe, Mickey Mantle, Tiger Woods, and now Lance Armstrong. Even those who conduct their private lives properly will live to see the day when their heroics have been brought to a halt by age-related limitations or infirmities. Most professional athletes are considered over the hill by age 40. In some sports, it's earlier than that.

What becomes of them after their sports career has ended? Some handle it well, while others have a hard time adjusting to the fact that it's over. A few embark on a new, not so admirable, lifestyle – hard living, womanizing, or shady business deals. Unfortunately, these things stain their reputation and forever damage the foundation of their once-great legacy. For these reasons, later reviews aren't always as complimentary of how they've lived their lives as were the reports written at the time of their successes "on the field." One can only conclude that a person's legacy isn't static – rather, it's dynamic. Over time, it may become subject to different intensities or modifications, even propelling that legacy in an entirely new direction. Many come to realize that non-physical activities and pursuits provide for a potentially greater "shelf life." In this area of non-physical accomplishments, some people have devoted their lives to the perfection of a skill or the creation of a service. A recent art auction catalog listed a Howard Terpning painting for sale. The catalog suggested its expected value to be in the $1,000,000 price range. The remarkable thing about this is that Howard Terpning is still alive! If he cared about money, all he has to do is sit down in front of a canvas for a few hours and turn out another $1,000,000 masterpiece. Very few artists have ever been able to claim such a monetary confirmation of the value of their art…while they were still alive.

The great evangelist, Billy Graham, was voted the most respected man in America for fifty-five years, 49 of which were consecutive. Certainly, his preaching, though simple, was spell-binding. But, Billy isn't the only great preacher. There have been a lot of great preachers. So, what was it that made Billy Graham so different? To start with, he lived what he preached. There were no skeletons in his closet. As a handsome, dynamic man, women would have been readily available to him. Recognizing that potential pitfall early on, Billy would never meet with a woman alone or behind closed doors. All his financial records were open to inspection by the IRS at any time. He had the respect of and an association with every U.S. President since Dwight Eisenhower. No matter their political differences, he remained true to God. This enabled Billy to be an effective counselor to each one of them.

Steve Jobs, the legendary founder of Apple Computer, was responsible for vaulting the company he started into one of the greatest business success stories to have ever been written. Yet, given the fact that Apple once fired him, it's evident that he wasn't always as appreciated as he had become at the time of his death! Unfortunately, also mixed with the rave reviews of his visionary prowess, were stories of the mistreatment of his staff and employees. He could be curt, dismissive, and insulting. Imagine the increased dimensions of the legacy created by his unmatchable business accomplishments that could have been realized had he *coupled* those accomplishments with a reputation for being loved by all those who helped him achieve that success…loved, not just for his genius, but also for how he treated them!

If a life of notable achievements has eluded you, take heart. You don't have to be a Steve Jobs, Howard Terpning, Billy Graham, or a sports hero to create a legacy that will make those you leave behind proud. You can depart this world with a reputation that speaks to your character, one worthy of acclaim.

Not so widely known as Howard Terpning, Billy Graham, or Steve Jobs, my father, nevertheless, was just such a man. Everyone liked him… and for good reason. He was one of the most honest people I've ever known. As a businessman his reputation was sterling. Moreover, he was a great golfer, having been inducted into the Colorado Golf Hall of Fame. Despite all the things he could have bragged about, he never did… because he was also a *very* humble man. These character qualities can be yours. You don't have to be a star; you can joyfully settle for just being pure gold.

This leaves the third category of legacy-building qualities: your interactions with people. Those are best exemplified by my wife, Janet. Her legacy is already being written. While she may well establish a legacy for her work as a bible teacher, author, and speaker, she has already created a most enviable reputation for her treatment of people. She's enthusiastic, positive, and cheerful. She is a great friend because she's a great listener. A conversation with her will be mostly about you. As you might guess, she's very generous both with her time and her things. In short, she loves people and they know it. Predictably, they respond in kind and eagerly return that love!

If you would like your legacy to revolve around your achievements, the development of your "A" skills is the most assured way to that end.

If you would like to be remembered as having been a person of stellar character, revisit the principle, Traits Of The Successful and Great." But if you'd aspire to a legacy of having lived a life marked by the quality of your interactions with people, then, review the principle, Invest In Others…And, take a page out of my wife, Janet's, book.

While your character may not extend above the heads of the crowd, and your achievements might not be particularly noteworthy, *you can develop a reputation for how you've treated others.* Of all the things to have been known for, isn't this the one you'd cherish most?

EPILOGUE

Why do some people's lives turn out so well – everything going according to plan? For others, the total of their experiences is merely a string of disappointments and failures. Shattered dreams define their existence.

In the beginning, your life probably looked very much the same as those in your neighborhood. Everyone lived in a similar size and style of home. They all attended the same schools and possibly belonged to the same church. The majority of the people in your community were from a common racial background and the household incomes were roughly the same. What could explain the wide divergence in their futures?

Allow me to explain what I believe to be the reasons behind this mystery through the use of an analogy. Imagine, for a moment, life's experiences as a tree…with its trunk, limbs, branches, and twigs painting a picture of a complex web of different paths for the sap to follow (you are the "sap"). Now visualize this tree sitting on a ridge. The sunny side of the tree overlooks a beautiful valley with snow-capped peaks in the distant background. The other side of the tree, however, looks down on a busy freeway. A huge retaining wall defines the edge of the outside lane of traffic. Since that wall came very close to the tree, many roots were cut during its construction. As a result, that side of the tree is sparsely populated with leaves and has a withered appearance. Moreover, the view from that side of the tree is of the incessant traffic below, a cemetery, a hospital, and a junkyard. That side of the tree gets no direct sunlight, is smothered with exhaust fumes, and has terrible views.

So, let's begin by characterizing your childhood as the trunk of that tree – everyone sort of lumped together in that tree trunk. That beginning begs the question: "How then did everyone become so separated when they all started so much the same?" **The answer lies in the decisions, or choices, each person made along the way!**

Everyone is constantly presented with choices – to go forward, go backward, turn to the right, the left, or stand still. A decision is made – another juncture, another decision. In a rather short period, many of the members of that original group had traveled very different paths and lived very different lives than that of any of their former friends. As you grow older, like the tree which begins to grow branches that separate from the trunk, you also travel away from your beginnings, forming your own identity, assuming an existence shaped by your decisions.

Early on, some people's decisions move them to the freeway side of the tree. Others, however, make decisions that move them to the sunny side of the tree. This is the side with the view of the beautiful valley where life is blossoming. Sometimes, even those who end up on the healthy side of the tree intersperse their good decisions with some bad ones. In so doing, they may destine themselves to remain in the lower branches of the tree – where the views aren't as good.

Only a few make consistently good decisions and find themselves at the top of the healthy side of the tree. At each juncture of a limb and a branch, or a branch and a twig, a decision must be made. Which path should you choose? Where you end up is of your choosing. It all depends on the quality of the decisions you make.

But there are so many complexities…so many decisions…so many choices to be considered. Selection of college, marriage partners, careers, selection of friends, pastime preferences, residence location, moral convictions (or their lack), etc. All of these influence your life's journey.

Never dare to think otherwise – your decisions *do determine* the course of your life. And like the analogy of the tree, each of your decisions can move you ever higher up the sunny side of the tree or further out on a limb overlooking the chaos of life.

But why…why do so many people make one bad decision after another? Is it a lack of intelligence? Do their emotions get in the way? Or, do they allow others to influence their choices? I think the answer lies in three areas: impatience, pride, and a lack of understanding.

A habit of impatiently jumping to conclusions, without ever considering the consequences, can't help but lead to some poor decisions. Some perfectly intelligent people do this very thing.

When pride enters the picture, it's pride that defends a bad decision – the damage of that poor choice is allowed to spread and deepen.

However, the pitfalls that accompany impatience and pride can be offset by a thorough understanding of the principles of good decision-making. You have now been exposed to such principles – study them, employ them, and expand upon their wisdom.

As you travel the road to success, you will be making more and more good decisions, as you leave more and more of the bad ones behind you.

Maybe you feel that up to this point your life has largely been a waste and you see yourself as nothing more than an ugly sucker, springing out from the trunk, awaiting the gardener's pruning shears. Or if you have moved away from the trunk, maybe it's only to have moved to the unhealthy side of the tree…and moving back to the other side of the tree (the sunny side) is not an easy task, since all the traffic is flowing against you. But it isn't impossible!

You're never too old, or too lost, to begin to reclaim your life and start moving in the right direction. It's never too late to put into practice the principles you've just read. This is your opportunity to *break the pattern of failure and discouragement and begin a life that pursues excellence and healthy thinking.*

Take the subject of decision-making seriously! *The ability to make consistently good decisions while avoiding the bad ones is one of the most important skills you could develop.*

www.ingramcontent.com/pod-product-compliance
Lightning Source LLC
LaVergne TN
LVHW041746060526
838201LV00046B/926